Advance praise

'Attachment theory is everywhere, but is everything you've heard about it right? Laura Mucha explains it all. Learn how to better understand yourself and your relationships, and how to improve them.'

Fearne Cotton

'An impressive and much needed book that explains attachment theory in an accurate, accessible and engaging way. Not just the best book on attachment theory for a general audience, but the best by far. Captivating reading and completely up-to-date, informed by the latest research.'

Dr Robbie Duschinsky, University of Cambridge

PLEASE FIND ATTACHED

PLEASE FIND ATTACHED

How Attachment Theory
Explains Our Relationships

Laura Mucha

BLOOMSBURY SIGMA
LONDON · OXFORD · NEW YORK · NEW DELHI · SYDNEY

BLOOMSBURY SIGMA
Bloomsbury Publishing Plc
50 Bedford Square, London, WC1B 3DP, UK

First published in 2023 as an original audio book by Audible
This edition published in 2025

A catalogue record for this book is available from the British Library

Library of Congress Cataloguing-in-Publication data has been applied for

ISBN: HB: 978-1-47298-8-003; e-book: 978-1-47298-8-041

2 4 6 8 10 9 7 5 3 1

Typeset in Bembo Std by Deanta Global Publishing Services, Chennai, India
Printed and bound in Great Britain by CPI Group (UK) Ltd,
Croydon CR0 4YY

To find out more about our authors and books visit bloomsbury.com
and sign up for our newsletters

For my mum

Contents

Contents

Introduction

Which parent did you feel closest to? Why? Did you ever feel rejected? Frightened? Were your parents ever threatening in any way? When you were upset as a child, what would you do?

These aren't questions we often ask. You may not know how those closest to you would answer some of them. Maybe even all of them. And if someone started busting those questions out on a first date, you'd probably find them a bit intrusive.

But these are just a handful of the questions I asked the people I interviewed for this book. They're not my questions – they're taken from the Adult Attachment Interview, or AAI, a one- to one-and-a-half-hour interview designed to surprise the unconscious. It's transcribed, with every breath, stumble and pause noted, before being coded for 6 to 10 hours by someone with at least two years' training.

I conducted the AAI with seven strangers. I asked extraordinarily personal questions of these people, but without being able to respond in the way I usually would. There was no 'I'm sorry for your loss', no hugs when interviewees cried as they spoke about difficult things they'd suffered during childhood. Instead, I asked the required questions and followed the strict guidance. Did the beatings cause bruising? Okay, next question …

The unnatural nature of the interview is partly where its power lies. Not only do the piercing questions build over time, but without the usual patterns of normal conversation, the interview somehow dislodges us from the everyday, the familiar. It brings up experiences that may have lain dormant for decades in the locked boxes and cobwebbed corners of our minds. The people I interviewed said 'Wow, I'd totally forgotten about that', 'I'm not sure where that came from' or 'I've never told anyone that before'. And they very generously allowed me to share their stories with you.

Why? Because they – and I – think we all need to talk more openly about the impact our upbringing has on us in later life, as well as the people along the way who can change the paths we find ourselves on.

To do this, we need to understand attachment theory. Attachment theory tries to explain how and why we pay attention, manage our emotions, remember, think and reflect when it comes to close relationships. It's used by psychologists, psychotherapists, social workers, teachers and nurses, by biological, foster and adoptive parents and in forensic work. But research suggests that while many professionals are familiar with the word 'attachment', they don't know all that much about what the theory and research say – even when they're claiming to base their work on it.

To make matters worse, many, many people misunderstand it. I regularly meet people who have done a quick online quiz to figure out their attachment 'style' and then acted on this by questioning, blaming or ditching their partner accordingly. Meanwhile, when most people read words such as 'attachment', 'insecurity' and 'anxiety', they can't help but infuse them with their everyday understanding – even though in attachment theory they mean something different.

This misunderstanding of attachment theory is partly down to its founder, John Bowlby. He was determined to change the lives of children and families, and in order to do this, he needed his theory to reach a wide audience. So he deliberately used everyday language in a simple and emotional way. He also built on stereotypes and prejudices from the 1950s, like the idea that women should be full-time mothers who are always available. He did this to make the theory fly – and it did.

It became incredibly popular – and Bowlby succeeded in changing the lives of children and families. Thanks to his work, children were no longer separated from their parents when sent to hospital. But the downside of his marketing strategy was that many people came to understand attachment theory based solely on his early public writing or speaking – a simplified summary that overemphasised the role of mothers and used evocative words without clearly explaining what they meant.

Like the word 'attachment', for example. Bowlby used it to mean two things: the first was all and any intimate relationships. Nice and simple. But the second was a set of beliefs, desires and behaviours that help us ensure that Someone Important is there to care for us when we need help. Not so simple. And very, very different. The broader, simpler meaning (intimate relationships) made attachment theory seem more user-friendly, more intuitive, more appealing. But from the late 1960s, Bowlby switched to mainly using the second, more convoluted meaning. And this has led to endless confusion and miscommunication by and between academics.

Meanwhile, people interested in attachment around the world relied – and still rely – on Bowlby's early scientific thinking, even though he changed his mind about a lot of important things (including the meaning of the word 'attachment' itself). He came to regret some of his earlier thinking – in particular, implying that children needed their mothers to care for them 24/7. But Bowlby's later regrets and qualifications are often overlooked.

This is not all Bowlby's fault. The researchers that followed him haven't always been brilliant at sharing new ideas with the public, so it's all too easy to rely on Bowlby's accessible early ideas. And he's not the only one to mislead by using everyday words that actually have technical meanings – other researchers have done the same. If that wasn't confusing enough, different groups of researchers use the same words to mean different things. Oh, and no other psychological theory has spawned more research in the past 30 years, making it very hard to get a handle on it all. So, is it any surprise that most people misunderstand attachment theory?

When understood and used in the right way, the theory and research can transform lives for the better. Used in the wrong way, it can be misapplied in phenomenally important decisions – like taking children away from their parents. Attachment has become a buzzword but, given how easy (and dangerous) it is to misunderstand it, my aim is to put the nuance back in.

So, that's the 'why' of the book. A bit more about the 'how'. Seven interviewees took part in this project. They weren't just generous enough to go through the AAI with me – they also allowed me to interview them over four years. In order to do this, I went through their AAI transcripts and codings, prepared pages and pages of questions, discussed them with world-leading thinkers in attachment, then spent up to 25 further hours with each interviewee, asking them about every detail of their lives. I took the 200,000 or so words from each person and condensed, shaped and organised them down into 7,000-word subchapters.

Reading about seven different people can get a bit confusing at times, so I've given each interviewee a small summary. For example, I describe Ray as 'the boy who was sent away'. Being sent away was only a tiny part of Ray's life, but I've added this and other summaries to try to help you follow which of the interviewees is speaking or being discussed at any one time.

There are seven chapters, and you will hear from every interviewee in each. The chapters may sound like fiction – but they're not. They're made up of the interviewees' own words. I occasionally needed to add a line or two, for example when merging things they'd said at different points in time. When I did this, I discussed these with the interviewees, who checked or reworded my changes. The interviewees had full editorial control at all times.

I've tried to be as faithful to the interviewees' words as possible because language is very important when it comes to assessing adult attachment. As is silence. That's because silence might mean a person is pausing to remember,

for example, or   quietly

reflecting.

But if someone stops halfway through saying something, then starts a new sentence after a long silence as if nothing happened, this is important for AAI coding. It's seen in a similar way to a child physically freezing, which is part of the fear response in both humans and animals. Because of this, I've included silences and pauses wherever they've happened in interviews. So where there's blank space on the page, don't worry — it's deliberate. And the white space I've used is roughly equivalent to the amount of silence.

As well as hearing from the interviewees in each chapter, you'll also hear from me as I discuss the theory and research and apply it to the lives of the interviewees. In order to do this, I joined the Child Health and Development Group at the University of Cambridge, where I am now Author-in-Residence at the Department of Public Health and Primary Care.

For six years I attended regular reading groups, talks and conferences on child and family mental health, and read and read and read about attachment theory. (I'd also read extensively about attachment theory for my first book, and as part of my undergraduate degree in psychology and philosophy.) I also had regular meetings with three world-leading experts: Robbie Duschinsky, professor at Cambridge University; Kate White, co-founder of the Bowlby Centre; and Linda Cundy, uber attachment psychotherapist. I'm HUGELY thankful for their input and research; there's zero way I could have written this without them.

When describing the science, I've tried to keep the language simple throughout. So I've used the phrase Someone Important or Important Person to refer to whoever is responsible for taking care of a child or who a child feels is important to them. This doesn't have to be, and often isn't, their birth parent. Occasionally I use the words 'parent' or 'mother' when this is specifically who was involved in research I'm discussing. But when I'm talking about one particular relationship, it's important to remember that attachment is about far more than our relationship with just one parent. Each Important Person plays a role.

The combination of research and the interviewees' lives may not always be an easy read. It'll probably make you question, consider, explore and reflect on your own life – and the lives of those around you. That's a good thing. Reflection can help understanding and, if necessary, change. But in thinking about all of this, it's all too easy to jump to conclusions about what classification you might get (or your partner, parent, colleague or friend) if you were to undergo the AAI. As you will see throughout the book, it's just as easy to get it wrong.

While putting people into boxes can help make sense of and organise the world, it can also lead to dubious judgements. So just because your life or the life of Someone Important echoes that of one of the interviewees, it doesn't mean you or they would be classified in the same way. On top of that, classifications can change over time.

The interviewees have a variety of attachment patterns and are invaluable in bringing the theory to life – and the role of our upbringings more generally. But they aren't the exemplars of the classifications they've been given. Just as there are different ways to be funny or clever or kind, there are different ways to have different attachment patterns. Of course, there are similarities across people within each grouping, otherwise they wouldn't exist. And hopefully hearing from the interviewees will give you a flavour of what those different groupings might sound or feel like. So as you read, it's worth thinking about how the different ways interviewees speak about their lives make you feel. Do different people make you feel more or less engaged, smothered or disconnected? If so, why? And what impact do you think this might have on their lives?

A quick word about structure. I've organised the book to follow the interviewees' lives from early childhood to adulthood – and I follow the development of attachment theory in the same way (although I do occasionally jump back in time to revisit some of Bowlby's earlier ideas). Attachment theory has a lot to say about early childhood, so the first chapter has more research crammed into it than the rest of the book. This chills out in later chapters.

All that's left to say is that I hope you'll find this an enjoyable and thought-provoking read. Attachment is a theory that can evoke strong feelings. It looks at human needs that aren't always met and experiences that aren't always easy to think about. It cuts through common assumptions about childhood and important relationships. It asks questions about these strong feelings, these human needs and how difficult it can be to think, *really* think, about our lives and the lives of others.

But asking those questions can be invaluable. Delving into attachment research can help us understand how we and the Important People in our lives think, feel and behave in close relationships. In doing so, it can help us understand who we are, and make more conscious choices as a result.

CHAPTER ONE
Early Childhood

Skyler

The girl wrapped in cotton wool

My earliest memory is being in the hospital when my sister was stillborn.

I remember eating a lollipop. I was 4.

There were red dots on her from things that were monitoring suction.

I hadn't really thought about this before, but …
                        that's a big first memory.

                  I don't remember any reaction from my dad.
At all. I know that my mom spent a lot of time in bed. And I
remember that she let go of any religious ties that she had.

                        That's the only time I ever remember
                                her looking sad.

I don't think they ever talked about it. And it was not something we were allowed to discuss.

So we told nobody.

I didn't discuss it with my sister.
        I didn't discuss it with my parents.
                For as long as I was old enough to make regular memories, I didn't discuss it with anyone.

I can recognise as I'm saying the words that that's not normal ...

                But it didn't seem abnormal because my parents never talked about anything.

I didn't know what my mom did for a living. I didn't know anything about her parents. I didn't know anything about her life before we were born. We didn't talk about it. That was normal.

I grew up in a house in the suburbs. I lived there my whole life. My mom was always the nice one and my dad was always the stern one.

I remember running a race at an athletics event where he was an official. I did something wrong, something very minor, and he disqualified me. On my birthday. It's not like it was going to make the difference between first and second ... I came in second to last and he still disqualified me. Because those were the rules and I broke them. On my birthday.

When I was young, I used to cry every single time I missed a goal in football. Every single time. And he would just yell at me and tell me to suck it up. It's not that my dad doesn't love me – it's just he has no idea how humans are supposed to show love.

Dad's definition of being a parent and showing that you love your child was to physically be at every sporting event ever. He came to every single soccer game, baseball game, every race I ran, everything.

He put a lot of pressure on me to win. It was pretty intimidating. He wanted so badly for me to run faster. And he was very much about the end goal. He would have never said, 'Well, you tried your best.' There are no points for competing in my house. If I lost, my dad would be disappointed in me.

I think he was desperate for me to be the best because sports are a concrete way to measure somebody's worth. If you run this fast, you are worth this much.

My mom's definition of showing love was being concerned about any type of danger in the world, constantly, and trying to micromanage and avoid all of those dangers. My experience of our relationship was her telling me to be careful.

I was best friends with the girl next door, Hannah. And if my mom wasn't home when I got back from school, I would go next door and play with her.

I probably spent at least two or three days a week at Hannah's house and went on holiday with them every year. It was better with them than with my parents cos there wasn't that overbearing need for me to perform well, as there was with my dad. And they trusted that I wasn't going to spontaneously die, unlike my mom.

Home was too coddling. It wasn't the right kind of comfort, it was illogical.

Mom would say, 'I don't want you playing in the backyard because it's too dangerous.' So I'd ask her why it was dangerous and she'd say, 'Well, there are snakes and bears.'

It's probably not something that I should admit, but from a very young age I realised that you couldn't reason with Mom using logic or emotion. So I would make up facts to win arguments.

I would come back with something like, 'Actually, according to a document I read, there haven't been any bear sightings in the last five years and there aren't poisonous snakes in North America.' I would just make up stuff to counteract her irrational overprotectiveness.

When I was 9 years old, my mom asked Hannah's mom to pick me up from school because she wasn't going to be around. When this happened, we would usually go to Hannah's house to play, but this time Hannah had a soccer game, so her mom suggested we go and watch her play.

This is before mobile phones existed, so we called when we got there and left Mom a message on the answering machine: 'Hey Mom, I'm with Hannah's mom and we are going to go watch Hannah's indoor soccer game. See you soon. Bye.'

About an hour later, a policeman came in with a photo of me and said, 'Is this you? Your mom thinks you've been kidnapped.'

My mom had come home, seen and heard the message, but couldn't understand what I was saying because I was mumbling. She thought it was a cry for help, so called the police and had a search party out for me.

I was very unpopular in school, so it was horrible to have the police come into a soccer game in front of my entire class and search for me because my mom thought I had been kidnapped.

It doesn't even make logical sense. It's not like kidnappers are going to say, 'Well, before I kidnap you, you should probably call your mom and tell her what's happening.' It's insane. She went from zero to a hundred. I always went across the street, and I had only been gone for less than an hour.

I have spoken with her about it since, and to this day she says, 'Well, I heard your message, any mother would have thought that their daughter was kidnapped.' I said, 'No! No! That is not a normal response!'

So, I can safely say she's overprotective. There's a level of overprotectiveness to the point of frustration.

Growing up with my parents was like living in a box room with nothing in it. Other than cotton wool. With my mom, it felt like there was so much cotton wool that I couldn't breathe.

Ray

The boy who was sent away

I was a bit early, a bit unplanned. Bad timing. Unaffordable.

My parents had both just arrived in this country and were struggling to survive. Mum came from Kenya, a country so traumatised by conflict that it was a no-brainer to leave somewhere that couldn't offer her safety.

My dad lost his parents when he was 13, and his family were left with nothing. So when he turned 14, his aunt gave him 100 rupees to get a train to one of the big cities to find a job. A hundred rupees was not a lot of money. It's probably not even a penny now.

He arrived, got a job and worked very, very hard. Then one day, his boss's friend offered him a menial job in his Glasgow office. By that point, Dad had saved up just enough money to get him there.

He left Bangladesh when he was 15, with nothing in his pocket, nothing to lose. But he did have a job and a floor to sleep on.

When I came along, Mum and Dad were both doing low-paid jobs. I don't remember being poverty-stricken. Although they did live on cereal. Every now and then, Dad would take me out and buy me a tiny little car that came in a box from the tobacconist round the corner, and that was a big deal.

There was a wreck of a small lorry outside our first home. With hindsight, it couldn't have been the greatest street in the world if people were fly-tipping lorries on it. It became the den for all the kids in the street. We would meet there every night and sit in it, play in it, take bits off. We spent most of the summer breaking it up. We picked it clean to its skeleton gradually.

Dad was working seven days a week doing two or three jobs and my mum was similar. Dad wasn't completely absent, I do remember him being about a bit. And I remember being at Dad's office quite a lot, left there by the babysitter while he finished off work.

I was babysat locally in people's homes. And then when I was older, the kids from our street used to walk me to nursery and back.

Then Mum found me at a babysitter's in quite a state. I don't know exactly what the state was, but it was so upsetting that she immediately decided to change the babysitter, get my grandma over from Bangladesh and not leave me with anyone else.

And when I was 2, I was shipped off to Bangladesh for three years. My parents just couldn't afford to look after me and not work.

I don't have huge memories of it. I don't remember missing my parents, or Scotland, or anything, which is weird. But I do remember the school. I've got this vague memory of the check shirt and the name of the teacher. And the pencils.

My dad told me recently that it was so unbearable that Mum decided to change her job so she could look after me a bit more at home. So my dad went off to Bangladesh and brought me back.

I remember fighting and protesting while being put on the plane. I didn't want to come back. I wanted to stay there.

When I saw Mum for the first time, I said, 'I don't want to stay here because that's not my mum, my mum's back in Bangladesh.' What a difficult thing for her to hear. I was talking about my grandma.

I used to keep going on about how much better Bangladesh was and pretending to be various characters from my life there. There was a man who used to walk around the streets with the big cart of vegetables every morning. People would come out like it was an ice cream van and buy vegetables – that's who I pretended to be for a few months when I got back.

My parents had a renewed vigour to spend time with me. I was suddenly absorbed and loved and hugged and not let go of a lot more. I've got very clear, fond memories of my dad taking me to iconic places in Glasgow together, just me and him. And my mum taking me with her to work so that I wasn't left with anyone. And being spoilt by her friends and being around both of them a lot more.

I think there was a degree of overcompensation going on.

I think my parents still carry a tiny bit of guilt for leaving me in Bangladesh.

I don't remember any major, emotional, loving connection with my dad. He was just unavailable. When we started to have more money, he used to buy me things – toys, cars and soldiers. A lot of his affection was shown through buying things. But I don't remember there being huge amounts of ... I feel very weird saying this, almost disrespectful ... but there wasn't much hugging or anything tactile going on.

I don't remember being held or carried around, I don't remember sitting on his shoulders. I don't remember holding his hand. I'm absolutely certain he did these things. I just don't understand why I haven't got a memory of it.

But I still felt I was loved.

I don't think I was ignored. But Dad never picked me up or dropped me off at school. He never knew what I was reading or studying. He just wasn't physically present because he was always working during the day doing one job, and then in the evening, setting up his other job.

He was never there at any sporting event, or anything I did at school. I don't blame him for it. I just think he was just really busy.

When I was upset, I would

either go to my mum or deal with it myself, quietly, or cry a lot in a corner or in my room. I am struggling to think of a time where I was hugged by my parents because I was upset.

Throughout all of this, my grandmother kept coming back from Bangladesh to help out, look after me, take me to school. She would come over for six months every year. I don't remember her leaving and it being sad. I don't remember traumatic moments at the airport or anything like that. When I think about some of the memories that come up from my childhood, I feel quite cold and almost callous, now that I think about it.

I don't have any memories of how I felt about leaving my grandma or seeing my mum for the first time, because I very quickly dealt with them and moved on and shut off. I don't know why I wasn't emotional about so many things when I was really young.

I just survived as a child. As long as I was fed and went to school and had some friends, I was kind of happy. I don't have strong memories of being attached to anyone.

I can't believe I just said that.

John Bowlby: the birth of attachment theory

John Bowlby was born in 1907. His father was surgeon to King Edward VII, and he had a very formal and distant relationship with his mother. When he turned 10, his parents sent him to boarding school because they thought the London air raids during the First World War would be unsettling for him.

Bowlby disagreed with their decision to send him away. He later said that he was strongly against young children being sent to boarding school, and that he wouldn't send a dog to boarding school at the age he went.

He studied natural sciences at Cambridge, then trained as a doctor, before becoming a psychoanalyst. But he found himself getting frustrated. At the time, psychoanalysts often failed to acknowledge how important family experiences were in shaping children's minds. For example, when he treated a distressed 3-year-old boy, Bowlby's supervisor, Melanie Klein, insisted that the child's mother sit outside the room. Then, when the boy's mum was admitted to a mental hospital, Klein wasn't interested in what impact this might have on the boy – other than the fact that it interrupted his analysis.

Bowlby thought it was ridiculous to treat young children and ignore their parents. He thought the job of a therapist was to help patients explore their past, thoughts and feelings, and discover who they were. To do this, he needed to focus on their actual experiences – but this was not how psychoanalysis worked at the time.

Instead, psychoanalysts believed that the way kids thought about their parents didn't reflect the truth, but a fantasy. Bowlby disagreed. His experience as a therapist wasn't that patients were telling him things they'd made up. If anything, they weren't telling him the important things, partly because they couldn't remember, partly because they didn't dare.

Even now, attachment theory isn't formally taught at the British Psychoanalytic Institute, and psychoanalysts can still sometimes fail to recognise the importance of children's actual experiences. For example, in a long-term study of children treated historically at the Anna Freud Centre (set up by Sigmund Freud's daughter), Peter Fonagy and Mary Target described cases where therapists saw children's descriptions of abuse as fantasy rather than things that had actually happened to them. Unsurprisingly, the children didn't do well in the long term.

So, Bowlby decided to move away from psychoanalysis, and during the Second World War he studied children who were evacuated. He wrote about their mental health symptoms, including tempers, disobedience, sleeplessness, bed-wetting and unexplained pains, and was convinced they were caused by the distress of being separated from their parents for a long time. He noticed that symptoms were milder among children who had caring foster parents and were common among kids who passed through multiple homes.

After that, Bowlby worked in a child guidance clinic, where he noticed that children who hadn't been evacuated, but whose parents were unkind or cruel to them, also often had mental health difficulties.

As well as children's well-being, Bowlby was interested in animals and devoured animal research, including the work of Nobel Prize winner Konrad Lorenz. Lorenz studied geese and found that, even though goslings weren't dependent on their parents for food, families still stayed together for at least a year. This echoed Bowlby's experiences of being a dad. At the time, most people thought a child's relationship with their parent came from the pleasure of feeding, but Bowlby had noticed that his children came to him when they were frightened or wanted affection, even though he didn't give them food.

Lorenz also wrote about how goslings followed the first thing they saw that moved. This could be their mother, or when they were hatched in an incubator, it could also be Lorenz himself.

Bowlby had intense discussions about this with his friend Robert Hinde, an expert in animal behaviour. Together, they concluded that the way young animals (including goslings) followed moving objects probably evolved to keep them close to Someone Important who could protect them from danger. And they thought young animals – including humans – were particularly likely to follow when they felt alarmed.

Bowlby also liked the phrase 'haven of safety'. Primate researchers Harry Harlow and Robert Zimmermann had used it to describe a child's desire to be close to Someone Important when they were hurt, anxious or alarmed, or when they thought they might be separated. They thought this desire to be close would chill out when they stopped being scared, or when they knew Someone Important would be there for them if they needed them.

Bowlby started using the phrase to describe the same desire in humans, although he thought that getting close meant different things in different situations and to different people. On hearing a loud noise, children who were confident that Someone Important would be there if they needed them might only need to look at that person to stop feeling afraid. Whereas some children might need to physically cling on to their parent.

Bowlby would have studied abuse, but he felt that this could only happen once society had become more honest about family life, and scientists had better tools to do better research. So he set up the Separation Research Unit at Tavistock Clinic. At the time, parents weren't allowed to visit children when they were in hospital, so a member of his research team, James Robertson, filmed the children's experiences of being separated. The films had a major impact.

One of the first was *A Two-Year-Old Goes to Hospital* – you can easily find it online if you're curious. It shows the sorrow of a 2-and-a-half-year-old girl, Laura, who was in hospital for

eight days without Someone Important. The film helped
people recognise the impact that major separations had on
children and played a key role in changing regulation around
hospital visits in the 1950s.

Bowlby, James Robertson and his wife Joyce and their
colleague Mary Ainsworth spent huge amounts of time
discussing their findings, and noticed patterns in the way
children behaved after being separated from their Important
People. When they were finally reunited, children were often
either over-dependent, 'clingy' and unable to settle, or they
angrily rejected and turned away from them.

Putting this all together, Bowlby started to formulate
attachment theory. He came to believe that children need to
have access to a 'safe haven', someone they feel safe with and
who can protect them when they're frightened or upset. He
called this need to be close to Someone Important 'the
attachment system'. He thought adults also have this need, but
that a phone call or thinking of them might be enough, rather
than the cuddles a young child needs to be comforted when
they're upset. By the end of his life, he thought what was key
was the feeling that Someone Important would be there when
we needed them.

Bowlby thought that our Important Person could be a
biological parent, or not. And they could be safe, reliable
and loving, or not – we'd still want to be or feel close to
them, to know they were there and that they would respond
if we needed them to. From an evolutionary perspective, it's
better to have an adult around to protect us – even if they're
not actually that good at it – than no adult at all. And as a
young child, being separated from that adult would be
seriously threatening, as our survival depends on them. By
separation, Bowlby didn't mean putting a child into day
care: he meant a situation where a child was scared by not
having their Important Person around, like a long-term
hospital stay.

Bowlby believed that we learn what to expect from Important People based on our past experiences. He also thought we could have a variety of Important People – grandparents, aunts, uncles and other relatives. He even thought our physical home could be a 'safe haven'.

He thought that, as a young child, our attachment system makes us behave in ways that help get Someone Important to be there for us physically and emotionally. But a child whose Important Person doesn't feel comfortable when they got close might learn to stay nearby and not let on how scared they are or how much they need a hug. Instead, they might learn to withdraw and rely on themselves. And that behaviour might actually help them stay physically, if not emotionally, close to Someone Important.

Bowlby's colleague Ainsworth went on to organise the different ways our attachment system makes us behave into three groups. The first group, 'secure', described children who could ask for help and were comforted when they did – in other words, children who could use their mum as a safe haven. The other two 'insecure' groups, 'avoidant' and 'ambivalent/resistant', described children who didn't seem to trust that their mothers would be there when they needed them.

The ideas of Bowlby, Ainsworth and others like Mary Main, Peter Fonagy, Mario Mikulincer and Phillip Shaver, are key if you really want to understand attachment theory. But I'm going to introduce them in more detail throughout the book to avoid it getting confusing. There's another advantage to learning about it in this way – it helps you understand how attachment theory 'grew up', just as the interviewees did.

Amos

The boy who couldn't remember

My earliest memory is playing in the snow with my dad. Which in Seville is insane, because it snows every 20 years.

I remember him doing a lot of things for me and being there for me. Although he wasn't as present as my mother, because he worked a lot more. I remember he was loving. I have no specific memories of it, it's a general feeling.

He always told me bedtime stories that he made up. He would develop them and had narrative threads over the nights. It was pretty cool.

Simple things. He doesn't cook, but would drive me places. Do things for me.

We played together, did things together. Like chess.

I remember my mum being there a lot in general. Hugging me. Buying me things. Cooking. Expressing her love to me. Stuff like that.

Sometimes she would say, 'If you don't do X, Y or Z, I'm not going to love you anymore.' I don't remember this, but my aunt told me that one of the times my mum said this, I answered, 'If I love you and you don't love me, what am I loving you for?' I was 2.

I remember our house, us being together, doing things together. We never moved. Always lived in the same house. It felt like a large house full of furniture, but very dusty. And there were not a lot of people in the house.

Very early, I have all good memories.

My mum was present. Always there. Literally. She would pick me up from school, that kind of stuff. She was home a lot.

She would read a lot to me.

I can tell you one time she wasn't present – she went to a conference. I don't remember any specifics.

I just can't remember anything when I was a child.

My mum got angry loads. She would come home and moan to my dad about people at work. And she was angry with my dad a lot. She had an explosive anger.

My mum would be screaming and yelling, and my dad would explain himself, being very controlled. In thousands of arguments, he lost his temper maybe four or five times in total.

There were also instances when my mum would say to me, 'You don't do anything right.'

I never criticised her back. I always accepted anything.

I just wanted to avoid drama.

I think my reaction when she was angry with me was instinctively to smile.

She was great, otherwise.

Generally, I would say my early childhood was positive. I feel like the relationships were positive.

Then I got sick. I was in hospital for a year and a half.

I spent a lot of time in hospital, like months and months. My mum was really anxious. She probably always slept in the room with me.

I probably wasn't going to die. But my parents were really scared that something could happen to me that was either final or that I might've had to live all my life with.

My grandmother was obsessed with puzzles. She got one every week in the newspaper and would cut it out, staple it so it was like a little book and brought it to me in hospital. And I would colour it in.

She died when I was in hospital. Although my mum never actually told me that she'd died. She said, 'Your grandmother has left to buy her medicine.' And I would ask, 'When is she coming back? Why can't we find the medicines for her?'

I don't, I don't, I don't have any negative memory of hospital. Just positive ones of people bringing me presents, having a room with toys. My memories are about the toys.

I had nightmares about dinosaurs eating me, people putting sharp things in my legs. And a recurring dream that my house would burn and I couldn't do anything about it. The main problem was that my books would burn. I remember being with my mum and dad and looking at the house and my books burning, and I tell them, 'My legs are shaking, I can't stop them shaking.'

It's very scary.

That's it. It was a nightmare. It ended like that.

But otherwise, I don't remember anything bad.

All right. So. That's the end of the hospital story.

So, it's all okay.

I've told you everything I remember.

My dad read to me from a very young age. He read me a story before bed every night with one arm round me and one holding the book. He would always fall asleep midway through a sentence. When I got older, I would try to take the book and read it, and he'd gasp and say, 'Oh, no! I was just reading!'

My mum would always help me with maths homework. She was the family rock. Everything was organised and consistent, and she was always there for everything. I can't even imagine a world, which I know is really common now, where my mum didn't drop me off at school, pick me up from school, ask me how my day was, and help me with my homework. To me, she was the model perfect mum.

That doesn't mean she wasn't annoying. Once, I refused to eat my cherry tomatoes and she wouldn't let me leave the table. My dad came home and thought, 'This is silly …' and ate them all. Then, with this big grin on his face, he said, 'Lily's done.'

And when I had just found out something new, like the capital of Peru is Lima, I would say, 'I've got this amazing fact!' And

Mum would say, 'Oh, I know the answer!' Whereas my dad would say, 'Tell me! This is amazing. You're so clever!'

As children, we were learning all the time. I remember asking who Eleanor of Aquitaine was one evening, and Dad got the encyclopaedia down and read to us about it. We'd often end up with about four encyclopaedias out at mealtimes. Dad would say, 'You can have as many books as you like. You get pocket money, but it doesn't have to go on books – I'll buy them.' I thought that was brilliant. All I really wanted was books.

My dad was amazing in not talking over me or my brother. He was always asking us what our view was, and if we didn't have one, he encouraged us to articulate our thoughts.

And he wouldn't let me go to bed angry or upset until I'd talked about it. He would ask explicit questions, like 'How are you feeling?' and 'Why are you feeling that way?' rather than assuming that if I was sad, I would actively seek support and know how to articulate it myself.

If my brother and I were having an argument, we would have to resolve it. And if we weren't resolving it ourselves, he'd come in, sit on the bed and wait while we cried. Sometimes we'd be up really late, even when we were little, and he would make us say sorry to each other, even if we didn't really mean it. He just wanted us to get to the point where we looked like we might mean it in the near future. Then we could go to bed. It was absolutely exhausting.

I think he was trying to get us to practise having those adult conversations in a juvenile way. He probably learned how to do it from my grandparents – they were very happily married for 73 years, and my grandma is quite open about her emotions.

My brother has a very serious condition called myelomeningocele, the most extreme form of spina bifida. He was in hospital the whole time when we were young. I have actually no idea how my parents stayed married given how stressful it must have been for them, never mind how they were so amazing for both of us. Not only did they care for Charlie full-time, but they made sure I felt safe, loved and remembered too.

I knew that my mum or dad would always read me a story before bedtime for as long as I was read stories, regardless of what was going on. And my mum always picked me up from school, which was a really good time to talk to her if I needed to.

My dad was adamant that, if we were all in the same house, meals were eaten together. That's what he had growing up. It was really reassuring knowing that I was coming home and sitting down to dinner, that I had this space that was sacrosanct, without any interruptions, where things could always be aired.

There was something about the security of those routines. There were a lot of things going on in the background with my brother's health, which I now realise must have been all-encompassing for my parents, but my routine didn't change. That stability meant I didn't worry about it.

It wasn't always easy. Mum was always, always saying, 'Be careful of your brother.' I remember feeling so frustrated because I just wanted to go and have fun and play with Charlie and I couldn't do that. I wanted to go kayaking when we were on holiday once – then Charlie wanted to do it too because he wanted to do whatever his big sister did. Mum said, 'He can't do that.' And that meant I couldn't do it either.

Although my brother took up a lot of my parents' emotional time, and I was very aware of that, my parents were very, very, very supportive all the time. I remember when the ambulance came once and I was really, really scared about the noise and hid under the sofa. Mum came to me and said not to worry and Dad gave me a ginormous cuddle – there was something about knowing I hadn't been forgotten and that it was okay.

The best way of synthesising my upbringing is probably being wrapped up in love with an absence of worry. I had permission to be free or happy, rather than fearing that someone may not be there when I needed them.

Strange Situations

Mary Ainsworth was a clinical psychologist and researcher who worked with Bowlby on his research into hospitalised children. She spent a huge amount of time discussing their findings and found it particularly fascinating that the two responses to being separated for a long time were completely opposite – anxious over-dependence on the one hand, and not showing emotions on the other.

Ainsworth and Bowlby worked together for four years, until Ainsworth's husband was offered a job in Uganda. She decided to follow and study the relationships between Ugandan mothers and their babies. She drove from village to village near Kampala to study 26 mother–child pairs, visiting families for two hours, twice a month for nine months. That's a *lot* of hours … One of the first things Ainsworth noticed was the different ways children behaved when their mum was leaving home. They would scramble on to their mum, nestle into her lap, raise their arms or clap to say hello or cry. They'd also cry, smile or make sounds to the person that was going to look after them while their mum was away.

Some babies seemed to be attached to their mothers but didn't cry, follow or cling when it looked like their mum might leave. It's as if the babies felt confident that their mum wouldn't be gone for long or that someone else would be there for them – they would be safe.

Another group of children were clearly attached and seemed to be worried about whether their mother would be there for them but didn't cry, follow or cling when their mother left. These were usually children whose mums didn't respond much when they were upset.

Ainsworth moved to Baltimore, divorced and suffered a miscarriage, and eventually decided to start therapy that lasted eight years. She described it as the most important positive influence on her career because it helped her understand emotions and the way humans try to defend themselves against them. She also thought her grief and longing for a child helped her become more perceptive in paying close attention to the way mothers and their children interacted.

Ainsworth's old mentor, William Blatz, also had a huge impact on her thinking. Blatz thought that, as humans, we feel secure when we believe that it doesn't matter what we do, it won't make it harder for us to get important things like food and rest. He thought that security allowed us to try and fail without worrying, and that by giving a child a secure base, a parent was ultimately helping them live a larger life.

Blatz thought that insecurity, on the other hand, was caused by a worry that our needs might not be met. And those worries would either make us feel anxious or lead us to use psychological defences to avoid the anxiety.

Having observed children and their mothers at home in Uganda, Ainsworth started doing similar research in Baltimore, US. It was incredibly ambitious – until then, most people thought theories about defence mechanisms in young children were something that couldn't be tested. And many thought that studying a child's ability to regulate their emotions was beyond the scope of science.

Undeterred, Ainsworth and her assistants regularly visited families and spent about 72 hours observing them when the children were between 3 weeks and 54 weeks old. As they did most of their visits during office hours, mums were often home with their babies while dads were at work.

The Strange Situation
As well as doing home visits, Ainsworth also created a way of observing a parent and their child in the lab called the 'Strange Situation'. She and her colleagues thought that you only really see the quality and strength of a child's attachment in certain situations. Having spent many hours observing families at home, Ainsworth thought one of these was when a child's mum left the room. And Bowlby thought that, thanks to evolution, being separated from your Important Person for

even a very short amount of time would be a threat. It makes sense – we wouldn't be much use fighting a panther at the ripe old age of 6 months ... much better to stick with an adult who has a better chance of protecting you.

Ainsworth brought the mothers and children into the lab. The children spent three minutes in a playroom they'd never been in, before a stranger entered. Then the mother would leave the room once, then twice, cranking up the activation of the attachment system each time.

Some children didn't seem upset when their mum left, and this reminded Ainsworth of her work with Bowlby and in Uganda. She and her colleagues concluded that the way children behave when they're upset provides an insight into whether they think their Important Person will be there when they need them.

Ainsworth started to think that these children could be put into three groups. Based on her research and the work of her students, 66 per cent of children were classified as secure, 21 per cent as avoidant, and 13 per cent as ambivalent/resistant.

Secure
In the Strange Situation, children in secure relationships generally tried to get (and stay) close to their mum when she returned to the room. And they didn't resist contact.

Instead, they could communicate when they were upset, be comforted and then calmly return to playing. In other words, they seemed to be able to use their mum as a safe haven.

When Ainsworth observed them at home, she saw that mothers of secure children were more able to understand and interpret what their child was telling them, and then respond appropriately and without too much delay. Ainsworth called this 'sensitivity' and believed that, as a result, the children learned that they didn't have to worry about whether their mum would be there for them or not. This meant the children weren't inhibited, angry or conflicted when it came to asking their mother for help or comfort and could instead get back to the important business of playing.

This reminded me of Lily (the girl who was wrapped in love) and her descriptions of how supportive, available and comforting both her parents were, despite also trying to cope with her disabled brother. She described herself as growing up with an absence of worry or fear that someone may not be there when she needed them. In other words, Lily grew up feeling confident that she had access to a safe haven when she needed it, or what Ainsworth called 'secure' attachment.

A quick word on language here. Bowlby told Ainsworth not to use the word 'secure' as it was 'shot through with value judgements', but she went ahead anyway. Subsequent research suggests Bowlby was right. One of Ainsworth's students, Everett Waters, found that psychology students assumed that 'secure' meant confident, and that when Ainsworth called a child 'secure', it meant they were socially dominant. But this is not what Ainsworth meant at all. And she didn't think that security came only from Important People. Instead, she thought we could draw security from a variety of places – like our country's welfare system or our community.

Avoidant

Children in avoidant relationships didn't try to get or stay close to their mother when she returned to the room. Instead, at exactly the moment when other children would show that they were upset, avoidant children focused their attention on toys. They didn't try to investigate the toys. Instead, they banged them about or threw them before picking them up again. It was as if they were using the toys to distract themselves from anything that might activate their attachment system.

This reminded me of Amos (the boy who couldn't remember), whose main memory of spending huge amounts of time in hospital was the toys. And I wondered whether he was focusing on the toys – both back then but also when talking to me about hospital – as a way of avoiding getting upset.

But the behaviour of avoidant children was not the same in the laboratory as it was at home. In the Strange Situation, avoidant children tried to limit showing how upset they were. At home, they became upset and frustrated more often than the rest of the children in the study.

They also tried to get close to their mum far more often, but their creeping, crawling or walking was usually tentative. They half-approached their mum before stopping, or went the whole way only to touch her, rather than go in for a full hug. And when they did manage to get very close, they didn't sink in or relax comfortably against their mother's body. In other words, they didn't seem confident that they could use their mother as a safe haven.

Ainsworth thought avoidant babies behaved in this way to protect themselves from experiencing the rejection, intrusion or frustration they'd come to expect when they tried to get close to their mum. Instead, they tuned into the neutral world of 'things' to avoid activating their attachment system. This helped them maintain some sort of balance by blocking out their worries and need for comfort – both from their mother and themselves. It also allowed them to be physically near, albeit not very close to, their mum.

Later research by one of Ainsworth's students, Everett Waters, and Alan Sroufe provided some evidence for this idea. When they took the heart-rate recordings of children with an avoidant attachment pattern, they found that their heart rates increased when they were reunited with their Important Person. Waters and Sroufe took this to mean that despite the unruffled behaviour of the children, they were having a strong emotional reaction – after all, if you were indifferent, your heart rate probably wouldn't increase.

Ambivalent/resistant

Ambivalent/resistant attachment was the fuzziest of the three groups, which led to some people criticising it. It didn't help that, when observing ambivalent/resistant children at home, Ainsworth and her colleagues didn't find many differences to secure children – except that they were upset more often both at home and in the lab. Even so, she defended its integrity.

Ainsworth and her colleagues thought that the ambivalent/resistant child worries that they won't get enough of what they want, and the avoidant child worries about what they want. In other words, the ambivalent/resistant child isn't sure their mother will give the comfort and protection they want, whereas the avoidant child is worried that showing what they want won't work, or worse, will irritate her. Either way, neither child is confident that they have a safe haven when they need it.

In the Strange Situation, ambivalent/resistant children were upset when their mum left the room, but when she came back, they continued to be frustrated, weren't comforted and couldn't find a way to get back to playing. Ainsworth suspected that these children had caregivers who had difficulty holding their child in mind.

They often failed to pick them up when they most wanted it, and often put them down long before they were ready. So the child knew that their Important Person could be available *sometimes*, they just didn't know *when*. As a result, their attachment system was activated more easily, at the same time as being harder to switch off. Then, when this strategy led to the child getting a response, it was reinforced.

Ainsworth thought that, while the child wanted to be close to their mum, this desire was also mixed with anger because they didn't expect their mum to react in the right way or at all. So they wanted their mum to be there for them and were angry if she wasn't.

This reminded me of Skyler (the girl wrapped in cotton wool). She described her mum as being overprotective to the point of suffocation – but when Skyler actually needed comfort, she didn't get it. In other words, she didn't get what she needed. And she found this incredibly frustrating.

What about the interviewees?
There's no way of knowing what classification each interviewee would have had if they'd taken part in the Strange Situation and were observed at home: we can't go back in time. There's also no way of knowing the attachment patterns of their Important People because, even if we carried out AAIs with them now, their classification may not have been the same back then. People change.

The same goes for the interviewees. We can conduct AAIs with each of them (and I did – which I talk about in Chapter Four), but that can only tell us what their classification is now. In fact, it doesn't even tell us that – it tells us what a coder thought their words on that particular day at that particular time said about the way they thought about attachment. It certainly can't tell us what their attachment pattern was as they were growing up. And that assumes that attachment patterns are fixed throughout childhood, when research suggests that's not actually the case.

Bowlby and Ainsworth thought that our expectations of how available others will be when we need them were pretty robust over life. But research suggests they aren't quite as stable as they thought. In a huge review of more than 21,000 Strange Situations, researchers found that there was plenty of room for change in attachment patterns over a five-year period. But this review only relied on research that was published, as reviews usually do.

And published research doesn't always paint the full picture. Researchers were less likely to publish studies where attachment wasn't stable over time – so when Jessica Opie and her colleagues reviewed published *and* unpublished research, attachment was even *less* stable and there was even *more* room for change.

Ainsworth recognised that attachment could change. If a parent were to receive more support and were then able to change the way they interacted with their child, she thought their attachment pattern would also shift. But Ainsworth also thought that a child's experience of having a safe haven might still be relevant to their later life, even if their relationship with their parent did change. And a review of research echoes this – as secure attachments were much more likely to be stable than insecure. If this is true, then children seem more likely to keep a sense of *having* a safe haven, than of *not* having one.

What could all of this mean for our interviewees? Well, when Ray was sent away to Bangladesh at the age of 2, it would have impacted how available he felt his parents were, as they were no longer in the same country. We can't be sure what he experienced or expected before or after. But we can infer that his expectations might have changed.

Ray didn't have memories of what it felt like to leave his parents for Bangladesh – which is unsurprising, given he was only 2 when it happened. But he also doesn't have many memories of when he came back, aged 5. He described feeling 'almost callous' because he didn't remember feeling anything when he left his mum or grandma, or strong memories of being attached to anyone.

Could this be evidence of him distracting himself from anything that might activate his attachment system? Of blocking out his worries and his need for comfort to maintain some sort of balance? If so, did he develop avoidant tendencies – at least by the time he arrived back in Scotland from Bangladesh – because he didn't think he'd have a safe haven when he needed one?

Bowlby, Robertson and Ainsworth noticed that some of the children who'd been hospitalised for long periods without their parents rejected their mothers when they were reunited. When Ray returned from Bangladesh and saw his mum for the first time, he said, 'I don't want to stay here because that's not my mum.'

But do we really have enough information to reach any conclusions, no matter how vague? The hospitalisation research was anecdotal. And in both cases, we're relying on Ray's memories, which may or may not be accurate. Plus, we're only hearing his side of the story, not watching him and how he reacts to his Important People both in a laboratory and at home. Also, children develop different attachments with each Important Person in their life, and as we've seen, these attachments can change over time. So there's unlikely to be a single, simple attachment story that can be crafted from Ray's life.

What about the relationships Skyler (the girl wrapped in cotton wool) had with her parents? She said her mum didn't give the 'right kind of comfort'. She wasn't allowed to talk about the loss of her sibling, and when she cried every time she missed a goal, her dad would tell her to suck it up. So when she was upset, it seems she didn't get the comfort or support she needed. Neither her mum nor her dad showed the sensitivity that Ainsworth thought was so important, and Skyler didn't seem to feel she had a safe haven.

And what about Amos (the boy who couldn't remember)? Did his descriptions of an angry and rejecting mum mean he didn't feel he could go to her when he needed comfort? And what about his focus on the toys during his hospital stints as a child … Was he distracting himself to avoid getting upset, to avoid wanting a safe haven he wasn't sure he'd get?

Or Lily (the girl wrapped in love) – when the ambulance came and Lily hid under the sofa, her mum recognised that she needed support, and both she and Lily's father comforted her. The comforting worked: Lily knew she hadn't been forgotten and it was okay. Both of her parents seemed sensitive to her needs and gave her a safe haven when she needed it. And as that happened over and over again, Lily grew up knowing that her Important People would be there when she needed them. This is Ainsworth's definition of secure attachment.

Whatever the interviewees learned to expect from their Important People when they were young, one thing we can probably agree on is that they wouldn't have come to expect the same thing. It makes complete sense that a child would come to expect very different things from Lily's parents compared to Skyler's or Amos's, or after being sent abroad like Ray. Even within a family, you can see how Skyler might develop very different expectations of her mum and dad – as they each responded to her in different ways.

Ainsworth's use of the word 'secure' has encouraged a general understanding that secure attachment is the ideal, something to be aimed for and compared against, the highest grade possible in the attachment exams, the all-clear when you've been to the dentist.

Even if secure attachment is better in the long term (which I'll discuss throughout the book), in the short term the other patterns might be the best option available to you as a child. Children have no control over the circumstances they're born into; all they can do is find the best way of responding to that environment and the people within it. If you realise that asking your Important Person for help leads to rejection or punishment, it's a wise move to stop asking for help. Particularly if that means that you can, at the very least, stay vaguely physically close to them.

It might be problematic decades later when you really do need to ask for help or express how upset you are because the difficulties coming at you are far too big for any one human to cope with alone, or there's a gulf between you and your romantic partner. You might find it shaming to ask for help, or worry that sharing feelings will lead to rejection.

But in that moment, in those early years, learning not to ask may be the best option available to you.

It might be the only option.

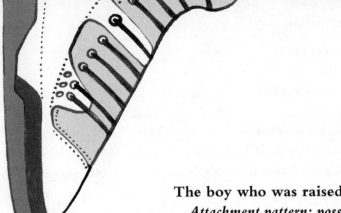

Elija

The boy who was raised by wolves
Attachment pattern: possibly insecure

My dad was my mum's first serious boyfriend. They were in the honeymoon period when the ... the mistake happened.

It's scary. Even now getting pregnant by somebody you actually like, no racism elements anywhere, that in itself is scary as fuck, let alone it happening by accident, there's a Black man involved – when Black men weren't allowed in the house – and Grandpa doesn't know you're sexually active.

I found out I was an accident when me and my mum was having a heated argument. And she says, 'You're the biggest mistake of my life, you was!'

I was saying some stuff that I shouldn't of, and she was hurt by that and wanted to hurt me back, as arguments go sometimes.

When things eventually calmed down, I said, 'What do you mean I'm a mistake? Was I a mistake?'

My mum and dad were having sex and the condom split. My mum talked to my grandma about abortion. My mum didn't want to, my grandma wanted it and my grandpa definitely did, he's a very racist man.

So that's how I'm here. And that's how I found out.

Heavy way to find out.

But accidents can be good …

I don't feel like it's affected me that much. I was 8 and it didn't plague me in any way. If you'd have told me when I was younger, it might've held substance in my life.

I wouldn't call my kid a mistake if it happened to me. 'Unexpected' is the word I would use. That's a nicer way of putting it. 'An unexpected surprise.'

Falling pregnant with me at 15 and having me at 16 was difficult. I remember my mum telling me stories of Dad not being around when I was a baby and never really supporting with money. So my mum struggled.

A lot of arguments were over money. They were earning just enough to survive – or Dad was earning more but wasn't telling. We were living month to month.

The first week if I asked my mum for sweets, she'd say, 'All right, what sweets do you want?' The fourth week, 'Mum, can I have some sweets?' 'No!' It's not that I'd done anything wrong or she was angry at me, she was probably frustrated that I couldn't have this 50p chocolate bar.

She had to pay for the gas and electric, if she didn't pay, we had to turn a key thing, back in the day, and it would just click off. 'Elija, go and push the emergency button.' And next day, 'Elija, run down to the shop,' after all night with no electricity.

I would say, 'Mum, I need some new shoes for basketball, can we go and get some?' Then we'd have to wait till the end of the month till she got paid. The end of the month would come and she'd say, 'You have to wait till next month or go and ask your dad.' Never went and asked Dad. Never went to ask him. I was really scared.

So at the end of the next month, I would get my basketball shoes, by which point, all the hype has worn off, they're not special anymore, everybody's got them already. So I was always behind in the hype of getting something new that I really liked.

My family was really strong, really stuck together. It was like a pack of wolves.

My mum was always strong on discipline. Usually when I was naughty, she would scream at me, 'Go to your room and watch gymnastics!' I'd go there and put the videos on, listen to the music and watch wicked moves. That was my punishment. I think that subliminally infused a love of the sport.

If I was really bad, acting up, Mum would say, 'I'm telling your dad.' And I'd say, 'No Mum, no Mum, please don't.' I would be so scared I'd straight away be on best behaviour, good as gold. And as my dad walked through the door, my eyes would be screaming, 'Please don't tell Dad, please don't tell him.'

Nine times out of 10 she didn't. She realised soon, and quickly, that telling Dad was not the best option.

'Ah, anytime I tell Dad, my son gets beaten the fuck out of. Maybe I'll stop telling Dad now.'

Matt
The boy with the stiff upper lip
Attachment pattern: possibly insecure

Zimbabwe 17c

BY AIR MAIL PAR AVION

Our house had a massive garden with a swimming pool that we played in all the time, it was beautiful. My older brother, David, would feed the monkeys – apparently we fought a lot when we were young, but I don't remember.

The dining room led out on to the garden, and because it was often nice weather I'd be outside, and Mum would be inside playing the violin or writing letters to her friends.

We had a live-in nanny – it was quite common for white families in Zimbabwe. Often the nannies stay in the house for 30-plus years. Her name was Ambuya. Well, that wasn't her real name but that's what we called her. Ambuya means 'grandmother' in Shona and she was very much like a part of the family. She was patient, loving, dependable, warm, calm and kind. And she liked to hang bread on the washing line to turn into toast in the sun.

My dad was in the navy and wasn't around as much. I can't remember weekends with him at all, I can't remember him being around. But I remember Mum more or less always being there if I needed her. It was reassuring to know that she was nearby, even if I was outside in the garden all day.

I wrote a regular diary throughout my childhood and when she's not there, I say things are really, really boring. When I was 8, I wrote this:

'This is just a boring old day, which normally happens when Mum's at the gym. I've got about a million questions for her, so I've got to wait until she gets back. We're hardly doing anything today, so I shouldn't bother taking my pyjamas off. Lunch was the remains of the chilli con carne.'

I don't know what I actually meant by boring, because I would be doing the same things whether she was there or not. Maybe boring was a word I used to replace a different word, like empty.

Mum laid down the law and we always listened (until we were much taller than her). Can you imagine six- or seven-hour car journeys with four boys in the back fighting the whole time?! We often had the threats of 'Stop fighting, otherwise we're going to drop you by the side of the road and carry on.' I always wondered if that would actually ever happen, particularly for Dave because he was the naughty one. It never did happen though, sadly.

I just don't know what Dad was doing as I don't remember him being there much. Maybe he stayed home when Mum was taking us places, or maybe he was out cycling a lot on the weekends.

We just wouldn't have any interaction with him. We never talked to him about anything on a day-to-day basis. It would always be Mum first and then if we got punished or did something really bad, we would go to him. It was a very old-school relationship.

Neither he nor Mum were proactive in showing affection or giving emotional support and nourishment. They never asked how I was feeling and I don't remember either of them hugging or holding me when I was upset or unwell. They both had incredibly stiff upper lips.

Zimbabwe was a pretty hairy place to live at the time – but there was no discussion around how we felt as kids living in a dangerous country. The violence was increasing and I clearly remember a story in the papers where a kid hid himself in a trunk while his whole family got killed. They didn't kill him because they didn't know he was in the trunk, and then he ended up living with his grandparents.

I was always hypothesising, 'If everyone did get toasted, where would I go and live?' Oddly, that seemed normal. Our neighbours got burgled, the people that lived opposite us got shot, I was acutely aware of the violence.

And my parents never asked how that felt.

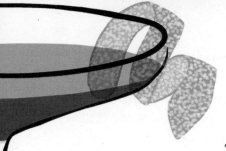

Zsa Zsa

The girl who walked into fire
Attachment pattern: possibly insecure

As a young child, I was in awe of my mother. She was this intelligent, fierce woman who used to wear fancy suits when she went to work. She was amazing. I always used to laugh, because she would pick me up from school and have the music really loud. She was pleased to see me and I felt grateful she was picking me up and that she wanted us both to have a nice time.

But when my dad was around, she wasn't like that.

Our relationship was definitely loving.
But at the same time,   insufficiently so.

I think a kicker is when I became acutely aware of how much she was drinking. Not just how much she was drinking, but how much it ended up in screaming matches with my dad,
        my dad throwing things and breaking things,
        my mum breaking things.

There's a definite memory I have of my dad picking up a wine glass and hurling it across a room, then swiping everything off the table. I've no idea how old I was …

I felt scared as a child when my parents argued. They argued a lot.

I don't know how I became aware that she was drinking, but I would come home from school and check the dishwasher and regularly used to find a tumbler that smelt of wine. And it was the only thing in the dishwasher, 'cause our housekeeper by that point had cleared it, so there should have been nothing in it.

I would find empty bottles – she kept them in the top drawer in the spare room, the same place where she'd hide my presents. As a child, you look for the presents. And regularly, I'd find empty bottles in there. Empty plastic bottles.

My parents had a big sort of   fucking, you know, crystal decanter fucking display of, you know, fine and rare whatever bullshit they had. You know, it was sort of like part and parcel of living in, you know, a fancy house that it had fancy drinks.

And yet my mum was drinking out of plastic.

As a child, I don't remember being worried about it. I just couldn't understand why my mother was acting differently, why she was somebody else. Finding the bottles and tumblers made me feel like she was definitely hiding something. And that made me feel distant from her.

It's really hard to know when I became aware that alcohol was the difference. It's really hard because as a child, you're not drinking alcohol. You don't know what effect it has.

I remember my mum crying. And I remember her crying quite a lot.

I remember one time hearing them shouting and screaming upstairs. My dad upended my mum's handbag, tipping out all the contents into the hall from the top of the staircase. She was crying. She was obviously drunk.

As a child I'm trying to get my dad to stop screaming, conscious that he probably just hit her prior to this and having no idea what to do about it, apart from just shout at them both to stop.

And I think to myself …
        'How on earth were they helping me with what I was going through at school, or my homework, or anything, if that's what the evenings looked like?'

I don't remember how often it happened, but I don't ever remember calm. I don't ever remember there
        not being that noise in the house, some sort of noise as to why things weren't right, or someone was unhappy.

I feel like our relationship was insufficiently loving because it was insufficiently aware of what fundamentally a child needs to feel confident and happy and able to go about their life, if   that's the environment they live in.   And with it happening not just once, but repeatedly. It almost felt …   feels   not premeditated, because I think that she probably doesn't have control over it, but at the same time,   'If you, if you love me as your daughter, why do you act like this?'

Every time my mum was abhorrently drunk, she'd write me a lovely note the next day, saying how sorry she was and how much she loved me.

As a child, when you're processing things you think, 'We tell each other we love each other, therefore we love each other. So this is love, yeah this is what it is, yeah I've got it.' You don't feel that same sense of threat with your mother drinking or your father potentially walloping you, because these are also the people who provide for you and look after you and are supposed to be there for you.

I hate being frightened now. I hate it. But as a child, I remember thinking that I wanted to put my finger in the flame.

My dad was constantly telling me I was fireproof. His philosophy was, 'Fuck you, I'm fireproof.' It wasn't a physical thing – it was emotional. The idea wasn't necessarily that the material that he and I were made of was fireproof, but that we were sufficiently fire-retardant that we could recover from any pain. We could deal with anything.

Why would anyone want to be fireproof?! Surely you would want to protect your children and keep them away from flames rather than encourage them to walk straight in?!

So when I was little, I always told myself I was so robust I could   walk into fire. Even though inherently I knew I couldn't. I didn't avoid situations that I knew would make me feel bad. I just fought fires as I found them, because I was fireproof.

There was an exhilaration in being frightened. And I remember being frightened quite a lot. I was fearful of my parents fighting. I had a deep-rooted fear that he would hurt her.

I remember being on holiday in Croatia once and being absolutely convinced that my parents were watching a football match in their hotel room. In fact, they were screaming at each other. When I woke up in the morning, my mum was in my bed.

There were actually quite a lot of mornings at home where I woke up and my mum was in my bed.

Saying it now, I think, 'Oh, that's weird.'

Throughout my childhood, my mum moved out and went to stay with her friend. I don't know how long she moved out for each time, but she definitely left the house. She left us with Dad.

I'm 100 per cent certain that I've just suppressed how all of this made me feel. Or maybe I didn't have the words to describe it as a child. My memories are all very factual, but I feel like it probably did make me pretty fucking distressed.

As a child, how do you deal with a situation like that?

I wonder if I ever thought, 'I shouldn't have to deal with this.'

I wonder whether or not it was the stress of having a child that made my parents fight.

I wonder if it was me.

My dad would say, 'She gets very stressed when she thinks about you, she gets very, very tense.' Then they would go on holiday without me, they did that a lot, and Mum would be quote, unquote, 'fine'. 'What, is it my behaviour that makes her drink? Is it my behaviour that makes you fight?' It's like, the person who's doing it almost tells you you're responsible, right?

Adverse childhood experiences: the Minnesota Study

The interviewees suffered a variety of what psychologists call adverse childhood experiences, or ACEs. Elija (the boy who was raised by wolves) grew up in a home where he both suffered and witnessed abuse; Matt (the boy with the stiff upper lip) grew up in a country overwhelmed by conflict; Ray (the boy who was sent away) was separated from his parents when he was sent to Bangladesh; and Zsa Zsa (the girl who walked into fire) grew up with domestic violence, substance abuse, repeated separations from her mum and potentially emotional neglect. Some also went on to experience their parents' divorce and mental illness.

There's no single agreed list of ACEs, but most would include the ones I've just described, as well as suffering other forms of neglect or the death or imprisonment of Someone Important. Another form of adverse childhood experiences is poverty, which Ray and Elija grew up in.

ACEs are common. In US research spanning 23 states, around 61 per cent of the 214,000 adults questioned said they'd experienced at least one type of ACE before turning 18 years old. Almost one in six said they'd experienced four or more. And as the number of ACEs increases, so does the likelihood of their negative impact.

ACEs are expensive. Research suggests that reducing them by 10 per cent in North America alone could save hundreds of billions of dollars a year. Hundreds. Of. Billions. That's because they're linked to chronic health problems, mental illness, substance abuse, teen pregnancy, cancer, diabetes, heart disease, suicide … and the list goes on. They can also have a negative impact on education, employment and earning potential.

That's not to say ACEs always lead to all these things. There are plenty of factors that can negate their impact that I'll discuss throughout the book. Similarly, there are lots of factors other than childhood adversity that can lead to these problems. But there is a link between each of them and ACEs, a link that comes up again and again and again in the research.

Most research into ACEs is carried out using questionnaires that ask adults about their childhood experiences. This has its benefits – it's cheap and simple to do and easy to repeat with huge numbers of people around the world. And decision makers love large numbers. But it also has its limitations – for example, some people may not want to admit to having experienced ACEs growing up because they're worried about judgement or stigma. And some may have buried their painful past in a way that means they can't consciously remember – or admit to – having suffered.

Remember Waters and Sroufe's research with children with an avoidant attachment relationship? They didn't try to get or stay close to their mum when she came back into the room as part of the Strange Situation – but their heart rates increased. If a child can learn to hide difficult feelings from themselves and others, an adult sure as hell can.

On top of that, questionnaires given to the adults of today relate to the childhoods of the past, so there's a limit to what they can tell us about childhoods right now.

The absolute best way to assess the impact of ACEs and attachment in the long term is to follow children from before they're born and get contemporaneous information from the nurses present at their birth, their teachers at preschool and beyond, parents, medical records, summer camps, observations of the children, films of them coded by multiple researchers, assessments, their romantic partners once they start dating, observations of the couples together, and then the children that these grown-up children go on to have themselves. It's complex, it's arduous, it's costly. But it's incredibly valuable because, as well as measuring virtually everything it can get its hands on, this sort of research looks forward instead of looking back. This is what the Minnesota Longitudinal Study of Risk and Adaptation did – and does.

The study transformed attachment theory. It was all very well Bowlby and Ainsworth telling the world that early relationships were influential in the long term, but they lacked the evidence to back that up. And many people didn't buy into the idea that early experiences had any sort of lasting impact.

By demonstrating that they did, the Minnesota Study showed why Ainsworth's findings mattered and forced people to take early childhood experiences seriously. It was such a game changer that in 1982 Ainsworth wrote to one of the key people behind the study, Alan Sroufe, to say that one of the very best things that ever happened to attachment research was his decision to take part in it.

The birth of the Minnesota Study
In his early work, Bowlby zoomed in on the importance of being separated from Someone Important in your life. In doing so, he deliberately avoided talking publicly about child abuse as it was such a taboo subject. It was the 1940s and Bowlby felt that a report on just how common abuse was among children referred to his clinic would be scandalous, and that the public and medical community wouldn't accept it. Separations could be documented more reliably, so would make it easier to persuade the scientific community of the importance of children's early experiences with their Important People, as well as their emotional impact.

Bowlby hoped that later researchers, who had better tools and lived in a society that was more honest about family life, would scientifically study child abuse – and how to prevent it. But it was a decision that weighed on him. In the last interview before he died, he said that he was appalled at how ignorant he and other psychoanalysts and psychiatrists had been about physical and sexual abuse.

By the 1970s, people recognised the possibility of child abuse and neglect. They were also increasingly interested in

the relationship between abuse and mental illness later on –
although astonishingly, some still questioned whether it was
actually harmful to children's development or not.

So, in the face of this debate, Byron Egeland, Amos Deinard
and Ellen Elkin began the Minnesota Study. It was the world's
first attempt to carry out a study of child abuse that looked
forward, rather than asking people later in life about their past
experiences. Decades later, their belief in the importance of
studying children from early on was backed up. As the
children that they knew had suffered abuse got older, only
half actually reported it when asked by the researchers.

Let me just repeat that to make sure you didn't miss it: the
Minnesota Group knew which children were being abused
because they had contemporaneous evidence of it, often in
multiple forms – medical records, observations, teacher
reports, *etc.* Of the children that researchers knew had been
abused, only half actually reported it when they were asked
about it when they were older. This means that research that
relies on adults describing their childhoods is likely to
drastically under-report the prevalence of abuse.

Egeland and his colleagues enlisted 267 pregnant women
living in poverty and tried to measure the many adversities
they faced, including domestic violence, mental health
problems and substance use. The ages of the mums when
they gave birth ranged from 12 to 32 years old. An average
of just over 20.86 per cent of the pregnancies were
unplanned, 41 per cent of the mums hadn't finished high
school and 59 per cent were single when they gave birth,
when the national average was 13 per cent at the time. And
only 13 per cent of the dads were living in the same home
as their children by the time they were 18 months old. On
top of this, the mums were often isolated and had little
social support.

Ainsworth's former student Everett Waters carried out a
parallel study of 50 mothers and their children in Minnesota
who were better off. Having this comparison group meant

that on top of everything else, the researchers could explore the impact of poverty.

Egeland soon brought his colleague, Alan Sroufe, on board. And together with their students, they carried out the Strange Situation with the mother and baby pairs. In line with Ainsworth's findings, Important People who were sensitive when playing with their babies or feeding them were more likely to have infants who behaved in secure ways towards them in the Strange Situation. The link was not as strong as it was in Ainsworth's research, but it was there, and it backed up her findings.

The Minnesota Study Group also found that children were more likely to have a secure relationship with their mums if their mums had fewer stresses or adversities. So if life stress was reduced, a child's attachment relationship and the care they received was likely to improve. If life stress increased, their care was likely to become less sensitive and the attachment relationship more insecure.

As a result, the Minnesota Group argued strongly against parent-blaming. When people think about attachment, they often think about the child and their Important Person. But the attachment between the two is massively influenced by family circumstances and the amount of stress and adversity they face.

Parents operate in a wider context. And without that context, you can't fully understand either them or their parenting. Much like you can't understand Ray's parents or their decision to send him to Bangladesh unless you understand that they were immigrants living in poverty and working multiple jobs in a country where they had no family support. Would they have sent Ray away if they'd had more money or support? I doubt it.

Maltreatment and neglect
In the Minnesota Study, 31 of the children were maltreated. And of these, a hefty 62 per cent had an insecure attachment

pattern. This was much higher than the 34 per cent of the middle-class mothers and children that Ainsworth had studied. And the earlier the maltreatment began, the more likely the child was to be classified as insecure.

This made me think of Zsa Zsa (the girl who walked into fire) and Elija (the boy who was raised by wolves), who were both maltreated from a young age. The Minnesota findings suggest that this maltreatment would increase the likelihood of having an insecure attachment pattern. And this makes perfect sense. Secure attachment means growing up with Someone Important who provides you with a consistent, reliable safe haven. A relationship where your Important Person is maltreating you is unlikely to give you that. Instead, the person who would ideally provide you with comfort and safety provides you with danger.

Ainsworth and the Minnesota Group were studying very different groups of people. Ainsworth had worked with comfortable, middle-class white women in stable relationships with fewer adversities. Whereas the Minnesota Study involved mostly young, single mums who had little access to education, were living in poverty and were often isolated with little social support. So it's no surprise that the Minnesota Group had way more insecure children than Ainsworth did in her research, and they explained this by arguing that poverty and other adversities made insecure attachment more likely.

The Minnesota Group also found that half of the children that were neglected had ambivalent/resistant relationships with their mums. When they looked at these in more detail, they found a high level of substance use, which made it more difficult for the mums to hold their child in mind.

People define neglect differently, but a common understanding is that it's the persistent failure to meet a child's basic physical and/or psychological needs. It can happen during pregnancy as a result of substance abuse. And it can happen once a child is born when an Important Person fails to protect them from physical and emotional danger, or does not ensure they're being looked after or given medical care and treatment when they need it. It can also include a lack of adequate food, clothing or shelter or the neglect of a child's basic emotional needs.

This reminded me of Zsa Zsa (the girl who walked into fire). Unlike the children in the Minnesota Study, Zsa Zsa grew up in relative financial privilege. But that doesn't mean she grew up with emotional privilege or that her home life was free from adversity. Zsa Zsa didn't ever remember calm. Her memories were mostly of her mother being drunk, things being smashed and her parents arguing loudly and violently. The people who would have ideally provided her with comfort and safety posed a threat.

Neglect can be difficult to spot because it's about proving a negative – the failure to do something, to act or to care adequately for a child. It's easier to notice when that failure is physical and visible – a child turning up at school with lice over and over again, for example. But when the neglect is emotional, it's harder to pin down. It can also be harder to identify or take seriously when a child lives in comparable financial privilege. But financial privilege and emotional privilege are very different and don't go hand in hand.

The Minnesota Study findings are relevant to Zsa Zsa's life for two reasons. Firstly, there was a link between substance abuse and neglect – and Zsa Zsa's mum was an alcoholic. But as well as growing up with more wealth than the children in the Minnesota Study, Zsa Zsa grew up with two parents, not one. This means that, theoretically, her dad could have buffered against the neglect that can come from a substance-abusing parent. Although, at least in Zsa Zsa's early life, the evidence suggests he was pretty neglectful and abusive himself.

Secondly, if her mum's substance abuse meant she struggled to hold her daughter in mind, this would have impacted her ability to make her daughter feel like she had a safe haven when she needed it. The Minnesota findings suggest that Zsa Zsa may have been more likely to have had an ambivalent/resistant relationship with her as a result.

The Minnesota Group tested children at both 10 days old and 3 months old. And they found that children that were neglected emotionally or whose parents were psychologically unavailable had average scores for mental and motor development. But by the time they were 6 months old, their development was delayed. Then, with every assessment, they went on to fall further and further behind from the rest of the children taking part in the study.

Knowing what we know now about neuroscience, this isn't surprising – the first years of life are fundamental to brain development. But back when the Minnesota Study began, people still questioned whether our early experiences actually had an impact or not. So these concrete, forward-looking findings were huge.

By the time they were 17 years old, most of the children that were neglected emotionally met the criteria for a psychiatric disorder. They were more likely than the other people taking part in the study to meet the criteria for an anxiety disorder, and more than twice as likely to meet the criteria for a conduct disorder or post-traumatic stress disorder (PTSD).

So, what could this mean for Zsa Zsa's life? Well, if her parents were unavailable or she was emotionally neglected growing up, the Minnesota findings suggest that she would be more likely to struggle with her mental health during her teens – and beyond. And she did.

Preschool
The Minnesota Group came up with ingenious ways of studying children, and one of them was to create a preschool that lasted 20 weeks. They made two classes from children who had the same Strange Situation classification at 12 and 18 months, and made sure they included children with each of the different attachment patterns.

Again, their findings were fascinating. Children whose relationships had been classified as secure had lots of positive interactions with teachers and asked for help when they were upset, ill or hurt. Those who'd been classified as ambivalent/resistant constantly tried to get close to the teacher and claim their attention.

Avoidant children, on the other hand, were the only children to frustrate the teacher so much that they were sent into a corner. They didn't try to get close to their teachers, except when it wasn't very intimate, like during large group time. And they often withdrew to a secluded spot when they were disappointed or physically hurt.

This reminded me of Amos (the boy who couldn't remember). As we'll discover, he regularly frustrated his schoolteachers so much that he was sent out of class. It also reminded me of Ray (the boy who was sent away), who said that when he was upset, he would either go to his mum, deal with it himself quietly, or cry in a corner or in his room. While he did sometimes go to his mum, he didn't always – and crying alone or dealing with it by himself suggests he didn't always feel he had a safe haven to turn to.

In the preschool, both avoidant and ambivalent/resistant children found making and keeping friends more difficult than secure children. Instead, they often hung around teachers during playtime. When secure children played or made up stories, they usually came up with positive solutions to serious problems. For example, if someone in the story was hurt, they were taken to hospital and felt better. Avoidant children, on the other hand, were less likely to come up with this sort of story. Instead, their imaginary play lacked almost any humans.

And when children were asked to draw their family, avoidant children's artwork featured people with more emotional distance, tension or anger between them, who were more likely to have their arms rigidly held at their sides rather than holding hands.

The Minnesota Study has now been running for over 40 years, and I'll be coming back to it throughout the book to follow the children that took part, in the same way that I'll be following the interviewees. It'll allow us to see whether the interviewees followed the same paths as children in the study that had similar experiences to them. And if they didn't follow the same path, it'll allow us to explore the events or people that may have changed their predicted direction in life.

The Minnesota Study raises all sorts of questions in relation to our interviewees' lives. Given Amos's and Ray's echoes of the avoidant children at preschool, would their relationships with their Important People have been classified as avoidant when they were little? Or perhaps the more pertinent question is: as children, did they think they'd have a safe haven when they needed one? Or did they think support from their Important People would not readily be available? Or that if it was, it wouldn't be helpful or comforting? And what about in later life? Would they be classified with the adult equivalent of avoidance in their AAI?

What about Zsa Zsa and Elija? Instead of providing a safe haven when they needed it, their fathers posed a danger and threat. Would they have been classified as insecure, like most of the maltreated children that took part in the study? And would this also be the case in their AAIs? And what about Zsa Zsa's mental health – would it suffer in line with the Minnesota findings?

We can never know the answer to some of those questions. But what we can be sure of, thanks to the work of the Minnesota Group, is that each of the interviewees' early relationships is likely to have had a vast and lasting impact on their lives.

Just as our own do.

CHAPTER TWO

Late Childhood

Ray

The boy who was sent away
Attachment pattern: possibly avoidant

As I got older, I started to realise how little money we had when I was little. My brother was born into privilege but when I was born, we were actually quite poor by modern standards.

By the time I was 8, things were reasonably good on the finance front. Dad had set up his own cleaning business and, thanks to a lot of luck, good management, and good friends and employers who were really supportive, it was doing quite well.

He and Mum bought their first house, and a kid called Luca lived next door. His dad used to shout and get drunk and beat up his wife and beat up Luca.

So Luca used to spend a lot of time at our house. He came round weekends, afternoons, school holidays, the works. Mum used to invite him to everything. He's the quiet, expressionless, beautiful child in all the family photos.

I don't remember being particularly close to him. He was just always there and around. It was later on that I worked out why.

I don't remember how often the shouting happened. I don't remember any bruising, but I know Luca was beaten up frequently. I don't know how frequently. I can't say weekly, but that's what it was in my head.

I've never spoken about Luca before.

I don't remember meeting Luca's dad. But I remember feeling lucky that I didn't have a dad who was about and drunk and shouty and abusive.

I remember his mum was soft-spoken but not frail. Just normal-sized.

Luca went along with everything we did. Same with all the kids in the street, he just went along with everything. If we were playing a game and wanted to dress him up as something, we knew we could because he would just do it. He would be whatever we wanted him to be.

As I got older, my life became tangibly more privileged. I started doing more and more things – taking up sports, going on holidays, going to a better school. It felt like I was leaving him behind.

Then, as Dad's business did better and better, we finally moved house. That was it. It was inevitable that we would move, and Luca wouldn't.

It was like we were on different trajectories and Luca was always how I could have ended up, under slightly different circumstances.

My parents did well. Got away. Did better for themselves and I benefited from that.

But I could have been a Luca. Not because of my dad being violent, which he wasn't, but because Luca represented a stage of our life that a lot of people didn't get out of: living in poverty.

I don't know what happened to him. But I often wonder.

And ever since, I've always been on the lookout for a Luca.

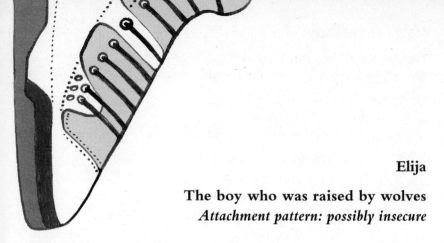

Elija

The boy who was raised by wolves
Attachment pattern: possibly insecure

My father was a very, very scary man.

I woke up in the middle of the night once to screams, bangs, crashes, saucepans. I was probably about 8. What do you do in that moment? Do you get out of bed?

You hear the saucepans flying around, glass in the kitchen. 'You fucking idiot,' 'Shut the fuck up,' 'Get out of my face.' Do you get up and run the risk of being hit by a saucepan as you walk around the corner? Do you run the risk of treading on glass? Is your dad gonna beat you because you shouldn't be out of bed?

As an 8-year-old, I just lay there. Your body freezes sometimes. Your body wants to go and your brain says, 'What are you doing? Stay in bed. It's not for you downstairs. You don't need to see that.'

So you just hear it. Which is almost more traumatising because then you start to imagine what's going on – and with imagination, anything's possible. Sometimes your imagination can portray it as worse than it is. If I heard glass smash, I would be wondering, 'Who's cut?' Whereas if I saw the glass fly across the room and smash on the kitchen floor, I'd know nobody's cut, it's just smashed on the floor. Your imagination can really mess you up sometimes.

The next day I wouldn't ask questions. Was I allowed to ask? Was I old enough to ask? Was it any of my business to ask? Mum never used to confide in me and say, 'Your dad beat me up last night,' de-de-duh.

When I got a little bit older, I remember Dad had been out late doing the dirty and Mum lost it. She knocked him out with a saucepan and I had to help her carry him up the stairs and put him in bed.

Mum told me he was cheating. It was obvious. I would hear arguments. 'Whose is this? Who's calling you? Oh you're going away again?'

You wouldn't think a kid my age could put two and two together, but when you grow up with it, you become accustomed to it – mannerisms, words, actions, reactions, you become wise as a kid.

The adults never see that coming. Parents don't realise that kids' brains are like sponges and they soak up everything.

I soaked up everything.

As I got older, I did intervene with my dad. There were moments when he just flung me off to the other side of the room like I was nothing. The rage, the strength that he possesses for a short skinny Black man is absurd. It comes from an anger inside.

A professional fighter would look at my dad and say, 'I'll snap you like a twig,' but if his rage gets released in a certain way, I wouldn't put money on the professional.

Dad didn't just beat Mum. I was made to sit in a cold bath, I was picked up and thrown across the room, he beat me with the belt.

I remember playing basketball outside, and my basketball bounced, hit the kerb, and rolled out into the road. I prayed it wouldn't hit the corner of the kerb and roll out, because I wasn't allowed to cross the road.

I looked both ways, I knew what I was doing, I was about 8, it was a quiet road, and I ran across the road to get my ball.

On my way back, how unfortunate is this, my dad is coming down the road in his work van. So I run across the road. My dad gets out of the van and he goes, 'Get in. Now.' I knew I had been seen.

He took me in and made me stand in the corner of a room for two hours with my trousers around my ankles and my hands on my head. At least five or six times he whipped me across the back of the legs with a bamboo stick. A really thin one that you put in a plant. When you hear that coming through the air ... It's like, whop, whop!

So I had lashes on the back of the legs, just for crossing the road.

My dad was an energy changer. Mum would say, 'Dad's gonna be home in half an hour,' and suddenly everyone would be on edge. Me, my sister, my mum, everyone was wondering, 'What mood is Dad going to come in with today?'

Make sure there's nobody sitting in his chair. Make sure no one's in the shower because if you're in the shower and he wants to go in, he's gonna go mad. Make sure dinner's ready for him, 'cause if it's not, he's gonna be pissed off that he has to wait. Make sure your room is tidy and your shoes don't have mud on.

It was always scary with my dad, always, always, always. I was always frightened as a kid.

I remember he bought me a pair of shoes for school and said, 'Don't play basketball in them.' They were a little bit suedey, I was young, I didn't know what suede was. So I decided to play basketball in the rain and they got a bit muddy. I saw them after I'd finished and thought, 'I'll clean them, no problem.' They looked okay when the suede was wet.

Dad came in from work that day, and the first thing he said to me was, 'Did you play basketball in your school shoes?'

'No, they were clean from when I put them under the bed.' This was about three hours before, but obviously when suede dries, you see what was on the suede.

He said, 'Go get me your shoes,' and I went to get my shoes. I was quite confident, I thought it was going to be fine, but as I looked at my shoes that had dried, they were absolutely muddied, stains everywhere. At that moment, I actually shit myself.

I came out, shoes behind my back. He says, 'Show me your shoes.' He always had a stern, deep voice, and he was always terrifying. I pulled the shoes from behind my back and showed them to him. His next words were, 'Go and get some books.'

That confused me as a kid. I look back now and realise, 'Ahh, he wanted me to protect myself.'

He beat me that day, I remember. He was not happy.

There was another incident where he picked me up, threw me backwards and nearly broke my elbow on the bunk bed. My mum run over to my defence, my dad's about to hit me with the belt, my mum puts her hand out to protect me and it hits her hand. After he dropped the belt and walked off, my mum sat in the corner with me for about an hour or two just holding me, rocking back and forth, crying her eyes out telling me, 'It's gonna be okay, it's gonna be okay, it's gonna be okay.'

She wasn't supposed to get hit, but she stood in the way of the belt. She put herself in my shoes that day, she felt what was actually happening to me. It hit her quite hard – and I was a lot smaller, so I think she imagined that belt hitting a 9-year-old boy.

From the age of 8 years old until I was a teenager, it was quite heavy at home. It was real heavy for five years, then it eased up a little bit because I wised up, learned how to avoid the beatings and stopped making so many stupid mistakes. But also I was getting bigger as well. The old wolf realised that the younger wolf was getting stronger, so he backed up a little bit.

But in the first five years … it was very heavy.

'Frequent' is a loose word. Kids go through this every single day, morning till night. Mum or Dad leaves in the morning, beats their kid, comes home at night, beats their kid. Did 'frequently' mean every day? Definitely not. Did 'frequently' mean regular? Yeah.

I had a few beatings once every week or two, just because he was in a bad mood and needed to release. My mum would take it some days, I would take it on others. But he would never touch my sister. Every single time he'd come home, he'd pick her up, even if she was sleeping, he would pick her up, hold her above him and then bring her down and give her a massive kiss on the forehead or on the lips. 'How's Daddy's little girl?'

I don't remember him ever giving me cuddles.

I'd never run away as a kid or self-harm. It was more internal. I suffered internally over the course of many, many years. I'd wonder,

'What did I do wrong? Why has he been doing this? How do I change it? How do I, how do I, me, I, me, I, me, me, me, me, me, me … what is it that Dad doesn't like about me?'

I ran over it a thousand times. I was indecisive, unable to concentrate. Emotionally, it was a rollercoaster. I mean, anyone can use a rollercoaster to describe feelings, but I'm talking about the biggest rollercoaster in the world.

I remember having crazy headaches, lying in bed, duvet up to my neck, head pounding. It was like my brain was expanding and hitting my skull and then shrinking again – continuous over a few hours. That was from taking beatings, being shouted at in my dad's tone. And he was absolutely out of it.

There were times when I used to cry to the point where I couldn't catch my breath, my eyes were bloodshot, tears streaming down my face, bottom lip quivering, I had a snot nose and couldn't breathe through it.

My dad would beat me, then he would ask why I was crying. I'd be so confused, 'What do you mean, why am I crying?! You've just beat me up! You know that it hurts.'

That was a bit twisted.

It's emotional torment. It's everything that a child is not able to compute or decode. He would play mind games, he would ask why I was crying, then stare at me. When I couldn't give an answer, he'd get more mad.

I've seen the emotion on my dad's face – it's like he needed an excuse to let his aggression out, to beat me more.

Then he beat me for crying.

Disorganised attachment: a disruption of the attachment system

As the Minnesota Group followed children from before their birth, they found that some of their results made sense. But some didn't. In particular, they were baffled by 12 of the 31 children taking part in the study who had been abused but who were classified as secure in the Strange Situation.

Except ... they didn't seem secure. Sure, the children didn't react to their parent in ways that were avoidant or ambivalent/ resistant, but there was something unusual about them, something that didn't fit with Ainsworth's coding for secure attachment. They didn't behave in a way that suggested they believed Someone Important would be there if they needed them. Instead, their behaviour seemed conflicted, confused or fearful.

Sroufe passed copies of the recordings to Ainsworth's student, Mary Main, who was already interested in these different ways of behaving. She'd worked with Ainsworth on her Baltimore Study and had noticed that some children seemed to be conflicted in the Strange Situation. They did things that seemed out of context – they flapped their hands, laughed inappropriately and were inexplicably scared.

Main had also carried out an ingenious study involving a clown who tried to play with a child whose parent was in the room. The clown approached wearing a mask, took it off and called to the child while somersaulting about. Then, after being asked to go away, the clown started sobbing very realistically for a minute.

Children with two secure attachment relationships seemed more sympathetic and were more positive when the clown invited them to play. Children with two insecure relationships, on the other hand, reacted less positively and sympathetically. And those with one secure and one insecure relationship were somewhere in the middle.

Main noticed that some children in the clown study also seemed to behave in confused ways. They would close their eyes and lie on the floor in the foetal position, rock back and forth while staring into space, show odd tension movements, laugh suddenly in an inappropriate or empty way, talk to the wall or wear a strange frozen facial expression. Main believed that these confused behaviours were more likely in children whose parents didn't like physical contact and were frightened or harsh.

She was amazed that so many of these strange behaviours echoed what Bowlby's friend, the ethologist Robert Hinde, had seen in animals. Namely freezing, confusion, awkward approaches, uncoordinated movements, contradictory actions when approaching their parent or tension when they were reunited. And as Hinde was spending a year in Berkeley, where Main was, she could very easily pick his brains.

By this point, Main had started her own long-term study with 189 families. Her aim was to replicate Ainsworth's findings, to show that they weren't just the science equivalent of a one-hit wonder. But after coding 46 children twice (with each of their mums and dads), she found that 12.5 per cent couldn't be classified using Ainsworth's system. And most of the kids who didn't fit Ainsworth's system behaved in conflicted, concerned or confused ways when they were reunited with their Important Person in the Strange Situation.

Main knew that Hinde, who had observed numerous animal species, had seen that lots of different factors could lead to an animal behaving in conflicting ways. There might not be one straightforward explanation.

But while Main and her colleagues didn't think there was a single cause, they did think that disorganised ways of behaving had one thing in common: a disruption or breakdown of the attachment system. They thought the conflicted, concerned or confused behaviour they were seeing reflected a contradiction in these children's expectations of their Important People. So, for example, looking away at the same time as crying and approaching their parent might suggest that the child wants to go to their Important Person but has also had experiences that suggest this isn't a good idea.

Main and her colleagues used the word 'disorganised' to describe these conflicted, concerned or confused behaviours. But this isn't what the word 'disorganised' means in everyday language, so it's easy to understand how people got confused about what they meant.

The Cambridge English dictionary defines disorganisation as 'the quality of being badly planned and without order', which basically suggests chaos. And very soon, the scientific idea was distorted by the everyday meaning of the word – just as it was with the word 'secure'. But implying chaos doesn't help anyone understand what disorganised attachment actually means or what to do with it.

So what does it mean? And why would a child behave in conflicted, concerned or confused ways towards their Important Person? Well, Main and her husband, Erik Hesse, thought that if that Important Person, who was supposed to provide their child with a safe haven, *also* often behaved in ways that alarmed them, that might lead to the child being conflicted, concerned or confused.

Main and Hesse thought that these children were trapped in a paradox. On the one hand, they'd want to escape the person alarming them. But at the same time, their attachment system would drive them to go to that very same person.

One thing that would clearly lead to a child being alarmed by their own parent was abuse. By this point, the Harvard Child Maltreatment Project was well under way, and 82 per cent of the children whose families were known to child protection services for abuse, neglect or both were classified as disorganised, compared to 19 per cent of those whose families weren't. The Minnesota Study also found a clear link between disorganisation and different forms of maltreatment and neglect.

But Main and Hesse thought that abuse wasn't the only way a parent could alarm their child.

They went back to footage Main had of children playing with each of their parents and looked at behaviours that were frightening to the child or showed that the parent was frightened. In doing so, they created the 'FR' coding system.

Frightening behaviour included bared teeth and lunging at or looming over the infant without warning or without being playful. Frightened behaviours included suddenly withdrawing from their child or having the startle response when they tried to get close, which suggested they were experiencing the child as threatening in some way.

They also included any behaviour that seemed dissociative. Dissociation is a way the mind copes with too much stress. Everyone's experience is different, but it can make someone feel disconnected from themselves or the world around them. Main and Hesse thought that dissociation might frighten a child because it meant their parent was inexplicably unavailable.

They later added more to their coding – including behaving in a timid, deferential or sexual way towards their child.

Research has since backed up Main and Hesse's ideas and found a link between these behaviours in parents and disorganised attachment in their children. A hefty review of studies involving more than 800 families found that children whose parent behaved in a disrupted, frightened, threatening or dissociative way were almost four times more likely to form a disorganised attachment than those whose did not.

And these behaviours might happen more often than we think. In one study with middle-class families, just 18 minutes of play was long enough for researchers to see parents behave in alarming ways to their children. One particular child very actively tried to get their parent's attention, but to no avail as they had completely frozen with a fixed gaze for 45 seconds.

Research has also found that children who witness violence at home are more likely to be disorganised – and the more violent the parental relationship, the more likely the disorganisation.

Context also plays a major role. Another review of studies including almost 5,000 children looked at the impact of socio-economic risks like substance abuse, family education level or income. The researchers found that children growing up in a family facing five socio-economic risks were *just* as likely to have a disorganised attachment pattern as those who were maltreated. Why? When families face quite so many challenges, it can lead to feelings of fear and helplessness, as well as being overwhelmed all the time. And this might disrupt the parent's ability to help their children feel like they have a safe haven when they need it.

Being frightened was something that came up a lot in Zsa Zsa's and Elija's interviews. Elija (the boy who was raised by wolves) described his father as 'a very, very scary man ... I was always frightened as a kid.' And Zsa Zsa (the girl who walked into fire) said, 'I was fearful of my parents fighting. I had a deep-rooted fear that he would hurt her.'

They clearly both found the way their fathers behaved towards them and their mums very frightening. But is that enough to warrant a disorganised classification?

Well, frightening or frightened behaviour doesn't lead to disorganised attachment 100 per cent of the time. Yes, research suggests that parents who behave in alarming ways are way more likely to have a disorganised relationship with their child. But at the same time, there are many who behave in alarming ways who don't. So it's not a guaranteed outcome, and there's a lot that researchers still don't know. But there's some connection between the two.

Zsa Zsa and Elija weren't just frightened of their fathers – they were also abused by them. And abuse has been linked to disorganisation too. As I mentioned earlier, in the Harvard Child Maltreatment Project, 82 per cent of children whose parents were known to child protection services for abuse or neglect were classified as disorganised. Although it's high, 82 per cent is not 100 per cent. And the percentage varied with age. Neither being frightened of your parent nor being maltreated by them necessarily leads to disorganised attachment.

But it does mean secure attachment is unlikely. In a review of studies involving almost 5,000 kids, maltreated children were *very* unlikely to be secure. And that makes sense. If secure attachment is about having a safe haven when you need it, that's unlikely to be the case when the person that's supposed to be your safe haven is the person maltreating you. The researchers also found that physical abuse and neglect were similar in terms of how likely disorganised attachment was.

Why does it matter if Zsa Zsa and Elija – or anyone else – were likely to have had a disorganised relationship growing up? Well, when a child behaves in disorganised ways, it can give us a window into their experience of how Important People care for them. And that window is hugely valuable. Both Elija and Zsa Zsa have already explained that they rarely had a safe haven because of their dads' frightening behaviours. They've already given us a clear window into their childhoods. So looking back at their lives and giving them a label doesn't tell us much more than we already know.

But their words are those of adults looking back on their childhoods and articulating what happened to them. It's much, much harder for a young child to describe when they're living it. That's why the window that the Strange Situation can provide can be useful. Although, studying parental behaviours directly is even more useful – and this is what researchers are doing more and more.

There's still value in doing the Strange Situation, and the research findings relating to disorganisation are pretty astounding. For example, research has found a link between disorganised attachment in childhood and aggressive behaviour and attention problems later on, as well as poor social competence and friendships. But it doesn't mean any or all of this will definitely happen.

First of all, timing plays a role. A large review of studies found that if you were 2 years old when you did the Strange

Situation, the assessment was better at predicting later aggressive behaviour and attention problems than if you did it when you were younger. That's probably because one of the things you're learning when you're 2 is how to regulate frustration in relationships. And if you're in a relationship with someone who behaves in alarming ways, you may not be learning how to do that very well.

But also, disorganisation is only part of a child's path. It's not something fixed, like their blood type. It's a reflection of their relationship with one person at a certain point in time. But if your relationship changes, your attachment is likely to change too – which is exactly what certain parenting interventions have found. And having a disorganised relationship with someone doesn't mean you'll have one with every Important Person in your life.

Context is *incredibly* important. The context your Important People are living in can lead to feelings of fear and helplessness and being overwhelmed all the time. And this has a giant impact on the Important People's ability to provide you with a safe haven. And that context can change – for better or for worse – over time.

This means that the impact of disorganised attachment depends on what else happens and who else steps in along the way.

Matt
The boy with the stiff upper lip
Attachment pattern: possibly insecure

Zimbabwe 12⁵

BY AIR MAIL
PAR AVION

I remember the day I went to boarding school, but I don't feel any kind of pain about it. If you think too much about the separation and anxiety, it's upsetting, but as soon as you see your friends and get stuck in doing stuff, you don't feel it as much.

My older brother definitely created a feeling of safety. He also meant I came into the school with a brand as he was well regarded and well liked. And I didn't have problems with bullying, because he was older and bigger – although I did have some bullying when he left.

Every weekend on a Sunday, we would write a letter to our parents.

'Dear Mum, I'm having a good time, unfortunately it is raining and there is thunder and lightning and hail stones. On Thursday I swam 48 lengths, 596 metres, and on Friday I swam 68 lengths.'

The letters had those thin blue envelopes that said 'air mail/*par avion*'. They took two weeks to get there, and two weeks to get back. So, I'd write and then wait four weeks for a reply.

> *'Dear Matt, I played golf with Miranda and I went to the gym, and my art class had seven people in it this week. How many will come next week I wonder? I'm really enjoying sculpting again.'*

It must have been quite hard for my mum to send her son away and be left only with letters. Now you can video-call, email, message, but not back then. Phone calls were about £3 a minute in today's money, so although it seems a privilege to go to boarding school, my parents weren't well-to-do and we couldn't afford those calls. So comms were pretty tough. In spite of that backdrop, she was always trying to keep the mood up in her letters, they were always cheery and upbeat.

Because Mum wasn't there for two-thirds of the year, when I think of our relationship, I think of those letters. I've still got them all – they're supportive, engaging, interesting, full of her drawings, and pretty comprehensive – two to four sides of A4. I was always excited to get them.

Dad didn't write anything to us. Which I guess is totally understandable because the same news would be transferred through Mum.

Each boarding house felt like a family in a way because the housemasters and -mistresses were married and often had kids as well. But housemasters didn't stay forever, and you'd only be there for a couple of years and then you'd move to a different house. So, there wasn't one consistent figure over a period of time.

There were matrons too, although some were better than others. I had a slightly embarrassing medical condition at one point and went straight to hospital to have it dealt with. I didn't even go to the matron about it, but she found out and told another parent, who obviously told their son, who told me. It then fed into the wider school group and I had the piss ripped out of me for it. So I didn't exactly go to her for emotional support.

I was often sick at boarding school. I would go to sickbay and be ill for a couple of nights, eat some toast and tinned tomato soup, and then go back. But you didn't want other people to see that you were angry or upset or emotional in any way. If you go to the matron, other people might be around there, and if anyone sees it, they take the mickey out of you. So what do you do?

I know this sounds nuts, but the safe place to go in boarding school when things have really gone downhill are the toilets, because you can lock the door. That's basically the only privacy you get.

I'm sure I must have cried in the toilets at some point, I'm sure others did as well. Even if you came out with puffy red eyes after crying, you could probably twist it into being something else – 'I've got eczema or hay fever' or whatever.

That sounds bleak, I think it was pretty rare.

I can't remember whether I went to my elder brother when I was upset. I wouldn't go and cry to the housemaster or the housemaster's wife because, even though they were a warm presence, it just wasn't encouraged. So I didn't know what to do. And that was coupled with peer pressure to show zero vulnerability.

So I learned to play the system and depend on myself. When I was bullied, for example, I was never going to tell on the bully. I suffered in silence, because I was living with them 24/7 for years, so it's a pragmatism.

That said, there was a general feeling of happiness and lots of running around and sport. My memory of school is an autumn landscape with big oak leaves falling down, a couple of feet deep, and once you've done all your classes for the day, you're off in these fields. We would play football for ages until tea, then if it was summer, we might go back out and play tennis.

Lots of elements were just like any other school – I went to a classroom and sat down and worked. But in the evening it was different. It was actually quite strict at prep school. We would have dinner, then sit down for an hour of prep, where we were supposed to do our homework and finish it within that time.

It took me longer than other people to do a really good piece of work, so if I went beyond the allocated prep time, I'd then end up in the toilets, again, finishing off. I'd be kneeling on the floor using the toilet seat to write up an essay, because you're not allowed to talk, let alone be up out of bed after bedtime.

Every term, we had two long weekends and a half-term break. So, three times a term, nine times a year, we'd stay with our maternal grandparents who lived nearby. So we spent 35 or 40 days a year with them. God, that's quite a bit, isn't it?

My grandfather liked talking about cricket. Other stuff, less so. But he was a visionary. He bought us a computer when we were really young and said, 'This is going to be the future, learn computer programming.' I look back and think, God, I should have listened to that!

He was very old-school. He fought in the Second World War, like most people of his age, and had a big shrapnel wound that ripped off part of his hand and had plastic surgery to reconstruct it. They did an incredible job because I didn't know at the time, I only found out when I was much, much older.

His flesh wound was from a bomb that wiped out his entire squad – only he survived, so he carried big emotional trauma. He was not someone you could discuss feelings with. The horrors of going through that war made him quite formal. My grandfather definitely had PTSD.

On the flip side, my grandma had a good sense of how we were feeling and was a really caring presence. There was a warmth to her. She was the one putting us to bed, cooking meals for us, looking after us, coming up with ideas. She was really driving the agenda for us as children, taking into consideration what we wanted and definitely overindulging us – not in a way that meant we'd turn out as spoilt brats, it was more just like a holiday. It was great.

They'd pick us up in the car and we'd get sweets straight away. Then once we were at their house, we'd have all the things we wouldn't normally be allowed to have – loads of fizzy drinks full of sugar, cooked breakfasts every day, and we'd go shopping for football stickers and toys.

Then when I was 12, Mum and Dad moved us back to England and we stopped seeing our grandparents as much because we started seeing them during holidays instead.

I felt sad about not seeing my grandparents anymore, but at the same time I'd got used to moving from place to place the whole time. So, it was just like another move. Between the ages of 8 and 18, I hadn't been in one country, place, home, whatever for more than three months. I was just always moving around.

I didn't know it at the time, but my grandma started with the early throes of dementia.

She didn't really drink alcohol when I stayed with them, until the last couple of times, when I remember she drank before going to sleep. She would basically get plastered and pass out. My mum claims she would hide bottles of vodka, but I don't remember. She definitely became big on alcoholism and I don't know why. It's possible that not seeing us as much exacerbated that. Who knows.

Either way, her alcoholism probably brought on early onset dementia.

She would still prepare these beautiful meals for us. One of my last weekends with them, when I was 13, she served up the food and we all sat down to eat. I got my knife and stuck it in to start sawing off a piece of steak and realised it was frozen. She put the food in the oven and forgot to turn it on. I looked at my grandad and was like, 'It's frozen …' and he's like, 'Just don't say anything.' He didn't say a word and sat there and ate it all.

That pretty much sums up my family's approach to anything emotional.

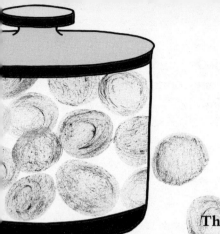

Skyler

The girl wrapped in cotton wool
Attachment pattern: possibly ambivalent/resistant

I don't know what my sister had that made her more confident than me. I don't know if it was because my parents treated me differently. You can hide being overprotective up to a certain age because that's parenting. And then, at a certain point, it gets ridiculous.

It became more noticeable from the age of 9 or 10, when other kids my age had a bit more independence. I never got that. But my sister did.

My sister was really popular at school, and I wasn't. At all. I probably could have hung out with the cool kids because my best friend next door, Hannah, did, but I never felt like I really belonged there. There were 62 people in my year and you could rank them. I was three or four from the bottom. I could name the people who were less popular than me.

I was probably 8 when the bullying started. I was very badly bullied by two girls, Sharon and Cally. They put a rotten egg in my locker and hid it, so all my belongings stank. Then Hannah had a party at her house. She invited everybody in the entire class – doesn't matter who you are, you're invited. But when Cally ran and gave me the invitation, she said, 'We have to give you this, but you do not have to go.' So I didn't. I was the only person that didn't.

There were certain tables I couldn't sit at, sports I couldn't play, movies I didn't get to go to, people I couldn't hang out with, parties I wasn't invited to. I felt so excluded and unwelcome.

I didn't provoke them, I didn't. I just was uncool. I don't even know what that means, but I wasn't cool. And if I'd failed, I would have been cooler. So at the same time as having parents who valued me based on what I achieved, I had this shame at school about being smart.

It wasn't only the cool kids that were mean. I remember once, my friend was eating candy and I asked her for a piece. She said, 'You know, Skyler, just because Princess Diana died, doesn't mean there's an opening for a new Princess of Whales.'

I had huge weight issues. It wasn't that I was morbidly obese, but I was never positive about my body, ever. I'm sure my friend didn't even think about how hurtful that would be, but it's these moments that you hold on to.

So I stopped hanging out with them, with anybody. I was never excited to go to school. I didn't want to go, I didn't want to be there.

The other problem was – when I was 8 or 9 years old, if I got yelled at by a teacher for not doing my homework, I would start crying. I was not one of those people that could hold in tears, which I'm sure didn't help with the coolness at all. If I wanted to cry at school, I tried to hide it. I would go to the bathroom.

When movies or TV shows depict bullying, it's usually a kid that always gets shoved in a locker. I was never beat up. That's not the way it worked. But that doesn't mean that it's affected me any less – it massively impacted my life and I'm still dealing with it today.

What was really sad was, the more I got bullied, the more I'd refuse to take a shower. Then I would get made fun of because my hair had knots in. The more I got bullied, the more I stopped caring about myself.

I didn't speak to my teachers about it. That probably would have led to me being bullied more. My sister wasn't at the same school as me, so I didn't talk to her about it either. And I never told the bullies to go away – I didn't have the confidence. My strategy was to move a lot. I was at one school when I was 10, another between 10 and 14, and another 14 to 18.

I decided not to tell my dad about it because I didn't think he would be helpful. My sister had an allergic reaction to a bee sting and it made her whole face swell up, and my dad, instead of being sympathetic, made fun of her. He told her she should be in a horror film. Dad was not someone to go to for empathy.

I told my mom, but she never knew how to comfort me in the right way. She'd say, 'Those kids don't know what they're missing out on, they're just intimidated by you,' or 'They're not worth it if they don't want to be your friend.'

That's not helpful. Of course I want to be friends with the popular kids, and saying that they're not worth your friendship is not helping a 13-year-old who is getting bullied at school.

But at the same time, I don't know what she could have done.

It's hard to convince somebody that they are enough.
They need to believe it in themselves.

Other than make unhelpful comments …
she didn't do anything about it.

Lily

The girl who was wrapped in love

possibly secure

Attachment pattern:

It wasn't as bad as I know bullying can be. It was
    jeering language, being left in a corner in a playground,
or children not wanting to sit with you at lunch. I remember
not wanting to go to school.

I was incredibly nerdy and my school wasn't exactly known
for prizing that. Teachers talked about pushing me up a year
– and I was really small and spotty. It wasn't exactly great for
being cool and I was bullied for it.

My parents spotted it quite early on. Dad gave me a cuddle
and found a way of asking about it that made me comfortable
to tell him what was going on. My mum was very upset by it
– as well as being comforted, I remember thinking, 'She's
finding this upsetting too.'

They quickly intervened with the schoolteacher and the head
and I thought, 'God that's embarrassing, I don't want my
parents to do that.' But they did and the bullying stopped, so
it was obviously the right thing to do. I remember it being
quite a short, sharp, dealt-with type of response. I suspect
that's not the norm.

My parents were there to see me crying under the stairs and wrap me up in hugs, rather than someone else having to deal with it or being left to cope on my own. Speaking to my mum or dad about what was upsetting me meant that by the evening I'd forgotten about it or worked it through. There was something really important about having that parental presence.

One of my strongest memories is crying underneath my pillow in bed and my dad coming and putting his arm round me and letting me cry for a bit, then talking to me about what was wrong. I must've been 8. I remember feeling better quite quickly after speaking to Mum too.

When I turned 9, I suddenly realised there are all these big things that are really, really scary, but I had no framework to understand them. I was really worried that my brain would stop working for a while, probably because of my brother, Charlie's, illness. Then, because a lot of my school friends' parents were getting divorced, I worried that would happen to my parents.

My dad would always have a bath at seven o'clock and if I couldn't go to sleep, I would go and sit on the bath and tell him what I was worrying about. He was probably thinking, 'I thought I was going to have a really nice bath.' But he would always talk to me until I felt better, which sometimes took quite a while.

Mum and Dad both had a strong sense of what it means to be a good parent, and I think that guided a lot of their actions. Their overriding aim was to provide us with love and for our emotional needs to always come first.

And they did.

Amos

The boy who couldn't remember
Attachment pattern: possibly avoidant

Primary school was pleasant. I had three, four good friends. It was a cool school and I loved to learn.

I was always very independent, quiet, interested in books, toys, fantasy. Even when I was very young, like 6 or 7, I never wanted my parents to help me out with homework. I was always doing everything on my own.

I think they were worried that I studied too much. But I really liked it.

I was always correcting the teachers. I remember a chemistry teacher once said that the symbol of potassium was P. And I said, 'No, it's K.' They would either send me to the library to do research, or down to a class the year below. It was very humiliating.

I can't remember much more. I don't remember any specifics.

Back then, if you had a child who was precocious, you sent them to secondary school early. That's just what you did. So that's what happened. There was no research showing it was bad.

Some of my teachers hated me in secondary school. I wouldn't do any work and they hated that.

Everyone else at school was older and from very different backgrounds. The other kids smoked. I was 9. So I didn't really have friends. They didn't invite me to parties. I felt very isolated, very excluded. I wasn't physically bullied, but I was never popular. I felt really weird and not liked and excluded. That was quite painful. It got me quite depressed.

It was a miserable time.

I don't think anyone noticed I wasn't happy. Pastoral care was not a thing.

I'm not glad I went to secondary school early.

I never told my parents that I was bullied.

I remember crying, but really not wanting my parents to help me out with it. And when they tried, they weren't good. My dad always downplayed what was going on or thought about something else. And my mum would collapse with anxiety that I wasn't doing well.

So when I was upset,

I would absolutely not go to my parents.

And I don't remember being upset.

I don't remember anything emotional.

I didn't realise that you could tell people if you had problems.

It's not that my parents were unavailable.

But they didn't have what I needed.

Being there: and what exactly that means

Bowlby originally thought that the aim of the attachment system was to get physically close to Someone Important. So if you were upset or frightened, all you'd have to do was get near them for your attachment system to chill out.

But as he got older, he changed his mind. By 1973, having studied the impact of separations on children, he decided the aim of the attachment system was to know that someone was 'available'.

He explained this as meaning two things – being accessible and responsive. He didn't think being accessible was enough on its own, because a parent might be physically present but emotionally absent. They also had to be responsive – or willing to comfort and protect their child when they were afraid.

Not only did he see availability as the aim of the attachment system, he also saw it as key to being secure. He thought security came from a confidence that our Important Person would be accessible and willing to comfort and protect us when we're afraid.

Bowlby thought this confidence was built up slowly during infancy, childhood and adolescence. He also thought that our expectations about the Important People in our lives were pretty accurate reflections of the experiences we'd actually had – and that those expectations could persist through the rest of our lives.

More recently, Harriet Waters and her colleagues have developed this idea of relationship expectations, and have likened it to learning a 'script'. In the case of secure attachment, the 'script' we learn is that someone will be there for us when we need them.

The pattern goes something like this: a child encounters a problem. The child gets upset, and communicates this and their need for support. Their Important Person promptly realises what's going on and offers support, which the child accepts. This support helps overcome the problem, and the child's Important Person comforts them, helps them regulate their emotions or both. Then they both get back to what they were doing in the first place.

How can all this help us understand the interviewees? Looking back on her upbringing, Lily described it as 'being wrapped up in love with an absence of worry. I had permission to be free or happy, rather than fearing that someone may not be there when I needed them.' And her expectations were proved right when she was bullied. She showed she was upset and her parents recognised this. They asked her what was going on, consoled her and intervened. Their support improved the problem. They were there for her when she needed them. And Lily could get back to going to school without worry or fear.

If Bowlby was right and security comes from knowing that our Important Person will be accessible and willing to comfort and protect us when we're afraid, then Lily's relationships with her parents were probably secure. Or in the language of Waters and her colleagues, she developed a secure script. She learned that when she faced a problem, she could ask for help and it would be there if she needed it. She learned that the help would actually be helpful. And she'd also be comforted too. Lily learned this over and over and over again, until it became something she expected.

But it was a different story for Skyler, Matt and Amos. Skyler (the girl wrapped in cotton wool) wasn't reassured by her mum's platitudes and didn't even bother going to her dad after The Bee Incident with her sister. Having been told about the problem, Skyler's mum didn't do anything about it. In the face of the persistent and damaging experience of being bullied, Skyler didn't feel she was or could be comforted or protected by either of her parents. This wasn't an example of a secure script. Nor was it what Bowlby meant by availability, as neither parent was willing to comfort and protect her when she was afraid.

Amos (the boy who couldn't remember) had conflicting memories. On the one hand, he didn't remember being upset. But then he did – and remembered his mother collapsing with anxiety, while his father downplayed what was happening or thought about something else. The upshot was, he didn't tell his parents when he was upset. As with Skyler, this wasn't what Bowlby meant by availability, and this wasn't an example of a secure script. When he told his parents he was upset, they didn't offer helpful support or comfort, and they didn't help him regulate his emotions. So Amos stopped telling them and kept his difficulties to himself.

Matt (the boy with the stiff upper lip) described his parents as not being 'proactive in showing affection or giving emotional support and nourishment'. He didn't speak to his father much, and when he was sent away to boarding school at 8, they had no contact at all other than school holidays. If he ever needed his mum, his only option was to write a letter and wait four weeks for a reply.

Four.

Weeks.

As with Skyler and Amos, Matt didn't feel comforted by his parents. They weren't emotionally available when he lived at home, and he had no communication with his dad, and very little with his mum, for most of the school year. This wasn't an example of a secure script, and the opposite of what Bowlby meant by availability. It also chimes with Bowlby's views of boarding school more generally, as he was strongly against young children being sent there.

In Bowlby's language, none of these parents were 'available'. He thought security came from feeling confident that your Important Person would be there for you when you needed them. And based on their memories, neither Amos, Skyler nor Matt felt that confidence with their parents.

But it's not just about parents. Bowlby thought we could have a variety of Important People in our lives, and research backs this up. Studies have found that each secure attachment a child has brings its own benefits in terms of their ability to understand language and use it to express themselves. Children with one secure relationship were significantly better at both than those with only insecure relationships. And those with *two* secure relationships were significantly better than those with one.

Did Matt form an attachment bond with someone at school? Well, his options weren't great: matron couldn't be trusted and 'it wasn't encouraged' to go to your housemaster when you were frightened or upset. And even if there was someone available, there was a peer pressure to show zero vulnerability.

For a few years, he stayed with his grandparents during school breaks. His grandfather was pretty old-school, and emotions were a no-go, but his grandmother was really caring – until he stopped seeing her when his parents returned to England, and she began to develop dementia.

Matt wasn't always in this situation. He didn't always have to wait four weeks to hear back from one of his parents. For the first eight years of his life, he lived with them (albeit with very little to do with his dad and hardly any emotional communication with his mum). So, would being separated from them impact their relationships with Matt? Almost certainly. To the extent that his mum had been available in his first eight years of life, would Matt be able to carry through a sense of that availability even though she was so far away? We don't have the research to know.

And what about Ray (the boy who was sent away)? He was sent to Bangladesh when he was only 2, so he could barely remember anything. Would it still have made a difference?

Bowlby didn't think it worked like that. He didn't think that just because things happened before we could remember them, they wouldn't impact us. And he didn't think we formed fixed expectations about the Important People in our lives. Instead, he thought that their availability shaped us throughout our childhood and teens. In fact, he thought the extent to which we felt they were there for us (or not) influenced how secure we felt for our entire lives.

Bowlby stopped thinking that being physically close to Someone Important was the sole aim of the attachment system, but he (and Ainsworth) still thought that being physically accessible was important. In fact, Ainsworth thought availability involved three things: believing that Someone Important was physically accessible, that there was open communication with them and that they'd respond if you asked for help.

Of course, it changes as we get older. We get better at understanding where our Important Person is and how to communicate with them even if they're not with us. This means that physical distance is less of an issue. But for Bowlby, the idea that we could reunite with Someone Important if we needed to was still fundamental to being available. He thought this was especially true when we didn't have open lines of communication – as was the case for Matt and his parents, and Ray and his father.

Having worked with evacuees during the Second World War and having been to boarding school himself, Bowlby was acutely aware of the impact of being separated from Someone Important. And he thought that, while the trigger for that feeling would change with age, the emotional repercussions were similar no matter how old you were. So even as adults, we can still feel just like little children who've been separated from their Important People.

It isn't just separations that can have an impact on how available Important People might seem. Growing up with violence, as Zsa Zsa and Elija did, can too. Its impact comes in lots of different ways – children in violent homes often worry that one or more of the Important People in their lives will be hurt, as Zsa Zsa did. On top of that, adults living in constant conflict and fear might have less capacity to be accessible and responsive as parents.

Homes with violence are also likely to be homes where open communication isn't allowed. In secure relationships, emotions like anger or sadness can be shared and talked about. But Elija (the boy who was raised by wolves) grew up in a home where sadness was punished. 'My dad would beat me, then he would ask why I was crying. I'd be so confused, "What do you mean, why am I crying?! You've just beat me up! You know that it hurts." … Then he beat me for crying.'

In Zsa Zsa's home, instead of being able to talk openly about difficulties, her father implied that her mother's alcoholism was Zsa Zsa's fault. 'My dad would say, "She gets very stressed when she thinks about you, she gets very, very tense." Then they would go on holiday without me, they did that a lot, and Mum would be "fine". It's like, the person who's doing it almost tells you you're responsible, right?'

In Bowlby's mind, the aim of the attachment system is to make sure Someone Important is there for us when we need them. But if that's the case, then for some children, like Zsa Zsa or Matt when he was at boarding school, their attachment system will never reach its aim. Instead of being comforted, Bowlby thought, they would feel yearning and dissatisfaction. And eventually despair.

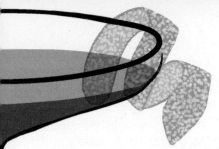

The girl who walked into fire
Attachment pattern: possibly disorganised

I bought a fizzy orange drink. When I smell that specific drink now, it's enough to make me physically want to be sick. I went to school. I waited until lunchtime. Then I skulled a whole load of pills in the toilet. And I came out and told somebody I'd done it.

Then I went to hospital and they pumped my stomach. My dad was furious. Don't know where my mum was, but my dad was furious. He'd had to drive a long way to get to the hospital near school. He wasn't happy.

I stayed in overnight. One of the teachers that came was very nice and kind and a nurse wrote me a poem. I've still got it. She was lovely. She was called Cindy.

She was just really nice and I remember thinking they were really nice people and ...   I'm really sorry that I'm taking up their time.

I can only imagine what you must think as a duty nurse presented with a 13-year-old child who's just taken a whole load of pills and had to have their stomach pumped, and whose father is obviously furious with them.

I remember him being told very firmly by my teacher who had come to hospital that his anger wasn't helping. 'She's your daughter and she's in a hospital bed, so get with the programme.'

I remember him pacing up and down, saying how he needed to get back to work. It was an imposition on his day that he had to drive for an hour to get there.

He must've been really stressed. He must've been ...
          he must've been feeling an enormous amount of
pressure. But the way it manifested was that I just felt like a
complete imposition and that he was angry with me for
ruining his day, because he had other stuff to do, because
mentally he was somewhere else.

I remember feeling dismissed. I remember feeling embarrassed.
I remember him looking very angry.

It's difficult, isn't it, when it's called a suicide attempt, and I
think, 'Well maybe it was me trying to find a voice and it was
a cry for help and it was a desperate measure to elicit a response
of sorts,' and when that response is   irritation
and not   'I love you, are you okay?'

After I ...   I don't like saying it in words.   After I had
taken my second overdose,   we went to
family therapy. It, it's hard to know how we'd ended up at it.
I mean, the idea now that my dad was able to take time off
work during a week,   like willingly take time off in a
week, and my mum, my dad and me went to these therapy
sessions ...   I have no idea how many we went to.

Something must've happened, because he started making
loads of effort to spend time with me. His way of dealing with
it was to take me shopping and to have my hair cut and just
throw money at the problem. But maybe it worked at that
moment in my life?

Previously my mum and I had spent time together. After that,
every single Sunday me and my dad would spend together. It
was almost like he had decreed that he was going to get to know
his daughter and be there for me. Clearly I must've said something,
or it must've been indicated to him that he was absent, or my
relationship with him wasn't intact. Or maybe it had something

to do with the fact that my mum was getting worse and he felt he needed to compensate for that. I don't know.

I suddenly felt like I had somebody who loved me, who, who understood me. I don't really remember us talking about stuff, but I know that I felt like someone was now looking out for me.

I think my parents found it really emotional. I remember one time when we were driving back from something and I had a tantrum and my dad pulled over and burst into tears.

And I remember thinking, 'I did that. That was shit. What a horrible daughter you are, what a horrible person you are, you make your dad cry.' And then it all wraps up in my head, I say, 'Well, I did this to my parents.'

How does it feel as a parent to have to deal with a child who's seemingly inconsolable and keeps taking overdoses? What do you do?

How does it feel as a child … ?

CHAPTER THREE

Teens

Matt
The boy with the stiff upper lip
Attachment pattern: possibly insecure

This is going to get very dark in a very weird way.

Just as I was hitting adolescence,

because I was at boarding school …

It's not that you conceal your feelings, you just don't talk about them. When people are crying because they're homesick, it's seen as weak.

I never was homesick because I had my older brother the whole time and I was okay with it.

But there was something about school that was clearly difficult for me because I started writing some pretty dark stuff. I still have the poems I wrote.

The dreaded dawn
Awakening from its dreary sleep
Without a creak.

Why was I such a fool
To come to this interminable school,
Where the days grow long
Without a bird chanting a song?

My teacher's note at the end summarises the school's attitude to emotion: 'A wonderfully gloomy poem – and the image of your sadness and depression while lying in bed really comes out. Clever to use the silent bird too. Please try to cheer up if this is really how you feel!'

I didn't cheer up.

Growing up, I didn't get a framework for relationships,
        a toolkit for how you interact with people of the opposite sex in a constructive way.   When I hit 13, I was suddenly aware of girls and I didn't know how to talk to them.

                        I was definitely more aware and more concerned about what girls thought of me because I started to see girls liking some boys and not others. There was just no interest in my direction.

I started having   well   suicidal thoughts of 'Does anyone even notice if I'm here or not?' Or 'If I kill myself, would anyone notice?'

It's not that I felt abandoned. It's more that I was aware of my existence but didn't know who actually cared.

My mum and dad were there if needed, but only if needed, not in any sort of proactive way.   You could argue that that manifests itself as ignoring.

If I did want their support, all I had was those blue letters. So while I had the support network of my parents, they were very distant from me.

I started thinking, 'There's no one I can talk to about any of this at all.'

So I didn't.

I had no emotional toolkit, I just bottled it up and carried on through. Stiff upper lip and all that. But I think it's very damaging.

And it was all coming out in my schoolbooks:

> Could I be saved
> by this weeny blip on the horizon,
> will it see me?
> If it saves me,
> I can get off this miserable
> low down castigating island.
> My lovely adorable family –
> will I ever get the chance
> to see their faces again,
> which brought me to life,
> and maybe, death?

I ploughed on, focused on different things. I don't know if this is an avoidant characteristic or not, but I've always focused on specific achievements and have been very achievement-orientated. I just refocused my energy on something else. Cricket, I think. I focused on doing well in that.

But it didn't take away from the general feeling … 'If I died, would anyone actually notice or care?'

And my writing got darker and darker:

> The smell of smoke filled the air as I came to from my concussion.
> Everywhere was up in flames with corpses
> and gore scattered around the shore.
> A small chunk of flesh was ripped from my hands.
> Small cuts and large bruises weren't scarce on my body.
> I was in complete agony.
> I tried to take my mind off it, but failure was there.
> I felt alone and terrified.
> My poor parents, they'll be extremely frightened that I'm dead.

Lily

The girl who was wrapped in love

possibly secure

Attachment pattern:

I remember Mum bursting into tears at Hong Kong airport the first time I left for boarding school in Ireland.

She's such a good nurse to my brother, she so looks after us. But that was the moment where I realised she feels things so much more deeply than she would ever let on. She did it several times – I remember her sitting on the sofa and crying when I came back for half-term.

I never felt like my parents were doing it to send me away, which I now know a lot of my friends at boarding school did. They were doing it because by this point my brother's health needs were all-encompassing, and they thought the best way for me to have any semblance of a normal life was to board. In the run-up to me going, Dad told me every day, 'You can call home any time you want. And you can come home. You can come home in the first week. You can come home in the second week.'

I was quite stoic, something which I learned from my mother and my grandfather. But I was so homesick. And really, really quiet. And a bit scared. And really, really homesick. And very sad.

Homesickness is like a constant ache. I imagine grief is like an extreme version of it. It's a constant, dull pain that you can't get rid of. It was brutal.

Knowing that I didn't have to stay any longer than I wanted to made it feel better. My parents spoke to me every day and came over at least every three weeks, so knowing that I had to get to those points every time was incredibly nice. And I had a lovely friend from almost day one who had an older sister at boarding school. So she was basically the cool kid who knew exactly what was going on.

After the first few years, I would say I was contented, if not overwhelmingly happy there. But the first few years, every time I had to leave my parents, I had terrible homesickness. It did wear off and it wore off increasingly quickly. But it was … It was just very sad.

I hated the flights. My parents gave me a phone and I basically only had my dad on there, who'd text me. 'Have you taken off okay? How are you doing?' Lots of messages to keep me feeling okay, I suppose. But the flights were awful. Then I got to boarding school and I was with my friends and it was fine.

Mum cried less as it went on, but every time I left to go back to school she cried. And then when I came back, she spoiled me mercilessly, which drove my brother mental. My dad would get very huggy. And they continued to call me every day, almost my entire way through boarding school. I think that was how they managed it for themselves probably as much as for my benefit.

My relationship with them changed quite a bit as a result of going away. It forced the time we were together to be much more emotional. I also learned to not rely on my dad. He had always been really involved with homework, but when I went to boarding school, I didn't really want that. I just got on with it. He took it very much to heart. He felt so keenly that he was no longer this all-knowing father figure and that was really sad for him. My brother's life was a collective effort, whereas mine became more independent.

My relationship with my mum became more mature. We became much more friend-like as she was very supportive around things like getting my period, having my first boyfriend. I remember the first time I had sex, she clapped her hands and said, 'So, was it painful?' It was so normalising – it made me feel much more comfortable about everything.

We also talked a lot about this stuff at school. I remember one girl would make us play truth or dare, and the truth was 'What did it feel like to start your period?' or 'Tell us about how you feel about your parents'. She would almost coach us in a really crude way to talk about our feelings, but it wasn't supportive – it was more interrogative.

I don't think boarding school fostered the sort of emotional security that would allow me to open up in a genuine way, except perhaps with my best friend, Elsa. Even though my parents did everything they could to make sure I felt loved, they weren't physically there and there was no safe space for me to go to. So when I needed support in the moment, I had to come up with mechanisms to cope with whatever was going on and endure it. I think that creates a very particular type of resilience.

No, that's an overly positive word. It creates a particular type of toughness.

My aunt lived near the boarding school and the idea was that I would see her regularly, she would be my guardian and could be the first point of contact in an emergency.

My aunt had no idea how to handle a teenage girl. She had been widowed a couple of years before I started school, had no kids of her own and was very introverted, but we got on brilliantly. I liked having a role model of someone who was very cerebral and a bit more internally focused. Even though she would have no idea how to broach emotional topics, like how I felt about the girls in my dorm, or the anxiety of not being included, we liked talking about similar intellectual things. She would talk about the book I was reading and I would feel at home.

There was never a meal on the table. Sometimes there was just marmalade on toast and we'd go out for a sausage sandwich, and that was the sum total of the meals for the day. It was quite refreshing. It wasn't at all like my mum. And I could go to bed when I wanted, which I couldn't at school.

One of the hardest things about boarding school was that I didn't get any respite from it. So if things were feeling a bit intense or a bit much, I couldn't leave. Whereas if you were a day pupil, you could just go home and think, 'Ah, I'm safe again.' That was quite hard.

There was a low-level stress and a sort of self-preservation that was needed to survive. You were either in the pack, or you weren't – but if you were on the out, where could you go? You couldn't go home, you couldn't find your tribe in your local pool or at gymnastics classes. Your tribe was dictated to you and they were there 24/7. And that was it. So there was a constant fear of not being included, a slight nervousness. It's really stuck with me in a way that I don't always appreciate.

There were definitely times where I needed to get out. There were definitely times when my parents picked up that I needed some support, and my aunt came and took me out.

I would stay with her and we wouldn't do very much other than get a sausage sandwich or watch TV or read or something simple. But the ability to be at peace, alone but together, was invaluable. She knew that sometimes I just needed to be quiet and that was nice, especially in a boarding school where being quiet was not an easy thing to do.

It was nice to have a haven on a Saturday afternoon. It was the next best thing to being safe at home with my family.

Amos

The boy who couldn't remember
Attachment pattern: possibly avoidant

My teens are a part of my life I don't find easy to describe. I remember very little.

I never had conflicts with my family because I didn't get angry. And I wasn't very talkative about my private life. So, there wasn't a lot of conversation.

My mum really wanted to talk more, but I didn't let her. She worried about the things mothers worry about – going out, *etc.* So, lots of lies to cover up as well.

I remember the first time I went out for New Year's Eve, I was supposed to stay out for the night. My dad said, 'Amos …   you got me.'

I think he meant – don't have sex unprotected. Or maybe don't have sex at all. That was my sexual education, basically.

When I was 16, my mum and I went to the surgeon I saw as a child, who had also done all the follow-ups since then.

He looked at all my tests and he said, 'He's really doing really well.' My mum was so happy. When we left, she said to herself, 'I've done something right.'

This part of my life is difficult to discuss. I don't have any specific memories.

Basically, I was in a rut.

So I decided to change high school.

I had top grades in everything, so everyone was really shocked I wanted to move. But I didn't feel that my personality fit me anymore and I wanted to change it. And you can't change it if you're surrounded by the same people. I didn't want to be discounted as somebody who's just good in school. I wanted to have a girlfriend, go to parties, do stupid things like drugs. I did a lot of things that I could tell others about.

Things improved in the new school because I felt more integrated socially. But there were also moments where I felt like I had been found out, where people saw through me. It was almost like I was trying to cover my tracks. 'How can people never see that I'm a weirdo, inside?'

That went on and on for many years.

But I did get a girlfriend, Martina. It was great until she cheated on me with her ex-boyfriend.
      I wasn't even in love with her, but it was so humiliating, I felt disgusted of myself. The break-up was physically painful.

I thought about killing myself.

One night I was really planning it.

That's the only time I actually thought about how I would do it.

I don't remember ever opening up and talking about it in a way that would give anyone the opportunity to give me support. I was like, 'I don't want to talk about this. I feel ashamed by it. Let's think about something else.' I wanted to show that I was hurt, but I couldn't convince others that I was.

Generally, in terms of mental health,
            I think I did pretty poorly. Especially given all the resources I had: a very available family, money, lots of education, no big adversities. So really I have to pat my back for messing it up so spectacularly.

I was depressed for a long time. Well, not clinically depressed. But it was very recurring. I couldn't feel any emotion, so depression was my main go-to.

I can give you a theory to explain. If I'm angry at you, in order to protect you, I'm going to be angry at me instead, so I don't have to hurt you. It really depicts what was going on with me.

You have to learn a number of behaviours to ask for help. You have to master language, anxiety, you have to open up, learn deferred gratification.

That's a lot compared to how easy it is to just keep it to yourself.

Mental health: summer camp studies

It's one thing doing the Strange Situation with young children and observing them at home, but how do you find out about their lives as they get older? How do you explore their relationships as they reach their teens, or assess what their mental health is like?

The Minnesota Group came up with a genius idea. Alan Sroufe and his colleagues set up summer camps, one the children attended when they were 11, and a reunion when they turned 15. Most of the young people that took part had also attended the Minnesota Study preschool years earlier. This meant the researchers had lots of information about each of them, including their attachment classifications when they were very young.

The summer camp for 11-year-olds lasted four weeks and involved sport, singing, arts and crafts and an overnight campout. The Minnesota Group observed the young people throughout and then interviewed them about their time there and their relationships with others.

When it came to physical tasks, there was no difference between young people who were secure or avoidant when they were little. On day one of the camp, at age 11, those who were avoidant seemed more confident and less vulnerable than others, but this first impression faded over the four weeks. They weren't as good at inferring other people's thoughts or feelings, and also saw others in a more negative light – both of which led to problems in relationships.

The Minnesota Group explained this in terms of our old friend, 'availability'. They thought that by growing up with Someone Important who wasn't available, these young people hadn't had a safe haven, they hadn't learned how to regulate their own emotions and they hadn't learned how to be with others.

When the young people turned 15, they came back for a summer camp reunion and were given group tasks where they were asked to choose a spokesperson. Out of 16 teens chosen to be the voice for the group, a massive 13 had been classified as secure when they were younger and only 3 had been insecure.

The Minnesota Group also found they could predict how good each person would be socially when they were 11 and 15 based on their attachment classification and how they behaved when they were only a few years old.

To explain this, the researchers turned to availability again – and emotional regulation. They thought that kids who'd grown up with Someone Important who gave them a safe haven and taught them how to regulate emotions could cope with group activities and handle potential conflicts with others. They thought all of this gave the young people better social skills. And later studies suggest they were right.

Mental health

When the young people turned 17, the Minnesota Group did more assessments, including a detailed psychiatric interview. And they found that teens who'd been classified as insecure as young children were more likely to have mental health problems. To be clear, insecure attachment didn't *cause* these problems. Instead, it provided a window into their experience of the care they were receiving. It was what led to their classifications – namely growing up feeling as though they didn't have a safe haven if they needed it – that made later mental health problems more likely.

As the first people to do this sort of long-term research on attachment, the Minnesota Group were just trying to get a rough sketch of the impact of our upbringings on later mental health. And they hoped that later researchers would refine and paint the detail. But the detail is far from simple.

The review of multiple studies I mentioned earlier found that having a disorganised relationship as a child was linked to 'externalising problems'. These include things like conduct problems or being aggressive or hostile. Zsa Zsa (the girl who walked into fire) grew up with parents who behaved in frightening or inconsistent ways, and this may have led to her having disorganised relationships with each of them. If so, that might explain why, as we'll see, she acted out at school, rarely doing homework, never handing anything in on time and being disruptive. Except it's not the disorganised attachment itself that makes those problems more likely – it's whatever led to the classification.

Avoidant attachment is also linked to externalising problems and attention difficulties, and (unlike disorganised attachment) internalising problems, namely anxiety and depression. So if Amos (the boy who couldn't remember) or Matt (the boy with the stiff upper lip) couldn't use their parents as a safe haven and had an avoidant attachment pattern as children, that might help make sense of their suicidal thoughts in their teens. And finally, insecure attachment of any kind was linked to having difficulties in social relationships. So if Amos and Skyler (the girl wrapped in cotton wool) were insecure, that might help explain how unpopular they felt at school.

But the picture is more complex than that. For example, almost all studies looking at attachment and internalising problems use reports from parents and teachers. But given that internalising problems are private by their very nature, parents and teachers might struggle to accurately notice and describe them.

There's still a lot we don't know. But we do know there are clear links between early attachment and mental health. We also know that secure attachment reduces the likelihood of mental health difficulties later on. So if Lily (the girl who was wrapped up in love) felt she had a safe haven with each of her parents, she'd be less likely to have mental health problems later in life.

What's also clear, and was clear in the Minnesota Group findings, is the link between child abuse and depression. Given that Zsa Zsa (the girl who walked into fire) and Elija (the boy who was raised by wolves) both suffered abuse growing up, this means they'd both be more likely to experience depression during their lives.

The Minnesota Group also found that insecure children weren't more likely to suffer trauma in later life. But those that did were more likely to experience symptoms of PTSD – an anxiety disorder caused by exposure to a traumatic, highly stressful or exceptionally threatening event or situation. Symptoms include recurrent and intrusive nightmares and memories; feeling isolated, irritable or guilty; having problems sleeping; and struggling to concentrate. Symptoms are generally severe and tenacious enough to have a significant impact on daily life.

Only 12 per cent of teens who had secure relationships when they were 12 and 18 months old developed PTSD after something traumatic. But that jumped to almost 50 per cent if they were avoidant, ambivalent/resistant or disorganised. So, to the extent that any of the interviewees didn't have a secure attachment growing up, they might be more likely to suffer PTSD following traumatic events.

School

By the time the young people in the Minnesota Study were 16, a few of the teens had dropped out of school, and the researchers wanted to explore why. Using statistical analysis, they could predict 77 per cent of the children this would happen to by looking at the amount of chaos in their home when they were little, their gender, their attachment pattern and how sensitive their Important Person was.

Once the Minnesota Group had factored these aspects into their analysis, later problems like being rejected by peers, conduct or disciplinary problems, truancy, low achievement or failing in high school didn't help them predict who would drop out of school. They concluded that all these things were actually just symptoms or warning signs telling us that someone was on a path to dropping out, which had actually begun much earlier in their life.

And they argued that the reason behind this was that to be successful at school, you need to be able to regulate yourself in lots of different ways. And we start learning how to do that in our very early years. But instead of learning how to regulate themselves, some children learn chaos.

The path isn't set in stone. Paths can be changed, and context plays a huge role in this. For example, in the Minnesota Study, when very isolated mums had better social support, their children's mental health and behaviour in school dramatically improved.

But the importance of context wasn't just about life at home. School was also a massive factor. The Minnesota Group found that some children's paths were changed by their experience of the school – including the teachers.

This wasn't the first time researchers had recognised the importance of school – years earlier, Bowlby had written that a school or college could be experienced as a safe haven. Now, decades later, here was the research to back him up.

And it's easy to see how school and the people in it could make a real difference in a young person's life. Take Matt: as a teenager, his suicidal thoughts were driven by the worry that no one cared. And when he tried to communicate this through poetry … no one cared.

Or at least, the only person who read his poetry, his teacher, responded by writing, 'Please try to cheer up if this is really how you feel!' At least his school helped his (defensive) coping in a different way – by allowing him to throw himself into achieving.

While our possible – or even likely – path might be set when we're very young, there are people and places along the way that can change our trajectories.

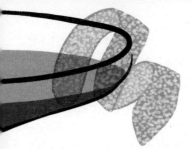

Zsa Zsa

The girl who walked into fire
Attachment pattern: possibly disorganised

I grew up around a lot of screaming and shouting – so I learned to scream and shout. At the same time, my dad would lose his absolute shit if someone else lost theirs.

I remember being really worked up about something and crying. I remember going to my bedroom. I remember him following, and I remember him just squarely hitting me across the face to shut up.

I have no idea what I was upset about. But I know I was a child.

So I acted out terribly at school, probably because I was curtailed when I was upset at home.

I had a lot of friends, but I was a rebel child. I frequently didn't do my homework, I never handed anything in on time and I was disruptive.

But because I did well at school without really trying, I think teachers thought, 'Well, she's not really causing too much of a problem and she's not dragging the school down the league tables, so there's nothing to fix.' It wasn't really ever approached. Maybe they thought, 'If she's still managing to achieve this, maybe there's not really a problem.'

Apart from taking overdoses, it all felt to me relatively normal   but then I don't really know what normal was.

When you're living through something and that's your only experience of it, you don't have any context – you don't realise that other people were having really serious conversations with their families about what they wanted to be when they were older. And their parents were checking they did their homework, seeing how they felt, actively engaging in parents' evening, and worrying if they got reports that looked like mine, where there were definitely red flags of behaviour that were not consistent with a happy, well-rounded child.

But when does a sort of naughty, slightly roguish child's behaviour become a cause for concern? Maybe no one noticed anything was wrong because there was nothing anyone could have noticed. Maybe they thought, 'Oh, she was just a naughty kid.'

There were so many markers upon which you'd look objectively and think, 'Just the most perfect, entitled little childhood. How privileged, everything was fine.'

Even now I still want to throw a cloak of normality over it and think, 'But everyone deals with difficulty, don't they? We had lots of dogs and chickens! People came round to our house to play tennis!' I don't remember my whole childhood being terrible and full of fear, and my dad was a good dad in many ways.

I still feel like I should be really grateful for the upbringing that I had. The voice that shouts loudly is the one that says, 'Don't be so entitled. You're very lucky to have had what you had. Why are you so selfish? Why are you so spoilt?' Then I reflect on it and think, 'Well there must have been some reason that I decided I wanted to die.'

There must have been conversations among teachers after I took an overdose. But what do you do? Especially if the child comes from a 'nice' family … Do you toe the line – because who are you to start digging into the private life of a kid in a wealthy school? You're not being helpful. You're being intrusive.

There was no one I felt I could talk to about what was happening at home. When you're quite young, you don't really have an idea of how it's going to be taken by anybody. You don't know if that's perfectly normal and everyone's dealing with it. You don't have a scale of what's right and what's wrong.

Clearly, I didn't really feel like there were any opportunities to talk to somebody, because taking overdoses very rapidly in succession isn't the behaviour of someone that feels like talking is going to make things better. 'We could talk, or I could try to die.' Not indicative of somebody that feels like they have a voice.

There was eventually one teacher I could talk to, Ursula.

She and I began to spend time together when I was 15 because I was excluded from one of my lessons. It's unprecedented in a fancy school that kids get excluded from lessons.

They clearly thought, 'What do we do with her?!' And Ursula said, 'I'll take her.' So that period, when I was supposed to be in another class, was actually the time I looked forward to most, because she and I would go and chat.

Twice a week, we would go for a long walk and talk along the playing field. I can't remember what we talked about, but I remember knowing her for a long time and I remember us being allies.

She definitely had a hard time because everyone else in this old fuddy-duddy school was predictably fuddy-duddy, and she was quite progressive. The old guard of teachers really didn't like it when she said, 'Let's listen to the kids.'

But if you're not being listened to at home, school might be the only place you can have a voice. Obviously my pals were there for me but in the very limited way you can be there for each other as children. But as an adult, Ursula could see the bigger picture.

She could just have given me things to do that were related to the class I was missing. But instead, she chose, over and above her obligations, to have an active relationship with me that was about care and compassion. Her primary motivation was my emotional well-being. It was the first time I'd had that from someone that wasn't my age. She gave a shit when she didn't have to.

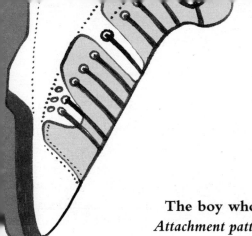

Elija

The boy who was raised by wolves
Attachment pattern: possibly disorganised

My dad was always, always there for my basketball games. He used to work away quite a lot, but whenever he was back, he would take me to training during the week, tell me what I was doing wrong, tell me how to do better, take me down to the park to practise.

But at 14, I decided I wanted to do gymnastics, and all of the support went out the window. He said, 'You want to wear Lycra and do cartwheels, I'm not having anything to do with you.'

I didn't talk to my dad for 15 years.

He also cut off any money. So I was going through gymnastics school and getting better and better and better. The gymnastics teacher would say, 'Can you come in for this? Can you come in for that?' It was just practice, practice, practice all the time, and you had to pay for these lessons. It got to the point where my mum couldn't afford it anymore and Dad wasn't paying, so I told my teacher.

She didn't want me to stop, so she gave me two years of free lessons to get me good enough to get into gymnastics college in London. That's how I went.

Two years.

Free.

I think Mum stayed with Dad for the kids. It was that generation of 'keep the family together'. Even if he gives £100 a week it's something, because without that £100 a week, she'd fall short on the food bill – but you can't fall short on the food bill because you've got two kids to feed. And with the domestic abuse, she was scared shitless. My dad was very, very scary.

That's why she stayed. Then I got to 15 and I got my first job cleaning offices at night. That's when I said, 'Come on, let's move out, let's go.'

She was crying in front of me, I remember her brown eyes shining in the light, her short blonde hair, I remember the sofa, the laminate flooring, I remember the layout exactly. She said, 'I'm with your dad because of money – and you need a father figure.' Anything is better than nothing in some cases I suppose.

Then she said, 'But I can't do it anymore, I don't love your dad, I haven't been in love with him for ages.'

I remember her looking me dead in the eye, and me saying, 'Come on, let's leave Dad, let's run away. Let him go to work one morning, we'll pretend we're asleep, then we'll get up, pack all the house up and move.'

A couple of weeks later we did it.

I think she was always contemplating it, always trying to find the courage. She just needed the support. There's no chance she would have left without it. I don't think anyone could.

We moved into a hostel. And I remember Dad rocked up at the door. I answered it and was so confused. 'You're not supposed to be here. We ran away from you. How did you find us? Why are you standing there?'

He said, 'Is your mum there?' And I'm like, 'Yeah, Mum's here,' but at the same time I'm thinking, 'I shouldn't get Mum because he's gonna beat her up.'

He didn't. He came just to be Billy Big Bollocks, cause aggro, show who's boss. He turned up that day to say, 'Yeah, I found you, you can't get away from me, still be scared of me.'

My mum told the council. They moved us to a different hostel and he never found that one.

I laugh about it now, but it's not funny at all. We didn't know how he found it, who had told him. We didn't know who to trust anymore – how had he got this information? Had he been watching us all day? Had he been following us around?

We was there for a little while, dingy cold place it was, I was sleeping on blankets on the floor, my mum and my sister were sleeping on a mattress. It was one room, we divided it up with the sofa – behind the sofa became the bedroom, and in front of the sofa was the living room. There was a toilet and shower room, a kitchen sink and an oven.

Fortunately, we got shipped on within two and a half weeks, so it wasn't that long. But it felt like two and a half years when we were there. Some people don't get as lucky. Some people were there for six months.

We got moved to a different area completely, and soon after, Mum fell for someone really badly. It was the first person she had dated after my dad. He moved in very quickly.

I never really liked him.

He'd been living with us for a few months when I had a big argument with my mum. She kicked me out and said, 'Don't come back' – and I, being a stubborn little shit, went to my friend's house and didn't come back for four days. But I didn't tell her where I was neither.

She probably knew where I was, but I felt good because I thought she didn't. After three days, I went home and knocked on the door, and he answered.

He just stood there, arms folded, legs spread across the door. I tried to get past him and he said, 'You're not coming in here.' And I said, 'What? What do you mean I'm not coming in – I live here.' 'Your mum doesn't want you in here.'

I said, 'Oh, okay, let me get some more clothes and see my sister and I'm going.'

'You're not coming in here.'

I tried to push past him, he gave me a big shove and I fell backwards on to the garden. So I got up and charged for him, and we got into a scuffle. He broke my nose. And he lost two teeth.

When Mum heard the racket, she came outside and immediately decided to take his side.   She picked her boyfriend over me and kicked me out.

From that moment, I went to live with the person I now call my second mum, Vanessa. She was my mum's best friend at the time. They don't talk anymore because of it. Vanessa is amazing, very small, very quiet, but doesn't take no shit. She's been beaten by men, she's beaten men. And her heart is absolutely huge.

So I went to see her and she stormed round to my mum's house and basically told her that she was bang out of order, 'This guy should not be here, who is he …' and so on.

I ended up staying with Vanessa for about two years – well, I was either staying on people's floors in London, or I was staying with her and bunking the train to go to the gymnastics college in London I'd got into.

She let me stay for free. She would feed me, get me up in the morning for college, and I didn't go through all the emotions I did in my own home. She was keeping me on track basically. She was there at the right time and she was there for a good amount of time.

Growing up with my dad, I felt like I was on fire. The beatings were red raw, the emotions were heavy, I was burning up, I was gooey, dangerous. I could have been a volcano myself.

Then when I moved in with Vanessa, into an environment where I wasn't threatened, it was like lava hitting the sea – *hisssssssss*. The red went away, I cooled off and I turned into this hard, solid rock. I turned into a shell.

The abuse gave me a high tolerance of pain, which was actually useful in gymnastics college. But I quickly learned the difference between tough love and love that's wrong. My teacher pushed me, but in a good way. She wanted the best for me, she knew that I had potential, so she pushed me to be the best that I could be. My dad didn't push me to be anything but somebody that might have cowered into themselves. It's different.

My teacher at college used to take me for coffee. No other students did that, it's not a normal thing for students and teachers to go for coffee, but she found out about everything at home because I came into college one day bawling my eyes out. I was broken. She said, 'Okay, we're not going to class, we're going for coffee …'

It became a regular thing. I used to confide in her and she checked on me every day, you know, 'How are you? How was today? How was your weekend?' Indirectly asking me if I was beaten the shit out of over the weekend.

I didn't ever find out if she had been through stuff like that, or whether she recognised it. You can see it in children sometimes. I do.

I was going through some pretty heavy stuff during that time. Without her, my story would have been completely different.

I finished college and got my first gymnastics job.

And I repaid my first gymnastics teacher by going back and teaching for two years, unpaid. I always said to her I would. And I did. So I paid my dues back and we were a great team together. The kids we taught did really, really well.

I took my second teacher out for dinner to say thank you for all the coffees. And I tried to give Vanessa some money for all the time I had spent living with her. But she wouldn't take it.

For people that go through anything like this, there must be some supportive people or support system that helps them. I don't believe that anybody could do it on their own.

Without that small amount of stability in my life at that precise moment, things would have been different.

I am from a council estate and it is not the best area. The friends I had from home, from the estate – some of them are not here anymore. Some of them are inside.

Without both of those teachers and without Vanessa, it would have been a whole different story.

It would have been a sad story.

I could have ended up in prison or dead.

The straight and narrow: developmental pathways

As he got older, Bowlby thought more and more about the paths that we follow as we grow, and the things (and people) that can influence them. In the book he was hoping to finish before he died, at least 5 of the 14 chapters were on these 'developmental pathways'.

He'd always believed that our early life had a major impact on us as people and our pathway in life, and that our expectations shaped those paths and how stable they were. He also thought that, because parents usually carry on the way they begin, vicious or virtuous cycles often continue. In other words, what we come to expect from Important People and what leads us down a particular pathway is likely to endure, keeping us firmly on the same route.

But Bowlby also recognised the importance of our environment, especially the people in it, and their ability to change our path.

If you were born into a 'favourable' family situation, you would start − and continue − on a pathway of healthy and resilient development. But if your family situation changed at any point, so too might your pathway. And if it became sufficiently 'unfavourable', your pathway might move towards disturbance and vulnerability.

Bowlby thought it also worked the other way. If you were born into an 'unfavourable' family situation, you might have an unfavourable pathway very early on. But if something changed for the better, so too could your pathway.

Bowlby provided two illustrations to explain what this might look like.

In each illustration, there is a series of vertical arrows all going up at very slightly different angles. Imagine a footballer standing before a goal − there are a number of different angles they can kick the ball and get it into the net. These are what Bowlby called the 'range of potentially healthy pathways'.

In the first illustration, there's another arrow labelled 'guilt-inducing techniques of discipline' that starts at the same point as the others but immediately veers away from them. Here, our imaginary footballer kicks the ball so far left that it's clearly not going to go in the goal unless someone else kicks it back in.

Then on this pathway, the child's mum dies, and the ball is kicked even further away. But then psychotherapy begins, and the line starts heading back in the direction of the others, back towards the goal.

In the second illustration, once again, an arrow with the label 'unstable home' swerves away from the others. Then, when the child's dad deserts the family, the line veers even further off course. As time goes by, the line goes further and further away until a helpful teacher does some fancy footwork and kicks the ball back towards the goal. But then the child has a major quarrel with their mum and the line veers off again – and the goal of developing in a healthy and resilient way seems more and more distant.

In both examples, while the pathways are changed for the worse (by guilt-inducing discipline, bereavement, an unstable home, a dad leaving, a quarrel with mum), they're also changed for the better – in the first by psychotherapy and in the second by a helpful teacher. And this feels particularly important given the role of family psychotherapy in the life of Zsa Zsa (the girl who walked into fire) and the teachers of both Zsa Zsa and Elija (the boy who was raised by wolves).

It also feels relevant to the life of Luca, who lived next door to Ray (the boy who was sent away). Spending almost all his time at Ray's house may have helped Luca move back towards healthy development. And when Ray and his family moved away, Luca may have found himself kicked back out again – unless someone or something else came along and helped him get back on track. But even if his trajectory did change once Ray and his family moved away, having their home as a sanctuary would have had a huge impact on his path for the time they were there.

Bowlby wasn't the only researcher to talk about the invaluable role of teachers. Alan Sroufe recognised their importance when describing a case from the Minnesota Study. 'EL' was only 4 years old but behaved in malicious, antisocial ways. He fearlessly went against what teachers wanted and seemed to be happy when others were upset. It would be easy to think that this child was beyond reach thanks to his deviousness and swaggering attitude. But underneath the swagger was a desperately needy child.

Thankfully, the teachers quickly saw ways to get close to EL and openly disproved his low sense of self-worth by showing him they cared. He formed a strong attachment to one teacher in particular and did brilliantly at learning how to meet his basic need for closeness.

Sroufe and other members of the Minnesota Group thought Bowlby's idea of developmental pathways was essential to understanding mental illness. The idea is that, when it comes to predicting mental illness, it's not just about our early lives – it's also about the quality of care that we're getting in the present moment, no matter how old we are. That's because how we adapt to a situation is always determined by a combination of our current circumstances and our early history.

This has been backed up by a recent long-term study: 125 adopted teens were assessed in the Strange Situation when they were 1 year old and in the AAI 13 years later. Researchers also observed how sensitive their mums were in supporting them during a conflict. Unsurprisingly, consistent, sensitive support was linked to consistent secure attachment from early childhood to teens.

But children that didn't get sensitive support when they were a year old weren't without hope. If their mum went on to provide it in their teens, the young people went on to be classified as secure in the AAI. In other words, what happens in both early childhood and adolescence are important. The problem is that parents usually keep doing what they're doing over and over again. So while parenting can and does change over the course of a child's life, it often doesn't. And, as a result, how sensitive (or insensitive) a parent is can be very consistent over time.

It's clear just how important sensitive, consistent care can be in adolescence in the interviewees' own lives. Elija suffered severe abuse as a child and was disowned by his father and then his mother. But thankfully other people stepped in and gave him sensitive, consistent care. Having a safe and secure home with Vanessa and the love and support of two teachers when he was a teenager was essential to his pathway in life and ultimately changed its trajectory.

Bowlby's idea of developmental pathways also implies that it's not just about our immediate context. Broader aspects of life, like relationships outside our family and the stresses and challenges we're going through at any given time, will also have an impact. Your Important Person – and their relationship with you – is probably going to be impacted if they have zero social support versus lots of stable, loving friends and family. And you might have the most secure and socially supported family in the world but if you're fleeing your home because your country is suddenly at war, that's going to have an impact on your path.

The Minnesota Group thought that another implication of Bowlby's theory was that living through lots of adversities over time is worse for mental illness than a single period of hardship in our early years – and the longer we follow a negative pathway, the more likely mental illness will be.

While Ray was born into deprivation and relative isolation, his parents were able to build social support around them and clamber out of poverty. By the time Ray was 8, things were reasonably good on the finance front, and when Ray's brother was born, his father described him as being 'born into privilege'. His parents were also far more available after Ray returned from Bangladesh – what Ray described as 'overcompensation' for sending him away.

Whereas Zsa Zsa didn't just live through a single period of abuse. She lived in a home with substance abuse, parental abuse, child abuse, repeated departures by her mum and possible emotional neglect. And these carried on throughout her childhood – until she cried for help in the form of two overdoses. For any human, living through all these adversities throughout childhood would harm mental health more than a single, contained period.

Mental health

For all these reasons, the Minnesota Group believed that developmental pathways were crucial to understanding mental illness.

But that didn't mean the relationship between the two was straightforward. They thought the same pathways could lead to different diagnoses. And they thought you could get to the same mental illness via different pathways. In their study, for example, there were two routes leading to teen aggression and conduct problems – one had risk factors that began in early childhood, the other had risk factors beginning in the teens.

This led the researchers to argue that by simply giving someone a mental illness diagnosis and focusing on it, you might miss the developmental pathway that led to it. It makes intuitive sense. Giving Zsa Zsa a diagnosis of 'depression' as a teenager wouldn't be that helpful without some sort of understanding of her family life – and what was leading to the mental illness.

The Minnesota Group also didn't think families were just another risk factor on our path in life. They saw them as fundamental in helping young people learn how to regulate their emotions. And as a result, family relationships were particularly important when it came to the start – and continuation – of mental health symptoms.

Looking at the interviewees' lives, it's easy to appreciate just how different children's experiences can be when it comes to being taught about emotion – and how that might impact mental health later on. For example, Lily (the girl who was wrapped in love) describes how her dad 'would ask explicit questions like "How are you feeling?" and "Why are you feeling that way?" rather than assuming that if I was sad, I would actively seek support and know how to articulate it myself.' She also remembers, 'One of my strongest memories is crying underneath my pillow in bed and my dad coming and putting his arm round me and letting me cry for a bit, then talking to me about what was wrong. I must've been 7 or 8.'

But instead of being taught how to regulate their emotions, Zsa Zsa and Elija were reprimanded for having any. Both their dads hit them for crying. So while Lily was being taught how to understand and articulate her inner world and ask for help when she needed it, Zsa Zsa and Elija were being taught that when they needed comfort, they weren't going to get any – and that instead they would get rejection, pain and punishment. Lily was learning a secure script. Zsa Zsa and Elija weren't.

Some say it takes 10,000 hours to truly learn something. But children usually spend far, far, far more than that with their family. And all those micro-moments add up and reinforce children's expectations. It's the way in which Someone Important does and says the ordinary everyday things of life that seems to help or harm their child.

Throughout her childhood, Lily's dad was teaching her over and over and over again that she had a safe haven when she needed it. It couldn't have been further from what Zsa Zsa's and Elija's dads were teaching them. The moment-by-moment support that Lily's dad gave her in feeling safe and understanding and accepting herself is a brilliant example of what the Minnesota Group meant by the importance of family relationships in mental health. And you can't fully understand Lily's mental well-being without understanding her relationships and the consistent emotional education, insight and safety they provided.

Resilience

As the children in the Minnesota Study had reached their mid-teens, both academics and the public more generally were starting to use the word 'resilience' to describe something internal, something individual, something that meant you could do better than expected in the face of adversity.

But Sroufe and Egeland didn't think resilience was something you did or didn't have, something that you were born with, that magically appears in your biology. They thought resilience was born out of relationships.

They defined resilience as two things: a child's ability to find ways and means to cope well in the present; and a child's ability to find the means, both internally and externally, to cope with future challenges. By including the word 'internal', Sroufe, Egeland and their colleague Tuppett Yates did acknowledge individual factors – but they didn't see these as something you were born with, something innate.

'Resilient' people were often described as having certain characteristics, like being calm or optimistic. But Yates, Egeland and Sroufe were adamant that these characteristics weren't inevitable. Instead, they thought they were hugely influenced by our upbringings and ongoing relationships with family and friends.

When Sroufe and his colleagues carried out statistical analyses on people who coped better with adversity, they could explain 80 per cent of this 'resilience' by looking at life stress and social support at different points in life. As a result, they argued that resilience isn't just a case of good outcomes in the face of bad experiences, but also the power of good past experiences to help us make the most of the situation. And as we accumulate support and are helped over and over again to manage difficulties, we develop attitudes, expectations and abilities to organise resources that help us cope better with whatever challenges we might face.

What does that actually mean in real life? Well, in Elija's upbringing, his mother's love (until she disowned him) and the support of Vanessa and two of his teachers helped him cope with the massive challenges he faced. Namely, a history of abuse, poverty, being disowned by both his parents, and a peer group where some had either died or were in prison. He managed to cope with working part-time to fund his studies while finding people's sofas to sleep on. He managed to trust that, despite his experiences, he could expect some people to care and be there for him. And he managed to work really, really hard to succeed in his career. He was adamant that he wouldn't have been able to do any of that without support – in other words, his 'resilience' was born out of the loving relationships he had with others at particular points in his life. Resilience isn't something he or any human just had – it was something that loving, safe relationships gave him.

The problem with seeing resilience as innate is that people who aren't miraculously fine having lived through difficulty are stigmatised. When, in fact, Yates, Egeland and Sroufe thought mental illness was ordinary and predictable if you didn't have enough support and if you suffered lots of adversities, especially through your childhood and teens.

The advantage of the limited view of resilience is that we as individuals and as a society can wash our hands of our responsibility for children living through difficulty. We can ignore or discount the necessity of safe, loving relationships in people's trajectories. We can sit back and think, 'Well, some children manage in the face of adversity – it's obviously possible. So we don't need to worry about it. The resilient ones will cope, and as for the ones who aren't resilient, oh well ...'

But it's our responsibility and we do need to worry about it.

As Sroufe explains, as members of society, we all share a responsibility when it comes to the care that's available to children. And if responsibility for a child's well-being doesn't exist in their family environment, then that responsibility is ours.

Ray

The boy who was sent away
Attachment pattern: possibly avoidant

Mum and Dad started arguing when I was about 15. I can't remember what would trigger it, but they would close the door and have a very, very shouty argument with very, very raised voices. And crying.

It became borderline violent. Things were thrown. Then pushed. At one point, Mum asked for intervention from me and my brother.

My brother would obviously find it upsetting. I distinctly remember him coming into my room and us shutting the door and having the dilemma of whether we drowned out what was going on or listened to it in case it got really bad.

I'd be comforting him and explaining things. But I found it really, really upsetting listening to them argue.

It got to a stage where I promised myself, 'I will never, ever be in a state where I'd argue like that. I'd never argue. I'd never argue.'

The arguments would happen every month. Then they'd calm down and Dad would disappear for a bit. He would go and stay somewhere else, then reappear a few weeks later.

I felt very responsible. I had a job to do under very difficult circumstances. It didn't feel heavy, it didn't feel onerous. I felt like a comic book superhero. 'I've got a purpose, I've got a role, I've got a job to do. I've got to make sure that Mum doesn't get hurt and my brother is okay.' I'd had it quite good until then, so that felt like quite a small price to pay.

But deep down I felt insecurity, immense insecurity. And fear.

I was scared for myself, I was scared for my mum, scared for my brother. I remember thinking, 'How are we going to live? What happens to us? Are we going to have to fend for ourselves? How are we going to survive?'

All I wanted to do was get away.

Around this time, I started dating Debbie. She was kind, generous, bright – she also came from a secure, loving family. In many ways, she was my escape. Plus I was thrilled to have a girlfriend in the first place.

But being in a relationship with a white girl wasn't a thing to do. So, I had to keep it secret.

We went out for a good 18 months before I was discovered. We were out one day when my dad spotted us. He didn't say anything at the time, but came in to see me that evening. 'I saw you going out with someone today. You can't do that. You have to concentrate on your work. It's a distraction.'

He was right, it was. But I knew it wasn't that that was bothering him. It was considered shameful to have anything other than an arranged marriage. That's just how my dad thought things worked.

Dad had no idea. He'd come from a cultural background which was suddenly alien in this new environment in the West. He didn't know what bits to hang on to, and what bits he should let go of. He carried a dilemma with him all the time.

So, we had this big argument about it and he effectively said, 'You've got to decide. Either you finish it or I'm going to disown you.'

I told him I wasn't going to finish it. So, I was disowned when I was 16.

We didn't speak for two years.

It was horrid. Absolutely horrible. It made me realise I had to survive on my own. I had to find a job and accommodation and become self-sufficient as soon as possible. Education was my ticket to doing that.

How do you survive, as a child? You are totally dependent on your parents for your education, food, shelter. If they decide not to provide that, what do you do?

I'd very nearly been kicked out, I knew I was on a short ticket. I couldn't wait to get away. So my university choices were all as far away from home as I could possibly find, including abroad.

By the time I left, Dad had left home and was living in a hotel.

Once I was at uni, I switched off completely. I did not want to know anything about home at all. I drank a lot. A lot. I didn't really think it was anything more than being a student. Then suddenly I became seriously ill and started suffering from what turned out to be the early stages of leukaemia.

My illness took away my ability to function as a human being. I couldn't do normal things. I was told that I wasn't going to do sport again, that the illness was potentially progressive and would eventually take me out.

It didn't. Or at least, it hasn't.

Then, as I very slowly started to recover, I became very curious about purpose and meaning in life, and other people needing help. I was also consumed by this desire to live and find out about myself. I started to spend a lot of time trying to work out me.

My parents got back together to get me through it. Dad moved back into the house. And for all intents and purposes, everything was okay. The whole dynamic changed because the job in hand was to get me through this and help me to survive.

Dad slept next to me in the hospital in the early stages. I remember him telling me about his life, but in a very selfish way, talking about how Mum had abandoned him, feeling sorry for himself and complaining about the marriage. I kept thinking, 'I don't want to be hearing this at the moment. I'm trying to survive.'

But even though he spent his time moaning, that was the first time I realised how much I meant to him, because he was there all the time. My mum was there too, but she'd always been like that. So I didn't feel the slightest bit of abandonment from my parents during that time. I felt incredible security from both of them.

Debbie also visited regularly. We broke up when I left for university, which was a devastating blow. But when I got ill, she travelled across the country to see me in hospital every week. She didn't leave me when I was falling apart. So I also felt incredible security from her. And because she and Dad were there together pretty often, they ended up getting to know each other.

Then out of the blue, one night when we were on our own, we went for a short walk together and Dad said, 'I want to apologise for the years of heartache I've given you. I can't believe I did and said all those things. And Debbie's wonderful. I'm sorry about how I behaved on that. I'd like to invite her and her family over to the house and make it all better.'

My dad wasn't stuck in his ways. He was a poor man who had no structure or education or coaching, who was being thrown at different life situations and dealing with them his way, reactively, belligerently. Then reflecting and coming round to the right way of dealing with them. The hard way.

So my dad and I reconciled. Everything was hunky-dory. I felt huge security.

But at the same time, I knew he was capable of disowning me, and that was always, always in the back of my mind.

So at some point I made a decision: 'I'm going to be totally self-reliant.

I'm never going to put myself in that position again.'

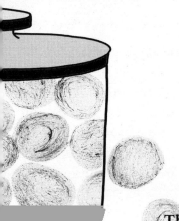

Skyler

The girl wrapped in cotton wool
Attachment pattern: possibly ambivalent/resistant

I was 18 when I noticed my dad listened non-stop to this really random band. So one day, I asked why he liked them so much. And he said, 'My brother was the lead singer.'

'You have a brother?' I said, and he replied, 'He died when he was in his twenties.'

My dad had a brother who died when he was 19, so before I was born.

And I had no idea until I was 18. If I hadn't asked him about that band, I would still have no clue.

I know nothing about his relationship with his brother. Nothing. I think it was an older brother, but I'm not even that sure of that. I wouldn't put more than £10 on it. I am also fairly confident that the death was related to the heart, but I don't know for sure. I don't even know if it was sudden or not, that's how little I know about it.

I've never asked my dad about him. It would be abnormal behaviour in our family if I were to sit down with my dad and go, 'So tell me more about your brother.' It would be very odd. So I didn't. And I don't.

My dad was raised in a very traditional way where you do things a certain way because we've always done them this way. That's the logic behind everything. He hated his job, but you don't change jobs, you do the same job with the same company your whole life, that's what you do. His parents were very strict and never talked about emotion. And he had a horrible relationship with his father.

But when I was in my teens, I discovered just how horrible. Shortly after I found out about his brother, my dad's cousin died. My grandfather was so upset by this that he decided he was done living and stopped eating. He was done.

I had absolutely no idea that my grandfather had always cared more about my dad's cousin than he did about my dad. It must have been horrible growing up knowing that. And then watching your dad decide to kill himself because the person he loved more than you died – when you were still alive. Horrific.

But my dad will never talk about it.

I really wanted to talk to my dad about all of this, I had so many questions.

But somehow just knowing that he had a brother who died so young and understanding how bad his relationship with his father was helped me be way more forgiving and compassionate for the way he is. It's totally transformed our relationship. It made me understand why he treated me the way he did as a child.

But I don't feel that way for Mom. At all.

CHAPTER FOUR

Young Adult

Surprising the unconscious: the Adult Attachment Interview

Five years after assessing children and parents in the Strange Situation, Ainsworth's student Mary Main was getting ready to bring families back to her laboratory for follow-ups.

She was reading Bowlby's book *Loss* at the time, in which he talked about the work of the psychologist and neuroscientist Endel Tulving. Tulving believed that there are three types of memory, two of which caught Bowlby's eye – 'episodic' and 'semantic'. Tulving thought 'episodic' information was made up of our own experiences of specific events – and the way these events relate to each other. 'Semantic' information, on the other hand, contained general descriptions or accounts about the world.

Bowlby thought that episodic information came mostly from our own personal experience, but that semantic information didn't necessarily – instead, he thought it could be made up of what others have told us, especially as a child. He also thought that this memory of what others had told us could trump our own memories.

This distinction between different types of memory was something that my interviewees recognised. For example, when I asked Lily to describe her early relationship with her parents, she said, 'It's hard to know what I can remember and what has been told to me.'

An example of semantic information might be Elija describing himself and his family as a pack of wolves – it's something he said over and over again in our interviews. But when he described specific events (episodic information), his family felt less like a pack of wolves and more like three vulnerable prey trying to avoid and survive the relentless attacks of an apex predator. There was a mismatch – Elija's specific memories were very different to the more general 'pack of wolves' story of his upbringing.

The idea of these different types of memory had a huge influence on Main and her colleagues, Nancy Kaplan and Carol George. First of all, they interviewed the parents in the families taking part in their study. Then they thought about whether the semantic and episodic information the parents shared during the interview matched up or not. The AAI was born.

In the AAI, you're asked to describe your early relationship with each of the people who brought you up, using only five adjectives. This is designed to get you to access your semantic memory. The adjectives the interviewees chose ranged from 'emotional' to 'empty', 'anxious' to 'absent', 'supportive' to 'scared'.

You're then asked to give a memory for each adjective to show why you chose it. This is designed to access your episodic memory (the memory that's grounded in specific events).

When I asked Lily (the girl who was wrapped in love) for a memory to show why she described her early relationship with her dad as 'happy', she said:

My dad read to me from a very young age. He read me a story before bed every night with one arm round me and one holding the book …

It was just us, I think that was the nice thing. Sharing something.

I'm trying to think of other memories that are probably more emblematic of who he is and how it felt. It just feels cheery around him.

I remember one where my mum sat me at a table. It's the only time I think I ever remember doing this.

I refused to eat my cherry tomatoes. I love them now. But I refused to eat them and she wouldn't let me leave the table. My dad came home and thought, 'This is silly …' and ate them all. Then, with this big grin in his face, he said, 'Lily's done.'

The AAI is packed with more questions like: when you were upset as a child, what would you do? Do you remember being held by either of your parents? What's the first time you remember being separated from your parents? Did you ever feel rejected? And each has a reason behind it. Main believed that avoiding physical contact was linked to avoidant attachment, and that how we cope when we're upset echoes what we do as a child in the Strange Situation when our Important Person leaves and returns. And separation and loss were prominent in Bowlby's thinking.

While you might theoretically ask these questions in ordinary conversation, you probably don't very often. And you probably don't know the answers for most people in your life. AAI questions are intimate and exposing, so much so that interviewees often said things like 'I've never told anyone this before' or 'You now know me better than most people in my life'.

The AAI is designed to 'surprise the unconscious' through repeated, insistent probing. It's relentless in dissecting the way you see your attachment experiences. Interviewers are given strict instructions on how many times to repeat or rephrase a question, and what words to use when they do. They're also instructed when to move on if they don't get what they're looking for – because not answering the question can say a lot in itself.

This is then combined with a total lack of reciprocation. When I was doing AAIs with the interviewees, I couldn't react in the way you might in a normal conversation. It's more like hurling a bowling ball at skittles than a game of tennis. It often felt incredibly awkward, even slightly inhumane – particularly after dredging up excruciatingly dark moments from someone's past. The AAI instructions are very clear on what you can and can't say. And you can't say much.

This was something Lily picked up on. When I asked her how she found the interview, she said, 'Going through the AAI was predominantly strange because, as the interviewer, you couldn't react to it and it felt like your questions were very formulaic. But it was surprising in that it generated a more visceral and emotional response than I would have expected from something so formulaic.'

Because of this relentlessness and lack of response, the AAI cuts away the patterns of speech that offer us a buffer against memory. So while you might be asked any one of the questions in ordinary life, put it all together and the result is an interview that can be very surprising, difficult and emotional.

But at the same time, taking time out to talk to someone who's interested in hearing about your life − without interruption or judgement − is unique. Everyday life is often so hectic that it's rare to get unadulterated time and attention from someone else, let alone someone you don't know.

Ray (the boy who was sent away) explained:

> *It was interesting to talk about all these memories and feelings and things. I only had limited 45-minute exposures to them when I'd dive in with a therapist, then after that it'd be left. So we didn't go into any serious depth. But the AAI went really deep.*

> *I was surprised at what I was bringing up. An example would be Bangladesh. I'd forgotten, entirely, that I was left there for years. Even now, I find it weird to think of that. But now it's come into my conscious. I don't know whether I packaged it up and put it away and whether that was a good or bad thing. In some ways it might've been good because I didn't remember it and I just had fond memories.*

> *But now that I am aware of it, when I do meet my parents, I can understand little things about why I might be irritated sometimes in their presence. Before, I couldn't work it out.*

Secure−autonomous

So far, I've talked about security through the lens of Bowlby, Ainsworth and, more recently, Waters. For Bowlby, security comes from a confidence that Someone

Important will be accessible and willing to comfort and protect us when we're afraid.

For Ainsworth, it's when Someone Important is sensitive to our needs as children. By sensitive, she meant they could understand and interpret what we were telling them, and then respond appropriately and without too much delay. She thought this would give us access to a safe haven when we needed it.

For Waters and her colleagues, security meant learning a 'script' where we expect someone will be there for us when we need them. This script is learned over time, as patterns of behaviour are repeated – namely that we show we're upset and need support, our Important Person offers it, we accept, the help is helpful and they also comfort and help us regulate our emotions.

For each of these researchers, security is about our expectations of how Important People will behave when we're upset or scared.

But when researchers refer to 'security' in the AAI, they mean something different.

Main and her colleagues noticed something unusual about the people whose children were classified as secure in the Strange Situation years earlier. When these parents were asked in the AAI about their early experiences, they described both good and bad aspects in a balanced way – even when these relationships had been tricky.

Main and her colleagues thought that these parents seemed able to access both semantic and episodic memory and could respond to questions that were designed to get at either. Just as their secure children could focus their attention on either their parent or their toys in the Strange Situation, these parents could turn to both positive and negative experiences, both semantic and episodic memory, in the AAI.

Main, Hesse and their colleague, Ruth Goldwyn, described the way these adults spoke as 'secure–autonomous', which I will call secure. This didn't mean they thought that the adult was independent. Instead, it meant that the defining feature of their interview was the freedom with which they talked about their experiences of Important People. They didn't restrict information in any way. They recognised the value of relationships with Important People but were also independent enough to assess them.

The AAI involved two tasks: to reflect on memories of experiences that relate to attachment, and to talk about these in a way that keeps the interviewer's questions in mind. Secure speakers could focus their attention flexibly between the questions they were asked and their own memories. This meant that they could let go of those memories to get back to what the interviewer was asking. And no matter how difficult the topic, they were able to generally collaborate with the interviewer.

The rules of conversation

As well as having evidence to back up their generalisations, people who were secure answered questions in a complete but succinct way – as we saw with Lily (who was classified as secure). They didn't veer off-topic. Their accounts were orderly, clear and fresh.

And this was something that a colleague of Main and Hesse's, Paul Grice, had thought a lot about. Grice was a philosopher of language and thought that there are four rules of conversation – to be:

1. truthful and have evidence for what you say;
2. succinct and yet complete;
3. relevant to the topic as presented; and
4. clear and orderly.

In everyday life, we might give someone permission to break these rules. For example, in the wake of a break-up, you might allow your friend to talk for most of the time you saw them to help them process what had happened and how they felt about it. But on the whole, Grice thought that these four rules applied to conversation. And Main observed that secure people usually complied with these rules.

Complying with them meant that an interviewee's story was coherent – that the different parts fitted together to create a logical whole.

Bowlby, Ainsworth and Waters saw security as believing we have a safe haven when we need it. But Main saw it as something different. For Main, security reflects the freedom with which we can focus our attention and talk about attachment experiences. For Bowlby, Ainsworth and Waters, security is about what we expect from Important People based on our experiences so far. For Main, it's about how we process information relating to those people. Research suggests the two are linked, but they're also very different.

Preoccupied attachment
Goldwyn noticed another pattern in the AAIs – some people focused on complaints.

They were angry and preoccupied with their relationships with Important People to such an extent that they often lost track of the question they'd been asked. They seemed to get sucked into vivid descriptions of their childhood relationships. Sometimes their main aim seemed to be to make a case against their parents, instead of responding to the questions. They couldn't go between episodic and semantic memory. Instead, they focused on the negative aspects of episodic memories – even when events could've been interpreted in a more balanced way.

They seemed to focus their attention on things to do with attachment, even if this was at the expense of cooperating with the interviewer. Main and her colleagues called this pattern 'preoccupied'. They thought the way that preoccupied adults spoke was akin to an ambivalent/resistant child in the Strange Situation who was worried about their Important Person leaving, who was scared and upset and couldn't focus on the environment and instead focused constantly on their Important Person.

In her AAI, Skyler was classified as preoccupied (the adult equivalent of ambivalent/resistant). And she recognised some of these ways of behaving when it came to romantic relationships:

> *I have looked for relationships everywhere.*
>
> *Like, three in the morning, passing a kebab shop and I'd think, 'That's the one.' I've given out my number on night buses. Why? That's not where you're going to find the love of your life.*
>
> *Everybody I met between the age of 22 and 70, I'd think, 'Could they be the one?' Literally.*
>
> *Relationships take up a lot of my brain space.*

The main way in which preoccupied adults broke Grice's rules of conversation was by just how much they talked about things that weren't direct answers to AAI questions. They also quickly switched their point of view, didn't finish sentences, said vague phrases like 'sort of thing' and 'this and that' and used nonsense words to end sentences, like 'dada-dada-dada'.

For example, when Elija was describing hearing his parents having a fight, he said, 'The next day I wouldn't ask questions. Was I allowed to ask? Was I old enough to ask? Was it any of my business to ask? Mum never used to confide in me and say, "Your dad beat me up last night," de-de-duh.' And this 'de-de-duh' was relevant to his AAI classification.

Preoccupied adults were often not very orderly in the way they described experiences. They didn't signal that they were talking about the past when they quoted conversations with their Important People. They spoke in a wild way, with highly entangled, confusing sentences that ran on and on.

To try to illustrate these points, I'm going to provide two AAI excerpts, one from Lily (the girl who was wrapped in love) and one from Skyler (the girl who was wrapped in cotton wool). This is from Lily's response when I asked her what her relationship with her parents felt like now:

We're still all really close as a family … I think my relationship with my dad is interesting because sometimes I feel like he is much closer to my brother and that we are more distant than we used to be.

With my brother, he's very much the first person on call for him. And I find that sad because I think, 'You prefer my brother. You spend more time with him. You call him.' He doesn't really call me in the same way. He likes it when I call him, but he doesn't want to impose. My brother doesn't have a partner or any prospect of a partner in the near future, because of his health. I think my dad is my brother's anchor point. My dad likes to be needed, and probably feels I don't need him in the same way anymore as I get older.

What Lily is describing isn't a totally perfect situation. But, as is the hallmark of the way someone secure speaks, she describes the negatives (and positives) in an open and balanced way. She doesn't try to recreate the conversation or address her father as if he's present. She doesn't get tangled in her speech or have sentences that run on and on. Her words are clear, orderly and fresh. As the coder commented, Lily's AAI 'suggests an awareness of the humanity in the flaws of her parents, and unpleasant or unfavourable experiences are described with forgiveness, balance and humour.'

This is an excerpt from Skyler's answer to the same question:

The more time that goes on, the more frustrated I get with my mom because she doesn't use facts. Or she'll use them incorrectly, or she doesn't trust that I can survive on my own, or she doesn't think things through, and that's why I get so frustrated.

For the past four years, we used to talk on the phone a lot, and then she has a horrible phone and the thing is, my parents are not poor. I mean, they're not loaded, but they're not poor. And my mom's phone just can't handle international calls. So I'm like, 'Just get a new phone.' But there's a seven-second delay every time I call, and it's so infuriating that I just can't do it.

And then I'm like, 'Why can't you get a phone?' And every time it's like, 'Well, you know, Bill said iPhones are $2,000.' I'm like, 'You don't need the latest version, also you can get it in contract, or you can get an old iPhone for $300, and you can afford that. Even if you had a number that was just so you could call me …' Because she will sit there and go, 'I never talk to you.' And I'm like, "Cause I can't talk to you. Because it's so frustrating to talk to you.'

And she just won't believe me. She doesn't trust me because one of her friends says something. And I'm like, 'Why do you not trust me over Bill? Don't you think that your 72-year-old friend is probably more out of tune with what technology costs than your daughter?' And she just won't believe me.

It's frustrating for her to go, 'I miss you so much, why do we never talk?' And I'm going, 'This is why we don't talk.'

'But I don't want to learn a new iPhone.'

I keep on trying to break down why it makes me so angry, and I think she won't acknowledge her feelings.

She would come up with excuse after excuse after excuse that I would solve. I know it sounds crazy to get so angry about it, it's so frustrating that she doesn't think things through. So our relationship is breaking down, which is sad.

The coder gave Skyler a rating of 8 out of 9 for anger for her answer to this question. And anger was the reason that Skyler was classified as preoccupied overall. She seemed angry with her mum about lots of things, and this pulled her away from keeping the AAI questions in mind. Skyler even remarked on it when I asked how she felt about doing the interview, saying, 'I was surprised how much I had to say and how angry I am at my parents.'

On her copy of the transcript, the coder jotted down next to this excerpt that Skyler used 'excessive quotes'. It's as if Skyler wanted to recreate the conversation, and she addressed her mum as if she was with us in the recording studio.

Skyler's full response to my question was twice the length of the excerpt I've included here. The rest of her answer was similar in tone and style but went on to describe a number of other things her mum did that frustrated her.

What I found striking about Skyler's full unedited answer was that most of the things she complained about related to wanting to be in contact, comforted or protected. And this is also what came up in Lily's answer to the same question.

Maybe that's not surprising. Knowing that your parent is on the other end of the phone is essential to their being available – which Bowlby thought was the aim of the attachment system. And he didn't think this was something we grow out of. Instead, no matter how old we are, he believed that when we're hurt or scared, or in an emergency, we're driven to look for Someone Important, and feel all the more troubled when they're not available.

In other words, even when we're adults, we still need to know Important People are there for us if we need them.

Skyler

The girl wrapped in cotton wool
Attachment pattern: preoccupied

My mom did not really cope with me growing up. There was never any change in the way that she treated me – she didn't give me any more freedom, there was no sense of independence. Nothing. I don't think she has actually treated me any differently from when I was 10 years old till now.

It was insulting that by my early twenties, she didn't trust me enough to take care of myself. I still had a 10 p.m. curfew when I was 21. So in the summers when I was home from university, I was legally allowed to drink but had to be home at 10.

And she always made me feel guilty whenever I complained about it. She'd say, 'Well, I'm sorry that I love you so much.'

She just kept piling on the cotton wool.

So I moved country to escape.

Even then, she would tell me on the phone to wear my seat belt. That is a level of micromanaging that should not be applied.

If I was heading home from a performance late at night, I would call other singers or musicians in the industry who were also awake and let them know where I was. I had certain safety measures in place. But still Mom would say, 'Call me when you get home.' And if I forgot, instead of just calling me back, the next day, she would say, 'I didn't sleep at all because you didn't call me and I thought you'd been kidnapped or murdered.'

She was so overprotective and unbearable. Unbearably overprotective.

When I first moved to the UK, I had a rocky start. I became very close with a girl named Amy. That was not a healthy friendship. At all.

Our friendship was a good example of how my attachment pattern means I think I don't deserve better, so I just let people take advantage of me and bend over backwards to make people happy.

It's like putting a frog in water and then slowly boiling it … I don't always recognise that it's happening, until it's gotten too far.

It's a similar story in romantic relationships. I have been single most of my life and   I, I don't want to be single.

I often say I would rather be single than with somebody I'm not in love with. And I think that I believe that. But equally, I have tried to fit so many triangle men into round holes, like, forced, with a hammer, shaving off the edges, shoving them in there. So that has to say something.

Like Frank. We went on one date – I thought it was a great date, but he told me I didn't have 'it', whatever 'it' means. We ended up hooking up off and on for two years. Every so often, he would end it and say, 'We have to stop hooking up because I need to find a wife and you're not it.' Then every single relationship he got into across those two years, he would either cheat on the girl with me and then end it or call me immediately after they broke up.

One time, he called me while walking home from the house of the person he'd just dumped. He didn't even make the 15-minute walk home after breaking up with her before calling me. My dog knew his house, I would stay there so much. But I was never good enough to date.

Then there was Karim. He was born and raised in Ghana and would constantly tell me that he was going to go back, even though he never did.

He moved in with me, which he lied to his parents about – I don't think he ever told them about me. From then on, as a singer, I was supporting both of us.

I wasn't allowed to post about us on Facebook. He wouldn't go to weddings with me because he 'hates weddings' but really, just didn't want to invest in getting to know any of my friends. Then one day, I walked into my flat after visiting my sister in the US, and he was waiting for me, having already moved out.

'Don't freak out, but … we're breaking up. I'm moving back to Ghana,' he said. But at least two years later, he was still in England.

Amos

The boy who couldn't remember
Attachment pattern: possibly avoidant

I decided to be a chess player. My mum and my dad were really against it. They thought I didn't have enough talent.

I didn't realise it back then, but they were right.

If you want to live well as a chess player, it's really, really hard. So I spent a lot of time trying to make it work.

There was a lot of studying on my own, which I loved. But I was also travelling a lot, playing all around the world.

At 21, where I lived, most kids didn't work. So, the fact that me and my chess friends had money and could spend it made us really cool. I was going out every night, having my own money, getting to know a lot of people that were really different from me.

We always had girls around. We rented this huge place with six rooms and sublet them to students for a year. After a couple of months, I would start a relationship with one of the women in the house. There was Jenny, who was French. It was one year with her.

Then I was learning Italian, so I dated Laura. Then Norwegian with Veronica. In attachment language, they were mostly preoccupied. As were my best friends.

For a few years, it was one girlfriend every year, one language every year. It's horrible. But at least I'm candid about it. And I got burnt more than the other person every time.

Raz, from Germany, for example … She was so beautiful, every time I was out with her, people would say, 'Oh my God, your girlfriend is stunning,' and that made me feel really special. But we had a lot of fights and she didn't really have any interests, so I don't think we were right for each other. She left me for another guy and it was very traumatic. I didn't have sex for a whole year after that. I was completely down for months and months.

For most of my life, I had the feeling that no one would want me. I think all my girlfriends were in very much love with me, and that was very satisfying.
                    But most of them weren't
                              exactly what I wanted.

I don't do it consciously, but people could probably feel ignored by me or put down by me. I don't think I criticise people directly … I don't think.

                    I'm maybe not a modest person, but at the same time I don't feel like I am really good. But I don't think anyone is really good. So I don't feel superior.

Then I started dating Milena from Colombia. It was my first actual relationship. I wasn't in love with her, but I cared about her. I think she was in love with me. Then when she went home for the Christmas holidays, and someone set me up with a friend of theirs and we started hanging out. I thought, 'When Milena comes back from holiday, I'm going to leave her.' But I couldn't. So, I had two girlfriends for a few months.

That's when I started psychotherapy.

I didn't feel the first therapist had anything to teach me. But I wasn't able to tell him. So, after a month, I started going to another therapist. I kept doing therapy with both for a while. And I still had two girlfriends. It was very funny. Very expensive.

In the end, in both cases I invented an excuse. I said I was moving to Chile.

Then one day I found a book by Marie Curie on a bus, and started reading it. I was engrossed. I wanted to know everything about her. So I started studying physics. After a few months, I quit playing chess.

I had tried to construct this picture of somebody who was very precocious and intelligent.
   And I think I succeeded. It just didn't give me really what I wanted.

That's also why I decided I really needed psychotherapy. I was psychologically weak. I wasn't feeling emotions. I was like a shell abandoned in the world and couldn't shoulder the power of my unconscious. I wanted to know myself.

I saw my second psychotherapist for five years. She would tell me that I was rejecting her, keeping her away. But I wasn't doing it consciously. And she didn't help me work on it. I really wished I could have learned from her, but I couldn't. I don't think we really connected. I was extremely difficult to connect to. A bit like now, except I was completely unaware of anything, including this avoidance I always talk about.

But at least I started to realise, 'I'm feeling angry. I'm feeling disrespected.' Until then, I'd never consciously experienced anger.

I remember having a fight with a roommate,

and the anger must have been so intense, that my heart was pounding in my head. I remember going to psychotherapy and saying, 'I guess this must be anger.'

'Yeah, that's anger,' she said.

I had headaches constantly during my childhood. Constant. It must've been related to it. That lasted until my late twenties. And I had diarrhoea every morning. So chronic.

I think it was anxiety.

Anxiety is about feelings you're scared of expressing. So I would withdraw. And I would get depressed. But at 26, I started having feelings. Now I never have headaches. Ever.

Even so, I don't talk about stressful things. When I have a problem, I think about it. I'm not really a guy who seeks help. I try only to rely on myself.

I definitely try not to think about things that make me anxious or depressed. I try not to get too activated, for sure. I totally avoid things the whole time. I have avoided difficult questions you've asked me.

Even in therapy. When something difficult came up, I would say, 'This happened, but it's okay.

Let's not talk about it.

Fine.'

The Ray conundrum: dismissive attachment

To code an AAI, you have to train at a two-week course and then pass a reliability test. For each AAI, you then have to spend 6 to 10 hours poring over every word, stutter, stumble and pause, focusing on the way the interviewee pays attention to and talks about their experiences with Important People.

Your job as coder is to look at the transcript as a whole and compare what someone says about their experiences generally ('semantic' information) to the evidence they provide of what actually happened ('episodic' information).

A good example of this comparison is provided by a mum from Main's Berkeley Study who I'll call Sarah. Sarah began by saying that her own mother was a 'good one' and that they had a 'fine relationship'. But later in her AAI, Sarah described how she painfully broke her hand as a child. She was in agony for weeks but didn't tell her mum as she would have been angry. Sarah's positive description of the relationship didn't chime with her lived experience – there was a memory mismatch. When Sarah was seen in the Strange Situation with her child, their relationship was given top scores for avoidance.

As she went through the AAIs looking for patterns, Main's colleague, Goldwyn, noticed that some people described their childhoods as perfect – they had zero problems, everything was glorious. But when she looked at the Strange Situation classifications five years earlier, Goldwyn was surprised to discover that these radiant descriptions belonged to people who had avoidant relationships with their children.

When Goldwyn examined their AAIs, she found that their memories either contradicted their flawless accounts (as with Sarah) or they couldn't supply many or any concrete memories of caring moments. Instead they often dismissed the idea of depending on other people and didn't think much of missing and needing others – or being missed and needed themselves.

Main and her colleagues concluded that these people were idealising their upbringings. In doing so, they were relying on their semantic memory (memory in the form of stories that may have been told to them as children) at the expense of remembering specific events that could've qualified their descriptions of impossibly perfect upbringings.

Despite their idyllic accounts of childhood, they also talked about specific, episodic memories of rejection. When Main used statistics to analyse this, she found a link between idealising and being rejected. She also found a link between people describing rejection in their AAI and avoiding physical contact with their child when being observed in the lab. The link was stronger where the rejection was something that the coder picked up on rather than something the interviewee clearly described themselves.

Goldwyn and Main thought that, like the Strange Situation, the AAI created a scenario that turned someone's attention towards attachment. In the Strange Situation, a child in an avoidant relationship focused their attention away from their Important Person. And in the AAI, their Important Person did the adult equivalent – they focused their attention away from their childhood and any feelings that it might bring up.

Main believed that shifting attention away from Important People as well as any attachment experiences or feelings stemmed from being rejected in childhood. For Main, rejection could mean different things, like a parent criticising, failing to understand or avoiding physical contact with their child. Main and her colleagues decided to describe the way these people spoke as 'dismissing'.

A decade later, Mary Dozier and Roger Kobak measured 'skin conductance' as people answered AAI questions. Skin conductance is when skin becomes better at conducting electricity because someone is sweating and 'physiologically aroused'. The idea being that if they're physiologically aroused, it's likely to be caused by emotion. Dozier and Kobak found that these interviewees who described their upbringings as wonderful had higher levels of skin conductance when answering questions about separation, rejection and threat. While they were able to hide their upset from their minds, they couldn't hide it from their bodies.

In the AAI, people with a dismissing attachment pattern tend to give very brief answers that lack detail. They don't have much episodic information to dip into – perhaps because they blocked this from their awareness as a way of protecting themselves, or perhaps they know about it but find it difficult to tell others. While they're usually orderly in the way they speak, they turn the conversation away from sensitive topics.

In his AAI, Amos (the boy who couldn't remember) described his relationship with his parents using lots of positive words but couldn't give any memories to back them up. He described his mother as loving, but instead of giving a specific memory, he said, 'Yeah, I guess she always showed her love towards me. She was very loving and attentive. Just in general. I don't know.'

The same happened when he described her as present:

> She was around a lot. I guess. Every weekend she was always with me. Then during the week, she was with me too. When I was sick, she was always there. Taking care of it. Taking care of the problem.
>
> I was in hospital for a long time. And she was just present.

There were no specifics, no images, no hooks, no stories. Everything felt very abstract and distant and brief. And sometimes his memories felt totally incompatible.

The AAI includes a question about whether you ever felt rejected as a young child – even if, as an adult, you realise it wasn't actually rejection. When I asked Amos this, he interrupted me before I could finish the question to say no. Then I asked him if he ever felt pushed away or ignored. And again he said no.

I was surprised by this as, less than half an hour earlier, Amos had described things in his childhood that were clear examples of rejection – like his mum telling him he didn't do anything right, or saying that if he didn't do certain things, she wouldn't love him anymore.

I was also surprised because, as I was asking the question, he started playing with the top of the water bottle on the table. I remember this very clearly, as the interview was being recorded and I was worried the sound might block the audibility of what he was saying.

When I did the follow-up with Amos, I asked him about it. 'Interesting …' he said. 'I didn't – I don't remember any of this. Are you sure?'

Thankfully, as it was all recorded and the transcriber had also picked up on it, I was sure. And Amos's response was, 'I have absolutely no recollection of this.'

It reminded me of Dozier and Kobak's skin conductance research – where people who said their upbringings were ideal had higher levels of skin conductance when answering questions about being rejected. But was this evidence of dismissive attachment? After all, it's a defence mechanism that anyone could have as a way of focusing their attention away from something difficult.

But Amos only did this once during the entire AAI and hours and hours of follow-up interviews I did with him: when I asked him to talk about rejection. And this echoes Main's belief that turning attention away from all things attachment stems from being rejected in childhood.

Amos wasn't the only person classified as dismissive (the adult equivalent of avoidant in the Strange Situation). Ray (the boy who was sent away) was also. Except his story is a little more complex.

Before I carried out his AAI, Ray explained that he and his therapist (who he had been seeing for nine months and who knew a great deal about his life and relationships) were convinced he had a preoccupied attachment pattern.

But when his AAI coding came back, Ray was classified as dismissing. The coder said that Ray was lively, talkative and generally engaged in the interview. He spoke at length about tangential, unemotional things. For example, his mother's comfort was reassurance and an explanation of how racism works, rather than a hug. He said his mother was 'quite tactile', but didn't give any specific memories to back this up.

The coder said Ray regularly steered back to racism and the historical context and the immigrant perspective. While this wasn't always off-topic, it was a notable feature of the interview. When Ray was asked about attachment, this is the topic he switched to, as if he used it to distract.

Ray also idealised his mum, in that he described her in very positive, gushing terms initially but then had no actual memories of supportive or loving behaviour to support this view. The coder gave him 7 out of 9 for idealising her. And in reaching this high score, the coder mentioned phrases like 'and then everything was reasonably hunky-dory' to describe life once Ray got back from Bangladesh. '[My parents] were both very lovely and very loving,' and they 'did everything for me,' he said, but when asked to give a specific memory for his mum's loving behaviour, he paused for 13 seconds

before saying, 'I can't actually, I'm sorry.' The coder gave Ray's parents the same ratings for loving as Zsa Zsa's – 3 out of 9 for each.

The coder's conclusion was that 'there is an unmistakable disconnect between the very positive image put forward and [Ray's] failure to recount actual instances of genuine comfort or support, beyond explaining racism.' Ray was classified as dismissive (the adult equivalent of avoidant).

But I wasn't 100 per cent sure of this conclusion. My hope was to explain dismissive attachment in a clear and simple way, but Ray's interview didn't feel like a classic or straightforward example of it.

There were times when he couldn't provide a memory to back up the five words he'd chosen to describe his relationships with his parents. And not being able to think of a memory to illustrate the word 'loving' felt particularly conspicuous. But at the same time, he valued attachment in a way that dismissive people don't tend to. He showed a lot of compassion and forgiveness for the way his parents behaved. His story felt coherent and fresh, and he balanced providing memories with answering questions.

So I arranged for it to be re-coded by the most experienced coder in the world.

This time, his classification came back as secure. To avoid bias, I didn't tell the coder he'd had an earlier coding, but as soon as she sent me his classification, I shared some of the first coder's notes. She reflected on it, considered all the points and concluded that Ray's classification was still secure.

It's not unusual for coders to disagree. They only agree around 80 per cent of the time. That means in one out of five interviews, they don't.

The second coder thought Ray valued attachment relationships, that he understood the influence of attachment experiences on him and that he was able to talk about them in a free-thinking, open and objective way. Referring to the coding manual, she wrote that his AAI suggested 'an awareness of the humanity in the flaws of his parents, and unpleasant or unfavourable experiences are described with balance and understanding'.

She went on to explain that secure AAIs can be quite varied. Some describe parents who provided a safe haven and secure base, while others describe parents who were rejecting, neglecting and/or abusive. Whatever they describe, they're able to give vivid memories to support the general picture, and the initial description holds up throughout the interview. Whatever story they tell, for their AAI to be classified as secure, it must be coherent.

The second coder acknowledged that Ray showed some dismissive tendencies. But she also pointed out that people classified as secure can show some lack of memory, as well as some idealisation of one or both parents. It just can't be too high.

One thing both coders agreed on was that Ray's father was very neglecting. The first coder explained that this was because Ray had described how his dad:

> *never picked me up or dropped me off at school. He never knew what I was reading or studying. He just wasn't physically present because he was always working during the day doing one job, and then in the evening, setting up his other job. He was never there at any sporting event, or anything I did at school. I don't blame him for it. I just think he was just really busy. And I went to Bangladesh. I was there for three years.*

In many ways, it would've made my life much easier if I'd just accepted Ray's first coding, as I would have had someone with a dismissive classification involved in the project from the start. And the path to finding someone dismissive was very long and painful – and involved years of arranging or carrying out AAIs, only to discover that people who were convinced they were dismissive, weren't.

Looking back, this shouldn't have been surprising. It was both ironic and entirely predictable that someone whose classification is defined by their dismissal of relationships wouldn't want to get involved with a project where they have to talk extensively about them.

What's fascinating, and also hugely important, about Ray's classification is this: his therapist, a trained professional, guessed his attachment pattern and came to a conclusion that was very different to qualified AAI coders. Ray, who had lived his life and read a number of books about relationships, did the same. The combination of these two assessments may have meant that, throughout their nine months of therapy together, they'd seen Ray, his childhood and his adult relationships through a particular lens – a lens that was apparently incorrect.

Or was it? An AAI coding can only tell you what your words on that particular day at that particular time say about the way your mind is processing your experiences of attachment relationships. If I'd done the AAI with Ray nine months earlier, before he had started therapy, perhaps his classification would have been different. But would it have been preoccupied? Given both coders commented on dismissive tendencies, that might have been his classification – but this wasn't what Ray and his therapist suspected. They might still have been wrong.

There's zero way of knowing what Ray would have been, as the AAI can't tell you with any certainty what happened in the past. It looks back instead of forward, it remembers and describes instead of following people into the future. And if the Minnesota Study tells us anything about looking back, it's that it's not always accurate.

Perhaps Ray and his therapist didn't independently come up with the idea that he was preoccupied. Perhaps Ray was influenced by his therapist's theory of his attachment pattern. Or maybe it was the other way round. And maybe the therapist's own attachment pattern influenced their assessment of Ray.

Ignoring how he might have been classified at a different point in time, what about the AAI he actually did? He only did one, yet he received two classifications. What happened?

The first coder, someone who had gone through the rigorous process of training and being approved to code AAIs, classified Ray as dismissive – and with good reasons. Then the most experienced coder in the world classified him as secure. They both had the same transcript, the same training, the same coding manual. But they came up with two very different answers.

So, two coders and one therapist – three professionals who I imagine have an advanced understanding of attachment theory reached three different conclusions.

And each conclusion has real-life repercussions. Before getting his AAI results, Ray would say things like, 'I'm very needy – it's because I'm preoccupied.' Or 'I spend all my time trying to pretend I'm not as needy as I am.'

The way he saw himself was influenced by this label. It altered the story he created of his life and relationships. It led him to blame himself for behaving in certain ways because he attributed them to an attachment pattern that his AAI suggests he doesn't currently have.

The stories we tell ourselves, the boxes we think we tick and the lenses that we and others choose to see us through can have an enormous impact on our lives. That's why we should be very careful when we choose which glasses to wear.

Ray

The boy who was sent away
Attachment pattern: secure

I first met Ayumi at a friend's fancy dress party. She was dressed as an anime character, and it took me an hour to gather the courage to go and speak to her. I waited and waited until she went to the bar and timed it so that I went to get a drink at the same time. She ordered a negroni. We immediately hit it off and spent the evening talking to each other. Then I asked if I could take her number and she said yes. I couldn't believe my luck.

Being beautiful aside, there was something about her elusiveness and the challenge of that which drew me in. She was fiercely independent and I was attracted to that.

I was about to leave uni, I had my dream job lined up, everything was going well – when Ayumi met me, I was sorted. I was self-confident. I knew what I wanted, I was doing what I wanted, and I was well and happy and set up.

I really didn't think I stood a chance. So, when we ended up together, it was a major achievement. Inside I was bursting, I wanted to high-five myself all the time. But I didn't. I was very cool about it. Having escaped my parents' unhappy relationship, having been in and out of hospital for years, I'd reinvented myself as the person I always wanted to be, but more resilient and emotionally tough. I was playing it out with someone who probably thought that's what I was really like.

Ayumi was cold and frosty and unfathomable. She did not want to talk about emotions. She was a woman of mystery who kept all her cards to herself. I found it really attractive. I didn't know that meant she was avoidant.

I remember one of my best friends at the time saying, 'I think you're falling in love with Ayumi — just be really, really careful.' But I found it exciting that I had to up my game and work at the relationship to keep it going, and it was addictive.

I worked out early on that compliments weren't taken brilliantly and were considered over the top, as were emotions. So I played them down because this was clearly a person who didn't want or seem to need that sort of thing. I played along with what she did seem to need and drip-fed the sorts of things people would say to each other when they're in love.

Had I been allowed, she would have been flooded. She would have run a mile if I'd said half of the things that were in my head about how much I loved her. But I was quite happy being the cool person with this cool girlfriend. I was just pleased that she was prepared to go out with me.

I'd be doing her a disservice if I said she was looking for faults or picking them out in me. I didn't feel belittled by her at all. But there was a lack of anything emotional. There was no bigging up, there was no putting down. I just felt ignored. It's as if I was irrelevant.

But on Planet Dismissive, there's only two things that you do to someone in your life — you either put them down or you ignore them. Ignoring means loving them, that was how I saw it. Being irrelevant was a compliment.

I picked up on the new language of the relationship. 'You're not going to get that much emotion and affection because that's not how this person's programmed. But if she's not slagging you off, that's good, that means everything's alright.' I adapted.

I worried my novelty would wear off for her at some point. And it did a bit. She called it off, called it back on again, and after some introspection on her part we were back together. But even then, I did feel vulnerable sometimes.

Then all the other things started to solidify around that, it's like they were cementing round the seriously weak joints in the structure of a building. A lot of glue was forming around these weak spots, making the structure reasonably resilient. Not the best structure in the world, but a reasonably functional structure that could survive quite a while.

The glue was time together, friends, family. We got on famously with each other's families, I mean utterly brilliantly. Her family loved me, and my family loved her. And it was much easier to spend time with my family when Ayumi was there.

My parents were still living together but their relationship was getting worse and worse. Their arguments were getting more extreme. And my dad had started to drink.

He'd never had a problem with alcohol. We'd always had it in the house, he would always offer it to others, but he didn't drink. So the fact that he took to drink wasn't good. He was doing it to anaesthetise himself. It was building up to something.

Then he couldn't sleep and the word 'depression' was bandied about. I remember clocking the word.

Then one day, when I was at home for the weekend, I walked into the bathroom and found Dad. He was out on the floor, next to an empty bottle of pills. I yelled at Mum to call the ambulance and I tried desperately to resuscitate him.

The paramedics came quickly, took him away, did their tests. He was all right. No serious damage.

But the suicide attempt was a shock to everyone – and to him.

He never tried anything like that again and decided to stop drinking. He also decided that was it. The marriage was over. He moved out.

There was no counselling. The way things worked then was your friends would intervene or help out. You had a doctor friend who would give you the right pills to help with depression and insomnia. But there wasn't any thought of seeing a counsellor or anything like that.

But I wonder what would have happened if they had seen one.

Both of my parents came from poor backgrounds and were very insecure about their futures, so they did everything they could to build security for themselves and then us. That was their major shared value.

As things got better financially, I think they worried that if they didn't keep moving forward, they would go back and lose it all. The insecurity was huge. Absolutely huge. It was as if they were in a war situation.

They lived their lives like that. They hedged, invested, did all the little things they needed to do to build security long term.

But you can't do that to that intensity, keep going, keep going, working, working, working, doing the job relentlessly without it taking a toll.

Their arguments became more and more extreme. They would say things to each other that people would only say in a movie, a violent, violent, unpleasant movie, horrible things that it's difficult for me to forget. Dad also said them to me.

'You're a disappointment' was the big one. 'You're the main source of my pain in life' was another. Or 'I've sacrificed so much for you and I don't get any thanks.'

Dad wouldn't do that in business. Just in his personal life. Maybe he thought he could get away with it safely, maybe he didn't realise there was damage caused when you did it.

I think happiness is a condition and he was never taught or shown how to actually be happy. He was only taught how to survive. There's a lot of people like that out there.

That's why I don't want the fight. There's no need for it half the time. And often it's not going to go anywhere.

So, if I ever felt like saying something like that to Ayumi, I knew that I'd be causing untold damage, that it would be remembered, even when I passed away.

So, you never say it. You just never say it. You never say things that you don't mean. I don't think my dad meant them, I genuinely don't. But he said them.

It could have been worse. He could have thrown things or beat people up … Other people do that.

But I didn't want to replicate anything that happened between my parents in their marriage. I didn't want my children to be hiding behind a door, listening to something play out. I didn't want to argue.

I think Ayumi was like that too. She didn't want to confront. She didn't want to talk about things.

So, Ayumi and I coldly calculated and agreed, jointly, not to argue, confront each other, or discuss seriously problematic or emotional issues about what we were dissatisfied with, and to just get on with it and try to have as good a time in the process as possible.

And that's exactly what we did.

And we never argued like my parents.

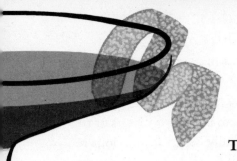

Zsa Zsa

The girl who walked into fire
Attachment pattern: preoccupied

I dropped out of school and the first thing I did was start taking endless amounts of drugs.

I felt lonely. I wasn't emotionally intelligent or wise. I was a firecracker. How I managed to sustain any friends is beyond me. I definitely had no sexual relationships.

I first had a girlfriend when I was 23. I really liked her, but she couldn't accept herself being gay, so that didn't last long. I had sex with men before then, but only when drunk and only because people did it. When I realised I was gay, I was like, 'Oh, well this explains why I'm not romantically attracted to anybody.' I genuinely thought I was pretty asexual.

I used to think I had a really liberal upbringing. My parents were the only parents who didn't give a shit what time you came home. I would happily have friends over, trash the house and clean it up again when they weren't there. They were frequently staying somewhere else, so weren't often around, and we were often left in the care of an au pair who didn't speak any English. I used to joke about how many au pairs I had, I counted two dozen.

I don't really feel like my home life contributed towards me having any sort of understanding of myself. I never really knew how hard life would be. I never had a wider understanding of what it means to deal with other people or have relationships.

I don't think I had any sort of emotional toolkit to be able to live my fucking life.

I definitely didn't have the toolkit to be able to discuss or troubleshoot anything when I was finally in my first serious relationship. I didn't know how to talk about things with a partner.

I feel like I have a,   a rage that lives in me. I'm a bubbler, I get quite furious.   My response to certain situations was always the same. I would lose my temper,   raise my voice or shout. Even though for me it's a deeply shaming experience.

                                        Even though I feel consciously aware that losing your temper isn't normal, I have crystal clear memories of really losing my shit, at both work and in my personal life.   I don't have vivid memories of other things that have happened in my life,   but I have vivid memories of those because   I just feel like I'm turning into my dad.

So even though I want to be in a relationship where I'm important to somebody,   I end up in situations where I feel worthless. I suppress my worth or disregard my own emotion because I think if I continue to walk into that fire, it'll get better.

But it doesn't.

And as I am now starting to recognise …
          I'm just burnt and empty.

The shadow of trauma: unresolved attachment

As she went through the AAIs looking for patterns, Main and her colleagues noticed something else. For some people, seemingly unconnected ideas seemed to interrupt each other, while other ideas were lost altogether. The way they spoke seemed to break down when they talked about their Important People – for example, they might go silent for a long time without seeming to notice. Others seemed to think about Someone Important in irrational or bizarre ways, like talking about a deceased relative as if they were still alive. Main and Goldwyn noticed that two experiences seemed to lead to these kinds of responses – bereavement and traumatic abuse.

Main and Hesse called these AAIs 'unresolved' and they created a scale for coders to measure physical abuse as a child. It also measured times when Someone Important behaved in a frightening way, which included sexual abuse or threatening to kill the child. Describing Someone Important as mean or hostile at times wasn't enough, unless the interviewee found it very scary.

Main and Hesse weren't just trying to measure any abuse that may have happened. They were also trying to assess how this had been processed by the person speaking.

Bowlby, Ainsworth and Waters thought of attachment in terms of our expectations in relationships. But that's not what the AAI measures. Instead, the AAI assesses how you process information relating to Important People. So it doesn't matter what went on in your childhood, or how you thought your Important People would behave when you needed them. What matters is how you process and talk about it now.

There are lots of ways trauma in the past can influence the present. You might, for example, block out all thoughts of it. Or you might become upset just thinking about it. In both cases, you're focusing your attention either away from or towards the trauma. Many would say that the trauma isn't resolved. But it's not 'unresolved' according to the technical meaning intended by Main and her colleagues.

Instead, according to Main, you're unresolved if your ability to pay attention to a traumatic event is disorganised or disoriented. The idea is that the way you talk represents the way you process it mentally – in other words, if your words are disorganised or disoriented, so is your mental processing.

According to Main and Hesse, signs of unresolved abuse include feeling that you deserved abusive treatment from Someone Important, confusing yourself with the abuser, and indications that you haven't finished mourning the abuse, for example if the topic invades your discussions of other things.

Another sign is describing abuse then denying that's what it was. The idea is that this could suggest a conflict between different views of reality. Although it might also reflect the tension between being honest about abuse and sweeping it under the carpet, as many societies expect you to.

Zsa Zsa (the girl who walked into fire) and Elija (the boy who was raised by wolves) were both classified as unresolved in relation to traumatic abuse they suffered when they were children. Elija was given the highest possible score – 9 out of 9, and Zsa Zsa scored 7. Their secondary classification was 'preoccupied'.

The coder thought Elija was clearly engaged and a bit of a talker. But he wouldn't talk about his early childhood, and only described a specific memory very occasionally. Instead, when asked about his early experiences, he said the family was strong 'like a pack of wolves' until his dad decided to stray – and that was when conflict began. Then Elija talked about his teens when his mum kicked him out and his dad disowned him – something he came back to throughout the interview.

The few times Elija did talk about early childhood involved intense physical abuse from his dad, as well as witnessing abuse between his parents. As the AAI went on, this eventually spiralled into long descriptions of physical abuse, where the coder thought Elija went in and out of talking in a disoriented or angry way. The coder thought these memories weren't open to being discussed or re-examined. Instead, they were closed.

When it came to Zsa Zsa's AAI, it took a while for the full extent of her trauma to surface. But once it did, Zsa Zsa struggled to contain it, and long angry rants about abusive experiences leaked in. The coder thought she was collaborative, lively, valued attachment and had lots of other signs of being secure, but trauma and anger ultimately overwhelmed her.

An hour and a half into the AAI, I asked Zsa Zsa to tell me about her dad hitting her mum. The coder gave a high unresolved score for her answer because it recreated interactions from the past, included vivid sensory descriptions, quoted Zsa Zsa's mum and ended with a 12-second pause. It also featured more than 20 vague or obscuring phrases – Zsa Zsa says 'you know' 17 times in just over two minutes:

It's really hard to know what came first, the chicken or the egg. My mum didn't end up as an alcoholic in spite of him.

I don't know if it's entirely because of him, because I don't know if you can blame other people entirely for those sorts of things. But … definitely …
He hit her when she was drunk.

And I remember the first time becoming aware that it had happened. I didn't see it, but she was drunk and struggling to stand up. And she was trying to tell me that he'd hit her. But she wasn't really making any sense.

I can still hear her saying it. She was going, 'And he pushed me and my head went uh-uh.' And when a drunk person is saying words like that to you, they sound almost infantile because they're not making any sense. 'And he pushed me, and I hit my head and it went buh-buh.' And I was like … You know, you don't, don't want really to believe that your father is – you see what I mean?

Even though you're not really conscious that it's as bad as it is, you also don't want to believe that like, you know, that this woman who's now crying in front of you and not herself for whatever reason has just been whacked by your dad. You know. You know, it, it, it, it's really hard to know, because, you know, again, my dad is ... my dad is a violent person. You know, I've seen enough rage to know the extent of the rage.

But you know, did my mum walk around with bruises on her? No. Would she have had bruises that I wouldn't have seen? Almost, almost 100 per cent. You know what I mean? But it's kind of like, you know, I don't know whether or not I'm filling in gaps with an untruth. But I, I'm sure ... You know what I mean? Like ... you know. He was a hitter. You know. And I don't believe in the lifespan of their relationship that the one time she told me, you know.

And they would also like – I mean I don't know how many times I saw him hitting her, but there was definitely holding of wrists and pushing and – you know, he, he would shove her, you know, when they would, you know. He would, you know. He would shove her in what I did see.

Now I always used to, as I got older, I became like really scared for her, that when she was drunk and they'd share a bed. I had a deep-rooted fear that he would like ...

hurt her.'

If Main and Hesse are right, the disorganised and disoriented way Zsa Zsa talked about her father's abuse represents the way she's processed it in her mind. And this is why she was classified as unresolved. But what does it actually mean?

Hesse's graduate supervisor, Marinus van IJzendoorn, carried out a large review of studies with his colleague Marian

Bakermans-Kranenburg, and found that almost all adults with PTSD were classified as unresolved.

Van IJzendoorn also did another piece of research where he carried out both PTSD assessments and AAIs with 60 conflict veterans. He also added a question to the AAI specifically about combat experiences. The lapses in thinking or speaking that are key to being classified as unresolved were so strongly linked to PTSD symptoms that it was almost as if they were the same thing.

Van IJzendoorn and his colleagues concluded that being unresolved and suffering PTSD symptoms shared something important – your thought, speech and actions are being interrupted, perhaps by experiences you still find frightening.

That doesn't mean that an unresolved classification and PTSD are exactly the same thing. But they're so similar that Bakermans-Kranenburg, van IJzendoorn and their colleagues wondered whether being classified as unresolved tells us anything more than we could find out using PTSD measures.

So perhaps another way of looking at Zsa Zsa and Elija's classifications is to see them as suffering from PTSD after having suffered relentless abuse as children, as well as being understandably angry and preoccupied with their relationships with Important People.

Most people think of PTSD as something that happens in the context of war. But as Elija and Zsa Zsa's interviews make abundantly clear, many children grow up living through wars inside their own home.

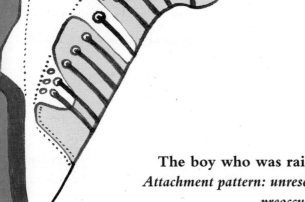

Elija

The boy who was raised by wolves
Attachment pattern: unresolved (primary),
preoccupied (secondary)

My gymnastics career was going well, really well, and for the first time in my life finances hadn't been a worry. My first two or three years, I was absolutely spanking money. I was getting paid really well, and every month I would buy myself two pairs of trainers. For two years in a row.

It's excessive. It's crazy. But that came from being deprived. Whatever you were deprived of, you buy in abundance.

If I'd been able to have the basketball shoes I wanted as a child, if I hadn't lived in poverty as I did, I wouldn't have wanted or needed to fill a hole when I got older. The hole-filling only changed when I got to 29. I finally started to reel my neck in and think, 'Hang on a minute, I need to have some kind of savings in the bank.'

I sold all my trainers. They were all brand spanking new because I used to clean them, put them back in the box and pick another pair at random. So they were all in very, very good condition. I put the money in a savings account. And I've only got about four pairs of trainers now, just for the record!

I was touring, I was dealing with girls, I was doing this city, that city, and I started casually dating someone. She was hot, funny, came from a background similar to mine – so we understood each other. But it ended up being an abusive relationship. And I vowed from that moment that I would never, ever accept it.

She had a bad temper, but this particular day, her sister had pissed her off.

All day she's ranting about it, so I go to hers, run her a bath, put some food on, start cooking.

She manages to let off some steam, we eat, we watch a movie and then we're going to bed. It's two in the morning, and she says, 'Ah babe, I haven't changed the sheets on the bed, do you mind changing them?'

My whole body's going, 'Why the fuck are you doing this at two in the morning? What's wrong with you? Just leave it, let's do one more night in these sheets and then let's change them.' But I didn't say that. I said, 'Okay, cool.'

You know when you change the sheets and you flick the duvet over the bed once you've finished to take all the creases out? When I flicked it, the duvet hit a vase of flowers and it smashed on the floor. And I hear from up the hallway, 'What was that?' And from her, and her mannerisms, I knew that I was in trouble.

'Why the fuck are you smashing up my house?'

That's how it came out, after I'd explained what it was. She started chasing me around the house and started launching plates at me. She lost it. It was her sister that had done it, but she was letting it out on me.

It got to the point where she put her hands around my neck and started to strangle me against the wall. I was very calm in the situation, very at ease, funnily enough. It's very strange. I looked at her eyes and watched her strangle me for two or three seconds. Felt like a minute.

Then I grabbed her arms off of my neck and bent them down by her sides – without any scuffle or anything, I was just stronger than her. I looked at her and said, 'Take your hands from around my fucking neck,' and she stopped. She went to the bathroom, I grabbed my coat and left.

I don't blame myself for it, I didn't mean to smash the bloody vase, 'I'm not trying to smash your house up ...' but it was that that made her flip. I felt like it was almost an outlet for her, the accident allowed her to do that.

That's the only abuse that I've received in a relationship other than with the parents. I won't ever tolerate it, never. I know the signs and I don't wanna be accustomed to that. That's not normal.

More instilled than seeing and experiencing abuse when I was younger are my mum's words, 'Don't turn out like your father.' Every day.

If you wanna be a basketball player, you've gotta play basketball every day. I didn't see beatings every day, I didn't see cheating every day, but every day guaranteed my mum would turn around and say, 'Elija, please tell me, promise me you won't turn out like your dad. Promise me, Elija, please, please, please.'

That's why I didn't end up hitting the girl.

Matt
The boy with the stiff upper lip
Attachment pattern: possibly insecure

Zimbabwe 17c

As I got older, my relationship with my parents became somewhat more disappointing. When they lived in Zimbabwe, I got it, I didn't really see them because of where they lived and instead our relationship consisted of blue letters.

But then when they were back in the UK, they only lived a short drive away so I thought they would suddenly start taking more of an interest.

But they didn't.

My relationship with my parents plus boarding school from 8 definitely impacted my ability to have romantic relationships. That became very apparent when I started going out with Jess. It ended very abruptly in carnage.

We broke up when I was 18 and it really knocked me. I didn't understand what was going on and I wasn't able to articulate it. Your first break-up is a classic time when you need support from your parents as well as friends. But I had no one.

So I went to my history teacher and sobbed my eyes out. He was very supportive and put an arm round me. I still wonder why I went to him versus other people. He was a really lovely, affable chap, but it's a bit bizarre to be telling your history teacher about your first break-up.

It was so painful I thought, 'Right, I don't want to go through this again.' So I went into my next relationship even more emotionally unavailable.

When that ended after four years, I was very sad – in spite of my protection mechanisms. So the mechanisms didn't really work. Then, probably because I had private health insurance with work, I thought, 'Let's go to a psychologist and see what happens.' I went and he was phenomenal. He helped me reflect on everything and gave me good insight into what was going on.

I wrote notes about it at the time:

> *I put the girls through a difficult time until the relationship is over. Maybe it is only then that I feel I am in a safe place to display my emotions. I'm afraid to display them before …*

> *We focused on the lack of emotional support I received as a child.*

I don't know if I knew this when I was younger, but my mum also went to boarding school from the age of 8. And Dad lost his dad as a young child, so neither of them had role models to show them how to give affection to me. They both had upbringings lacking in any sort of emotion. Then as adults they joined the navy, where they met. That's part of it too.

Mum was warm and present, which I don't take for granted, but questions about how I felt, any sort of emotional discussion, never happened, and I definitely would have benefited from those. But while my parents ignored my feelings (and their own), it wasn't intentional. It was just something they weren't aware of because it's not in their skill set or capabilities.

Neither of my parents had an emotional toolkit of any sort. Whereas my grandmother probably did have one and we didn't know it.

It makes me sad that my mum didn't see or understand how important her mum was to us and how brilliant she was with us. The pain she has from her mum is too massive. She can't get over it.

But I have no idea what that trauma is because Mum bottles things up. She hates anything on TV that's vaguely emotional – she will leave the room. Any kind of conversation involving emotions and she visibly gets fidgety and wants to get the hell out. She can't deal with it in a really bizarre, extreme way that I haven't seen in anyone else. Then it gets repressed and explodes out either through temper or massive bursts of crying.

That bred a problem that, amplified by boarding school, meant that growing up, feelings weren't permitted. So I've always found it difficult to express myself emotionally. That's something I've worked on quite a bit in therapy but also more generally.

I also trivialised relationships and the trauma that they give you because I thought, 'There are wars and children dying, so this is not that big – stiff upper lip, crack on.' Which is completely the wrong approach.

As well as discussing my upbringing, I talked to the therapist about whether breaking up with my ex was the right thing – and I decided it was. The sessions gave me a very clear image of the person that I wanted to be with, and also what I

was doing that was unhelpful in relationships. My notes from
the sessions say:

> *Don't be afraid to let go and take risks with a relationship. When I
> hold back, it's worth saying to my partner, 'I'm protecting myself ...'*
>
> *Maybe I should ease up on protecting myself a bit.*

Lily

The girl who was wrapped in love

Attachment pattern: possibly secure

When I was younger, I don't think I was aware of how lucky I was to have such a loving mum and dad. They were just my mum and dad. Then when I was in my twenties, I started seeing the role my friends' parents played in supporting them through different relationships and break-ups. It made me realise that I had grown up with a pretty secure mode of attachment.

My mum and dad have consistently provided me with support and wrapped me up in love. Consistently.

And I think that has made me resilient.

I feel very secure in myself, like I have an inner strength that others can trust. My brother can lean on me. My mum and dad can lean on me. And I can lean on me.

I think that's something growing up in such a supportive and loving family has given me.

And I've always felt a strong sense of self-worth. It's why I've never felt trapped in a relationship that I didn't want to be in.

That's not to say I had the world's most amazing dating choices. I dated someone who lived with his parents and regularly left me waiting alone upstairs while he argued with his mum for hours. Another guy I went out with was very, very kind but spent his weekends watching TV from the moment he woke up until the moment he went to bed. Breaking up with him was like kicking a teddy bear.

I remember one guy who I really, really, really liked, and he was just not behaving well. In hindsight, he was almost certainly a stalker. He always wanted to know where I was. Always. And he turned up uninvited to my home in the middle of the night on more than one occasion after we broke up. Thanks to the model my parents gave me of what a relationship should be, but also the value I place on myself, I knew I didn't have to put up with it because I was worth more than that. And I knew that being in a relationship was not the be-all and end-all. So I broke up with him. The stalking didn't stop – when I eventually got married (to someone else) I saw him waiting at the door of the registry office. But breaking up with him was one of the best decisions I ever made.

Then I met Matt. We got chatting in the elevator of an outdoor clothing shop, spent ages choosing and buying bikes together and decided to go for a cycle straight after. It went so well that we agreed to meet the next day for an official date.

We started spending all our time together and would regularly stay up chatting until 3 a.m., which was a big deal as I'm a 10 p.m. bed person normally. I remember lying to him and telling him that I went out until 1 a.m. so that he would think that I was interesting.

I thought he was extremely hot and liked how blunt he was from the outset. I also thought he was one of the kindest people I'd ever met. He had strong integrity that I found really attractive. He always wanted to do the right thing and thought carefully about what that was.

We also had similar interests and values. We were both clearly into cycling and I loved how open-minded he was. There was not a single topic where he had a fixed view. His response was always, 'That's really interesting, let's think about it.' He was stimulating but not judgemental, and I soon noticed I didn't want to be with anyone else. Everyone was boring compared to hanging out with him.

He was incredibly independent from the start. And I liked that because it meant I could be very independent myself. I didn't know anything about attachment theory at the time but I think he was almost certainly dismissive. And it wasn't a bad thing. It felt very empowering because I had no restrictions, I could still see my friends, I still had the same career ambitions and he saw them as equally as valid as his. Our lives were coexistent, but independent of one another. In the early days, my life didn't change a whole amount except I had a best friend who I shared all the highs with.

I know lots of people who enter relationships and suddenly start seeing their friends and family much, much less because their whole future and lifestyle becomes embodied in that one person that they're dating. Going out with Matt was different. He had a whole life planned and I had a whole life planned, and when they overlapped, great, but if they didn't, that was okay too.

And he was totally happy for me to spend five months working in Brazil, whereas I know many other relationships where that wouldn't have been the case.

I'm sure that by giving him space early on, I didn't trigger dismissive behaviour. Whereas if I'd had a preoccupied attachment pattern, that definitely would have. But I do think his attachment pattern was changing over time because he wasn't happy for Brazil to be an indefinite move. The idea of a long-distance relationship where we really did

lead completely separately lives was something that we agreed
was not going to work.

I could see that we were slowly becoming more coexistent,
and I knew all the fundamentals were there.

So when he proposed, I said yes.

CHAPTER FIVE

Settling Down

Lily came along and I was still … and she knows this …

I was still in the middle of, well not in the middle of, I don't know how quite to say this, but I was in conversations with multiple other women. Nothing was happening with them, but I was, you know, actively engaged.

Whereas before I might have thought, 'Well, let's see how each of them goes,' I cut all of them off and focused on her because she was just incredible. I wanted to give it a proper shot, so I decided to risk everything and make myself completely emotionally available.

It was really scary, really scary, because I was completely vulnerable and it made me very anxious. I'm pretty sure I was dismissive when I met her, probably because of my upbringing or boarding school, or both. But when I fell in love with Lily, it felt like I flipped from being dismissive to completely preoccupied because my feelings were so overwhelming that I needed regular reassurance – and she felt the same way and I could tell that.

So I proposed. I knew she was 'the one' after about three months, but my mum said, 'See how you feel after a year.' I thought that seemed sensible, so I waited. And when I still felt the same after a year, I asked her to marry me. Lily said yes, but I gave myself a bit of a safety net by saying, 'We won't do it straight away, we'll give it a bit of time so if things go belly-up then we can change.'

But things didn't go belly-up. They were great. We had a really strong spark and loads in common, there were so many things to talk about. Then over time I realised we had a similar outlook on life and shared values. I think her understanding my background and me understanding hers also helped.

We got married six months later. I wanted a massive wedding but we were broke, so we opted for drinks in a pub with our closest 200 friends and family. Lily looked amazing in a beautiful yellow dress and gave a brilliant speech. It was a really joyful day.

Finally, I was in a relationship where I felt safe and seen – and accepted.

Matt's story: earning security

Matt (the boy with the stiff upper lip) was convinced – as were Lily and his therapist – that he was dismissive. But after a solid 6 to 10 hours looking over his every word, stutter and stumble, the most experienced AAI coder in the world classified him as secure.

Was he always secure? Growing up, did he believe that Someone Important would be there for him when he was upset? Did he learn that if he asked for support, he'd get it, that that help would be helpful, and that Someone Important would comfort him and help him regulate his emotions? Did he feel he had a safe haven when he needed it? If so, if we went back in time and assessed him and his parents in the Strange Situation, their relationship may well have been classified as secure.

But this doesn't fit Matt's description of his upbringing. He said that no sort of emotional discussion ever happened with his parents, and he very rarely communicated at all with his father, except to be told off. So it's hard to see how either parent would have helped him regulate his emotions. He couldn't remember being held or hugged when he was upset or unwell, and when the people living opposite him got shot, his parents never asked Matt how he felt. So it doesn't seem like he felt he had a safe haven when he needed it.

Does this mean their relationship was actually avoidant? And if so, had Matt somehow shifted to being secure?

Or was his relationship with his parents, or at least his mum, secure until he went to boarding school? If he wanted his mum's support while he was there, all he could do was write a blue letter and wait four weeks for a response. This is not what Bowlby would describe as being available. And when Matt went through his first break-up, he felt he had no one to turn to and sobbed his eyes out to his history teacher. So it doesn't sound like he felt he had a safe haven at school.

Another possible story is that his attachment pattern shifted from security to avoidance when he was sent away, only to become secure again as he got older. And perhaps thanks to therapy and his relationship with Lily, he felt he finally had a safe haven in adulthood.

When Main and Goldwyn were looking for patterns in AAIs, they noticed that secure people fell into one of two groups. One group seemed to have positive relationships in childhood, and could back this up with specific memories, or at least avoid contradicting it. The other group, on the other hand, seemed to have the opposite – and described their relationships in childhood in a negative light.

Despite what looked like very different childhoods, both groups had the hallmarks of secure attachment in the AAI. They could focus their attention on the good and the bad, they were able to move between memories and talking to the interviewer, and they could recognise their own perspective and those of others. In other words, they were free in the way they talked about their experiences with Important People.

Main described the response of one mother, who I'll call Meera. When Meera was asked about her early relationships, she said, 'How many hours do you have? I have one of those families that they should write a whole book about. Okay, well to start with, my mother was not cheerful, and I could tell you right now the reason was that she was overworked.' Even though she described feeling rejected when she was little, Meera recognised the negative aspects of her upbringing and understood both her own experiences and those of her parents. In the Strange Situation five years earlier, Meera and her child were classified as secure, and given the lowest possible score for avoidance.

Main and her colleagues called this pattern 'earned-secure'. And they decided that, in order to get this classification, the coder has to decide that both of your parents were very unloving. The coder decides this by balancing descriptions, evaluations and memories against each other to see whether each parent seemed to be emotionally supportive and available, especially in times of trouble. The coder then gives a score out of 9 on the 'loving scale'. To qualify for being 'earned-secure', a coder has to give each parent a score of 2.5 or less out of 9.

The only interviewees whose parents made the cut were the fathers of Matt, Skyler (the girl wrapped in cotton wool) and Elija (the boy who was raised by wolves). No one I interviewed had *two* parents that were deemed unloving enough, so no one could qualify for earned security. And that includes Matt.

Incidentally, none of the 19-year-olds that Main followed up in her Berkeley Study were classified as 'earned-secure' either. That might be because 19-year-olds haven't had enough time in their life to 'earn' security. But it might also be because the criteria were so strict that few people would ever qualify.

But the classification is important beyond how many people qualify for it. Most researchers see it as recognition that the way you process information about childhood relationships can change over time. In other words, you can see and feel differently about things at different times in your life. And these changes can be hugely important.

Matt's path involved him seeing a therapist after a traumatic break-up. This made him reflect on how his upbringing had impacted him, but also how his parents' upbringings had impacted them:

[My therapist and I] focused on the lack of emotional support I received as a child … it wasn't intentional. It was just something [my parents] weren't aware of because it's not in their skill set or capabilities … I don't know if I knew this when I was younger, but my mum also went to boarding school from the age of 8. And Dad lost his dad as a young child, so neither of them had role models to show them how to give affection to me. They both had upbringings lacking in any sort of emotion. Then as adults they joined the navy, where they met. That's part of it too.

As a result of his therapy and reflection, Matt was able to forgive his mum and dad, and when I interviewed him years later, the AAI coder classified his transcript as secure. Does that mean Matt earned security? Technically, no – because only one, not both, of his parents were deemed unloving enough.

But that's not the only version of the story. The other is that Matt probably did become more secure, but that Main and Hesse's idea of 'earned security' is technical and incredibly strict.

The first people to actually study earned security were Carolyn and Philip Cowan. They defined it as someone who spoke in a secure way in the AAI but who seemed to have at least one parent who was very unloving and neglecting and rejecting.

In the Cowans' research, a quarter of the people that took part were classified as insecure, half were earned-secure and a quarter continuously secure. Continuously secure people had lower levels of depressive symptoms than the others, but those who were earned-secure were just as warm and structured when playing with their own children. People with an insecure pattern, on the other hand, were less so.

Under the Cowans' criteria, Matt still wouldn't have qualified as earned-secure. Even though his dad was deemed seriously unloving and neglecting, his rejecting score wasn't high enough for their requirements. But if we ignore this and apply the findings to Matt's life anyway, they're very interesting. If he'd been secure throughout his life, he'd be less likely to suffer depressive symptoms.

But when it came to being a parent and playing with any kids he might have, it wouldn't make any difference if Matt had earned or always been secure. In other words, no matter what your childhood is like, you can still change your path and provide warmth and playfulness to others.

Everyone loves a hopeful ending. But there was a key problem with the research behind these findings: it was retrospective. The Cowans hadn't followed these adults from birth. They were relying on what came up in the AAIs, but they couldn't verify what had actually gone on.

So the Minnesota Study Group, with their epic long-term study, stepped in. 170 people who'd been followed by researchers before they were even born did the AAI when they turned 19. When the Group used Main and Hesse's first very strict criteria, only 2 per cent were classified as earned-secure. But when they changed their criteria to something similar to that of the Cowans, 14 per cent were.

When I say it was similar to the Cowans' – it was mostly the same. But the way in which they changed the criteria was crucial to whether Matt would qualify or not. Under their requirements, at least one parent had to be unloving, and one had to be either rejecting or neglecting. Finally, Matt could make the cut.

He didn't according to two out of three sets of criteria, but he did in one – and that raises something important: criteria are set by a bunch of different people. Sometimes they're just a scientist's best guess at where the line should be drawn. And sometimes they're making that guess when they don't even know whether there should a line in the first place.

But it's all too easy to see criteria as the truth. For example, when I asked the coder if she thought Matt could have earned security, she said no, as his loving scores were too high. But as I delved into the research, I realised that that was just one way of looking at it. The coder was using Main and Hesse's coding instructions, but theirs was only one of three (or more) ways to assess earned security. And even their criteria had changed over time.

The Minnesota Group's findings echoed those of the Cowans', namely that earned-secure people had more depressive symptoms than those who had always been secure.

Then, when they observed these 19-year-olds with their partners, they found that people who were secure, irrespective of whether that was earned or continuous, were able to make their partner feel secure, share positive emotions with them and resolve conflicts. And they were much better at this than people who were dismissing or preoccupied. So in Matt's life, it wouldn't matter whether he had earned security or always had it, he was still more likely to behave in ways that benefited his relationship with Lily.

Except the Minnesota story wasn't that simple. When they looked back at their earlier research, they found that the people who were classified as earned-secure based on their AAI when they were 19 had actually been given the same classification in infancy as people who were continuously secure. But if that was true, and they were both secure in early childhood, how could some of them have 'earned' it as adults?

The Minnesota Group also found that the earned-secure people had received the most supportive care of any other children when they were 2 years old. And at 13, they'd had much more positive and supportive interactions with their mums than people who were insecure. The Minnesota Group concluded that the differences between the way earned and continuously secure people described their upbringings might not be caused by actual differences in their childhoods.

Instead, it might be explained by their tendencies to describe things in a negative way, which could be due to depressive symptoms.

So that means there's another possible story. Maybe Matt did have a secure and loving upbringing, but he described his parents the way he did because he has a tendency to describe things in a pessimistic light. Except Matt described plenty of other things related to attachment in a hugely positive way – like his relationships with his grandma and with Lily, for example. And at the time of our interviews, he wasn't suffering from depressive symptoms.

I doubt Matt was having more positive and supportive interactions with his mum when he was 13 than people who were preoccupied or dismissing, as she wasn't available in person or on the phone if Matt needed her. His only option was to write a letter and wait four weeks for a reply – and this meant he had to rely on himself for comfort and protection. So how does his story fit in with the Minnesota Group's findings?

Earned security continues to be controversial, and academics have even disputed what it should be called. The Minnesota Group thought it should be changed to 'evolved' security, because earned security isn't about rising above mean parenting using pure will – it's about being scaffolded by caring adults. Hesse and Main agreed, but by this point, 'earned-secure' had been used for so long that it was entrenched, and most researchers have ignored the rebranding.

Thankfully there is some agreement among researchers – namely that your history isn't what lands you with a particular classification in the AAI. It's the way you talk and think about your attachment experiences. And that means that, no matter how difficult your childhood was, while it may influence you, you're not rigidly bound by it.

But at the same time, our development as humans isn't a blackboard that we can simply erase and write on again. Even when we change in a major way, the shadows of our earlier patterns remain, and can flare up in times of stress.

As soon as we got married, Matt and I went through a rocky patch.

Matt was made redundant and was really, really struggling to get a job. Having a job made him feel validated, so he struggled with the lack of job offers, the prospect of prolonged unemployment and not being sure who he was, I guess. And he wasn't comfortable talking about it.

I didn't appreciate how lost and how vulnerable he was feeling, especially with the pressure of all his peers being employed. Matt has a desire to be perfect and to present that to me – and not to present the vulnerability that is engendered by being unemployed. Rather than discussing how he was feeling, which was the opposite of what he had learned to do growing up, he just went out more and more and more and more.

Then he kissed someone else.

He knew it was wrong, so he went to a therapist to say, 'I know this is not okay behaviour, I don't really know what's going on with me, I want to. It's my fault, how do I figure this out?'

Then I found the therapist notes that he left out and figured out what had happened.

It was first thing in the morning. I broke down into tears and didn't really stop. I missed a whole day of work. My boss was really understanding, although I obviously didn't tell her the reason I was taking the day off! Matt and I spent most of the day discussing what had happened and I was inconsolable for long periods. That week was a nightmare. I was really distracted at work and had absolutely zero headspace for anything else.

Either the day I found the notes or very soon after, Matt asked if I would go to therapy with him. Initially, I was pretty nervous and resistant. But Matt was really adamant and I was open to trying anything. I knew what he had done was wrong and even though I was devastated, I wasn't thinking of leaving. I wanted to do everything we could to make our marriage work, and so did he. So we went.

What was interesting was that the therapist didn't demonise Matt for kissing someone else. Society would think, 'He was the bad one, he did the bad thing.' Whereas in our therapy sessions, it wasn't so much about the thing, it was more about unconstructive behaviours in our relationship that led him to do the thing.

Instead of being vilified for kissing someone, he was vilified for the emotional detachment. He was in a tricky place and, rather than talking to me about it, he acted out. But then he'd had zero emotional support growing up, so it's no surprise that this was his go-to strategy at a time of stress.

Of course, I was not helping that conversation happen either – there is more I could have done to try to get us talking when he was feeling so low. It was much more constructive to have it framed in those terms, rather than to point the finger.

Unemployment was a major factor, but getting married also played a part. Matt describes it as going from an immature perception of relationships, where you coexist but focus on your friends and job, to then saying, 'Okay, this is the person I am with forever, who I really need to trust in every aspect because we're going to have to go through a whole lifetime together.'

That felt like quite a step change for him. We had to become much more intertwined than he had ever really allowed himself to be with anyone else.

He still struggles with it, to be honest, but now he actively tries to manage it and articulate the vulnerability. Now he can say, 'I'm feeling really down,' whereas before he wouldn't say anything. And I certainly didn't have the language to say, 'I'm not feeling great about this either, we aren't spending any time together, that's not okay with me.'

Instead I thought, 'I'm not sure you're alright, but I'll let you do your thing, I won't impinge on you, we'll just not discuss anything and I'll continue with my thing.' Even though I knew, 'It is not okay. It's a Sunday afternoon and we're not spending it together because you're out in the pub again with loads of people.' Which is something that would never happen now. That's definitely not how he would make himself feel better anymore.

There was no sense of support on either side. And there was no mechanism or track record in working it through.

It was an incredibly painful time, but I think being secure meant that I was able to ask for help from others. It also meant that I had very close familial and friendship support networks that would help, even without my asking, if I needed them to. It wasn't just knowing that I could call my parents or go down to their house any time for a gigantic hug, I could also call my best friend and she knew from the way I answered the phone that I needed to have a cup of tea with her and I needed it to be now.

I noticed that the friends who were more secure were the ones I turned to because they were much less judgemental. They were more open to the concept of therapy and working through the relationship. What I didn't want was friends who would say, in a way that they thought was supportive, 'Oh, he is a bad egg. Don't stay with him, what he's done is a terrible thing, you're so much better than that, we never liked him anyway.'

I don't think it would have been constructive, particularly given I was married. And it's not what I heard from my friends who I thought of as secure and who have gone on to have very secure, happy marriages. Whereas the ones who are, coincidentally or not, in unstable relationships would very often say more negative comments. So I resisted talking to them about it because they made me feel worse. They made me feel judged.

Divorce was only mentioned once. I brought it up by saying, 'Are you saying you want to get divorced?' And Matt said something ambiguous like, 'I don't know.' Then I exploded.

But it never came up again, so I don't know whether divorce entered his mind in any real way. Now he would say, 'It was never on the cards, it was never discussed.' So I don't know to what extent he's either rewritten history or whether it was never something that he explicitly thought of in his head.

Ever since we went to therapy, lots of people have asked about it and then used it as their licence to go themselves. Many were surprised at the time that we had done it and their response was, 'If you did it, it must be okay.'

Now, among Matt's group of friends, 80 per cent of them have been to therapy and acknowledged it to each other. They've either been alone or with their partner. But when we went, it was definitely stigmatised because it felt like an admission of failure. Whereas now it's an admission of strength.

I think it can be seen as an admission of failure because there is a desire to have a perfect relationship. And if you're seeing a therapist, it's not perfect, the person you are with may not be 'the one'. There is still such a strong aspiration to find 'the only one and the perfect one', with 'perfect' being defined as no real problems ever.

Having seen my parents go through better or worse periods together, I don't believe that marriages are perfect all the time or that everyone is always perfectly happy all the time. Instead, I saw that my parents were perfectly happy on average. I think that helped.

I remember a time when my mum stormed out, slammed the door, and didn't speak to my dad for two days, other than a couple of monosyllabic statements. And there was a period when we moved to Hong Kong for my dad's work, but his job was really uncertain and my mum didn't have any sense of stability or community.

They really struggled – Mum in particular was really down while we were there. So they decided to come home, even though that had a negative impact on Dad's career. Seeing that gave me a really good model of how you can have an amazing 50-year marriage, but it's not all plain sailing. Marriage is for the duration but is not always perfection.

I think if I hadn't been secure, our relationship probably would have broken. There was a fairly prolonged period of relying on my belief in the fundamentals being right, rather than my immediate emotional needs being met. Just because it isn't perfect, doesn't mean you're broken.

I don't know how much of it was having the patience to see it through, rather than run, when I wasn't getting very much. Maybe it's not patience, but grit because I don't require immediate gratification all the time.

I think I just had the firm belief that the foundations were there and they were really good, so although we were going through an earthquake, we were going to survive it. And we did.

Skyler

The girl wrapped in cotton wool
Attachment pattern: preoccupied

I met Liam at a 10K run. We got chatting at the start line, then after the race, he asked if I wanted to go for a drink. So I did. We hit it off straight away. He was kind, honest, hilarious, impulsive, we both loved running. We also loved travelling and volunteered for the same environmental charity. It was just massively easy spending time with him. And weirdly, he wasn't dismissive. He was probably even secure.

It was clear early on that this was serious but we didn't tell many people. His family knew, my family knew and his best friends knew. But he had an ex who had a lot of mutual friends and was really not over him, so we kept it quiet for her. He was about to move to my town, a few hours away, and hoped the distance would make it easier to tell everybody.

I stayed with him for a week to help him pack before the move. We went through loads of photos of him as a kid, got takeout, and danced all night. It was a dream week. In the middle of all of this, we had a massive talk about how, when we started hanging out it was just fun, but that we were both falling for each other and wanted to actually make it something. We were basically defining that we were in a serious relationship.

I left on the Wednesday and called when I was on the train home. We were both knackered, but we chatted for a bit until my phone cut out. And when I called back, he never picked up. I figured he was asleep because it was late and didn't really think anything of it.

The next day, I knew he had somebody coming over to help him pack as he was moving the day after. So when I called and he didn't pick up, I thought it was odd, but fine. I didn't want to seem too clingy and I figured that he was packing and that he would call me back. But he didn't.

When it got to Friday, I knew something was wrong. I spoke to one of my running group friends, who, looking back, was probably dismissive. She said, 'Look, you guys have just solidified the relationship, he is probably just freaking out. Give it some time, everything's fine, just give it another day.'

So it wasn't until Saturday afternoon that I called again. When he didn't answer, I phoned a mutual friend of mine and Liam's and he started calling around to see if anyone had heard from him. They hadn't. On Sunday, somebody went by his house and found him.

By then it was too hard to tell what had happened. They couldn't figure out a time of death, and that's always thrown me. I'd like to think that he died on the Wednesday, because … if he died on the Wednesday, it's not my fault. I couldn't have done anything. But of course, his parents want him to have had the longest life possible, so his official date of death is the Saturday.

But if he died on Saturday, I might have been able to prevent his death if I'd said something earlier. If I had just gone with my gut, and if he was only in a coma, he would still be alive now.

Liam's death broke me.

I couldn't do anything for months. I didn't know how to deal with it because I felt like it was my fault. I felt like that was like the only chance I was ever going to have to love because I was 29 years old and it was my first proper relationship. It was very early on in our relationship – we still weren't friends on social media – but it was a big deal to me.

At the funeral, I felt like I didn't belong. I didn't sit at the front and I felt intimidated because I didn't know if I had the right to cry.

There were lots of lifelong friends who had years of stories of how much of a great character he was. I was just this girl who didn't know most of them and who came on the scene a few months earlier. Then at the wake, his ex gave a 20-minute speech that ended with her saying she thought they would have ended up together if he hadn't died. She just started doing it, so his parents couldn't stop her.

I was next to her when she was doing it, and everybody was packed in so I couldn't leave. So I had to sit there.

I met his parents for the first time at the funeral. That's not a normal experience. Then Liam's dad got me alone towards the end of the day and said, 'Is there any chance that you're pregnant?' It was an awkward question to be asked, but you can't blame him – Liam was their only son and they desperately wanted his genes passed on.

I called my mom on the train back from the funeral, and, as always, instead of comforting me she made it worse.

She said I should be grateful, happy even. 'At least he didn't cheat on you. I've always told your father, I would rather him die than him cheat on me.'

No. Just no.

I think the logic there is that if someone cheats on you, then you've been rejected. But if they die then you haven't.   It was a horrendous thing to hear and say. It's essentially saying, 'My need to be validated and accepted is more important than your life.'

I have since asked her about it, which is very unlike me. She doubled down and said, 'Well that's just the way I feel.' And didn't give an explanation.

She still claims that that's the way she feels. If she experienced the death of my father before my father was supposed to die, I think she would then learn that she was wrong.

My dad thinks Christmas is capitalistic and purposeless so we don't really do Christmas presents in my family. But that year, my mom decided to give me one, a book about grieving. My only Christmas present that year was a book on grieving. Why make it a Christmas present?! Just give me a book!

It's not that my mom didn't want to be comforting, she just wasn't. At all. When everything was great in my life, she would pile on the cotton wool. More and more until I couldn't breathe or move. Then when I actually needed comfort, I didn't get anything – no warmth, no protection.

Instead I was left in a small, dark box room with no furniture and windows.

The truth about Skyler: unresolved loss

You might remember that in Chapter Four, Skyler was classified as preoccupied. Well, she was. But that was her secondary classification. Her primary classification was unresolved in relation to the loss of Liam.

When Goldwyn was looking for patterns in AAIs, she noticed that people whose interviews were splintered and incoherent had often been bereaved – especially before they reached their teens. Just like the unresolved interviews of people who had suffered trauma when they were young, in these AAIs ideas invaded each other and others got lost along the way.

Main and Hesse thought that, much like interviewees who hadn't resolved their trauma, some hadn't resolved their loss. At the time, the ideas of 'unresolved grief' or 'mourning' were becoming more and more popular, and psychoanalysts, including Bowlby, had written about the benefit of acknowledging and accepting a loss for mental health symptoms.

Main and her colleagues noticed two different ways of speaking in an unresolved way about loss. The first consisted of saying things that undermined credibility. Someone might, for example, say, 'I don't know where I want to live, but my mum [who died 15 years ago] says I should move to Scotland.'

In Main and Hesse's view, when someone talks in the present tense like this, it suggests that they believe their mum is alive and actively involved in their life, when she actually died a long time ago. Incidentally, you can't get an unresolved classification for loss for a year after being bereaved – the idea is that thinking and behaving in this way is a natural part of the initial grieving process. But not all slips into the present tense are significant. If, for example, someone said, 'My mum has been a lawyer for years,' Main thought the slip might just be minor.

The second pattern involved the way interviewees censored (or didn't censor) how they spoke. The topic of death might invade discussions about other subjects, for example.

Interviewees might suddenly use words that idolised the person who had died in an exaggerated way, or leave exceptionally long pauses that they didn't seem aware of. Or they might be absorbed by particular details of the death.

As with trauma, Main and Hesse thought that there are lots of ways a loss in the past could influence the present. But they only thought you'd be unresolved if your ability to pay attention to the death of Someone Important was disorganised or disoriented. The idea being that if you spoke in unresolved ways, it was because you were still overwhelmed by your unprocessed memories of loss – and this interrupted your mental processing.

So, simply grieving, taking a long time to grieve, or not grieving at all doesn't make the cut. If someone dismisses the importance of a loss and hasn't mourned, it's often called 'failed mourning' – but for Main and her colleagues, this doesn't mean you're unresolved. That's because failing to mourn is actually very organised: you're consistently focusing your attention away from loss. It's a bit like the way children in avoidant relationships focus their attention away from things that might make them upset during the Strange Situation.

The coder is looking at whether the way someone talks about the bereavement is disorganised or disoriented – specifically information relating to Someone Important. The way they speak has to be disrupted – it's almost like they have to be 'at a loss' when talking about their loss.

During her AAI, I asked Skyler whether she had lost any Important People, and then asked her to tell me about what happened. Her answer included an immense level of detail. It was clear that Skyler blamed herself for Liam's death, and she said the phrase 'it broke me' over and over again.

Skyler and I weren't surprised by her classification – the anger of her preoccupied classification resonated with her lived experience of her parents, and her unresolved classification resonated with the way she thought and spoke about Liam's death. Plus researchers have found that you're twice as likely to be classified as unresolved for loss if you experience and describe the loss as sudden – as Liam's death was.

But what does the classification actually mean? The idea is that when Skyler spoke differently compared to the rest of her AAI, memories or beliefs that she'd blocked off were interfering – and these memories or beliefs were incompatible. And when Skyler was unusually absorbed by memories about Liam's death, it reflected how poorly integrated those memories were with the rest of her experiences.

What does the classification mean for Skyler's life? Well, it's hard to say. That's because Main and her colleagues weren't totally clear about what disorganised or disoriented states of mind in adulthood mean. Not only does that make it hard to understand in the first place, but it's also made it harder for other researchers to develop or test the theory further.

One thing they did suggest is that people who are classified as unresolved are more likely to have disorganised relationships with any children they have – and early research found a strong link between the two. That means that unless her classification changes, Skyler is more likely to have a disorganised relationship with any children she might have. It also means that, if Skyler's mum was unresolved in relation to the unexpected and sudden losses she suffered in her life, she'd be more likely to have a disorganised relationship with her daughter, Skyler.

But as more and more research has been carried out, the link seems much weaker than originally claimed. There's still a link. But, for example, you're just as likely to have a disorganised relationship with your child if you're classified as preoccupied as if you're classified as unresolved.

It's seductive to do an assessment like the AAI, get the result and assume that what you've been given represents some sort of truth about you, your life or your relationships. But attachment research is about probabilities – something becomes more or less likely when we look at a group of people with a particular classification. But although they're important, these probabilities aren't gigantic and don't mean that any given person's fate is sealed.

It's also important to remember that measures like the AAI were created by researchers for specific purposes and they aren't perfect. One of the AAI's limitations is that it has quite artificial and strict limits on what counts as a trauma. Skyler can be coded as unresolved for Liam's death, a loss she suffered as an adult. But according to the AAI's coding system, you can't be coded as unresolved for abuse unless you experienced it as a child. So Elija dating someone abusive when he was an adult wouldn't technically count. The AAI also fails to register the effects of a parent leaving the family, emotional abuse between parents (unless there are stand-out moments) or chronic neglect by Important People.

And studying children who were hospitalised played a major role in Bowlby's thinking about trauma and loss, but this also wouldn't qualify according to the coding manual. So even though Amos spent significant chunks of his childhood in hospital and has continuous nightmares about it, he couldn't get an unresolved classification in relation to it.

Scientific measures, like the humans that create and assess them, have their limitations.

That's not to say the AAI isn't hugely valuable or insightful. The interview and coding can reveal a massive amount. I could undoubtedly feel the difference between the interviewees' classifications as I carried out their assessments. The unresolved and preoccupied interviewees, Zsa Zsa, Elija and Skyler, talked way, way more than the others, for example. Their loss or trauma spilled out into the interview like little geysers at first, before eventually growing into full-blown volcanoes. And I could feel Skyler and Zsa Zsa's anger at their parents. It filled the room and bounced around the cushioned walls of the recording studio. And I could understand why they were angry – they had plenty to be angry about.

But boy, could they tell a story. Their interviews were full of colour and taste and smell and detail and all the things you're taught to include in creative writing classes. Their words were filled with emotion, even if that emotion could be a little unruly at times.

Whereas Amos, who was classified as dismissive, spoke in the abstract. His interview lacked stories, pictures, hooks for me to hang his life on to. And he struggled to remember anything specific. Instead, he insisted that everything, including extensive stints in hospital as a child, had been great. Reading and rereading the 200,000 or so words of his from our interviews, I found his words harder to connect to. It was as if some of the emotion and story had been sucked out. This was something Amos recognised in himself, and he told me that he consciously tried to involve more emotion and tell more stories when he spoke, even though they didn't come naturally to him.

But at the same time, he had an impressive ability to communicate incredibly difficult things about life in neat, succinct nuggets, like, 'You have to learn a number of behaviours to ask for help. You have to master language, anxiety, you have to open up, learn deferred gratification. That's a lot compared to how easy it is to just keep it to yourself.'

The secure interviewees, Lily, Ray and Matt, were comfortable talking about their childhoods no matter what the question. They valued important relationships, but without seeing them through rose-tinted glasses. They were happy to talk about positive and negative memories, even the really painful and grisly ones, with honesty and balance. Their upbringings weren't perfect. Ray was sent away as a child, listened behind his bedroom door as his parents had borderline violent arguments and was disowned by his dad for dating a white girl. Then he developed leukaemia and found his dad shortly after he'd tried to kill himself. But Ray described the imperfections with relative ease, compassion, empathy, acceptance and forgiveness.

The interviews had a totally different quality to them – both while I was carrying them out in person and also when it came to poring over the transcripts again and again. There was something tangibly, viscerally different about the way each person thought and spoke about their childhood and Important People. And there are mountains of research to back up my anecdotal reactions and views. In fact, recent work by Alessandro Talia and his colleagues suggests that the different ways people use language when talking about Important People in the AAI are so significant that they also come up when they speak about other topics, like friends or work.

There's no doubt in my mind that AAI codings tell us something meaningful about the people taking part. And there's no doubt in my mind that it's incredibly potent. It led interviewees to tell me things they'd never spoken about before – like when Ray told me the story of Luca, which he had never shared with anyone else.

The AAI is an exceptionally powerful tool. But it's also flawed – both because of limitations in the measure itself but also because of the overwhelming complexity of the human beings it seeks to assess.

Zsa Zsa

The girl who walked into fire
Attachment pattern: unresolved (primary),
preoccupied (secondary)

I remember really losing my shit and shouting at my second serious girlfriend, Alex. She said, 'I'm leaving now, because if you raise your voice, I won't talk to you. I'll talk to you about anything. But if you shout at me, it's game over. I can't, I won't have you shouting at me.' And she left the room.

Alex made it quite clear at the beginning it was never going to work if I always responded that way. She forced me to think consciously about how I wanted to discuss things and how I was going to deal with issues. And we worked our way through problems that I definitely would not have been able to get through with my first girlfriend – or anyone else.

It was the first time anyone I cared about had given me enough time and space to say, 'This isn't normal … and you can't do it.'
I had always justified to myself that people are allowed to lose their temper because it shows that they care, I'm sure because I'd seen it in my dad. It's almost like not being able to control your rage is indicative of how much you care about something.

Alex wanted things to work, and in order to make them work she had to be brutally honest with me,
which is quite a scary thing. I reflect on it and think, 'If only I'd been able to have those types of

conversations and recognise my own behaviour growing up. Or to have somebody say to me, "You can't act like that – and what you want to say gets lost because you're dealing with it wrong, you're storming out, you're losing your temper.'" It's important to have somebody who cares enough about you to tell you those things without judging you.

I never didn't feel loved by her. Looking back now, I think, 'God, I was really secure in that relationship.' I didn't ever question it, I really loved her and I know she really loved me. Then, I have no idea why, but I subconsciously decided that we should stop having sex and I didn't tell her that, nor did I talk about it with her.

So, after quite a lot of months, she tried to discuss it with me, but I continued to push her away because I had no idea how to deal with or talk about it. Then I convinced myself that I didn't fancy her and I didn't love her and we broke up.

We started arguing a lot. It was horrible. It was really horrible. She always says, 'We broke up, it was because of us,' and I'm like, 'No, it was because of me.'

But when you're just starting to recognise your patterns of behaviour, you're not always able to stop yourself from reacting in a certain way all the time.

But your ability to catch yourself reacting in a certain way and think about things differently happens more and more quickly. So you can start to live with a greater sense of awareness in real time.

But no matter how much I've become aware of my reactions, I still see the same patterns coming up again and again.

I have a tendency to walk into unhealthy relationships thinking I won't get burnt. Then I walk in and think, 'Woah! A fire! Why am I pretending to be fireproof again?!'

I grew up with Dad constantly saying, 'Fuck you, I'm fireproof!' Now, as an adult, I will see a burning flame and know that leaving it alone   is the thing I should do. I should just move on.   But instead,   I can't help myself. I just put my diamanté goggles on
and walk right into that fire.

Like my current relationship. It's been obvious since day one that she's not going to be someone I can rely on.

And I don't think it's pure coincidence that I've ended up with somebody at the extreme. But I'm like, 'Maybe I can make this work still … Why don't I walk further into the fire? If I keep going into the fire, it's coolest in the middle, like a tornado is calm in the middle.' Then I get to the middle and realise it's terrible.

Maybe I look for care from people who I know I won't get it from   because I feel like that's all I deserve. People I'm close to, including male friends, just fucking disappear off the face of the planet when I need them. I say, 'I could … I need some – oh, no, you've gone, okay.' It's quite consistent. And my fears get magnified when people just fucking disappear.

I try to say to myself, 'Why do you judge yourself in terms of how available people make themselves to you?'

But it's hard to undo certain ways of thinking and reacting when you're conditioned to believe that you are less important than alcohol, let's say, or work.

I have a very childlike response in me that says, 'Why don't you love me enough to be there? Why aren't I important enough? Why aren't I loveable?'

And no matter how much I recognise my own patterns of behaviour, no matter how many mechanisms for dealing with certain situations I have, no matter how much I am able to talk about how I feel, I, I can't silence that little

       you know   wanting child.

Sounds pathetic, doesn't it?
                      I feel pathetic when I say it.
    But there is this weak, pathetic child who just wants to be loved. I feel like it's a weakness to need to be loved. Probably because …
               Well,

    I'm supposed to be fireproof, aren't I?

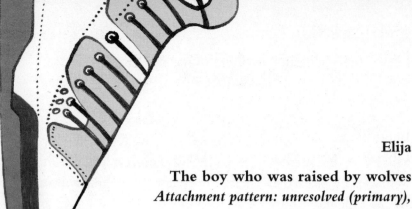

Elija

The boy who was raised by wolves
Attachment pattern: unresolved (primary),
preoccupied (secondary)

There is one person in my life that I kick myself for – Shelley.

I cheated. I did her wrong, and when I look back, she was open, she loved me, she did things for me that nobody else did, she didn't do things to me that other people had done. She cared, she was open-minded, emotionally available, she was there.

She was just very different, she was open. And I destroyed that completely.

I messed up because I was young. And I hadn't processed anything from my upbringing. Nope, not at all.

I didn't know it was something to do with my dad, that he was doing it, and now I was following in his path. It's only when I got to my thirties that I realised that's what was going on.

Shelley was able to talk about emotions. The mannerisms, the ease of communication … She always showed love and care, and it was in abundance. It was like it just flowed off like butter dripping off a knife.

And with it being in abundance, with her showing the love and the appreciation and being open and there … I took it for granted.

I was young. I thought I could have my cake and eat it, and I was being greedy and I missed the mouth. I dropped it all down me, didn't I? I made a mess of it.

But maybe I wasn't just being greedy. At that point in my life, I thought, 'You want to be with me? What? No, you're lying, definitely lying … what do you want? What are you doing this for?'

There's never been a safe element where my upbringing is concerned. The only safety I've ever had really is gymnastics. And so, when that person does arrive and they're like, 'Hi, I'm here to stay, I'll love you, come here, give me a hug, you wanna talk about it? Sweet, let's do this.' You kind of go, 'Who the fuck are you? You're not even real, go away.'

Shelley was like memory foam. At the time, I didn't know how to be supported. 'What are you doing? Why are you doing that for me? I know how to do it myself – I'm very capable and very independent. I can carry the world on my shoulders …' But now I'm like, 'Come and support me please!'

Five years ago I emailed her, 'I would love to meet up with you, just for a coffee,' knowing that I just wanna sit there and say sorry and then she can be on her way. But she doesn't wanna meet. Now there's no emails, no connection, no nothing. She doesn't want to see me.

I would just like to say sorry.

It eats me now, because it was beautiful, it was everything that I ever thought about and now, 10 years later, I think, 'Why can't someone like Shelley come around now?'

Everyone else I've dated has been closed off. Definitely. They had a lead barrier around them, like my dad.

One girlfriend cheated on me, and when I found out, she wasn't even able to give me an answer to why she did it. She said, 'It's just one of those things, Elija.' Definitely not acknowledging what's going on. And then two days later, she moved country ... She had that lead barrier where you don't let anybody in, you try to fly through life without giving anybody any answers – including yourself.

It's heavy work, looking for a girlfriend, I tell you. Wow.

I don't go on dating websites and say, 'I want a dismissive person.' It doesn't work like that.

It's more that I see something I can fix, maybe I feel like I can open that person up. Maybe I see potential.

But no matter what I do, that potential is never reached – and I'm coming to realise that the lead wall can only be knocked down from one side.

Romantic relationships: a new theory of attachment

By the mid-1980s, Ainsworth had done a vast amount of research using the Strange Situation, the Minnesota Study was well under way and Main had just begun to use her newly created AAI. But no one had delved into the murky world of romantic relationships. So even though Bowlby believed that our early childhood influenced us throughout our lives, researchers still knew very little about how the relationship we have with our parents affects the one we have with a romantic partner.

Until Phillip Shaver came along.

Shaver was a social psychologist. Developmental psychologists like Main and Ainsworth study the way humans grow and develop over their lives, whereas social psychologists like Shaver focus on social interactions. And Shaver was specifically interested in romantic relationships because he'd noticed that, in his own, he'd always have a woman waiting 'in the wings' in case his main relationship didn't work out.

Together with his student Cindy Hazan, Shaver argued that our romantic partners can provide us with a secure base and safe haven – much like our parents can. In order to explore their theory, Hazan and Shaver created a short questionnaire called the 'Love Quiz'. The quiz included three descriptions and asked people to decide which of them best matched their experiences in close relationships.

The idea behind the Love Quiz was to work out which of three adult attachment 'styles' someone might have. They called these three styles secure, avoidant and anxious/ambivalent (which I'll call anxious for short).

According to the quiz, you had a secure attachment style if you found it easy to get close to others, felt comfortable being depended on and depending on a partner, and didn't often worry about being abandoned or someone getting too close.

You had an avoidant attachment style if you were uncomfortable being close to others, found it difficult to trust them completely and allow yourself to depend on them, and found that romantic partners often wanted more intimacy than you were comfortable with.

And finally, you had an anxious attachment style if you thought other people were reluctant to get as close as you'd like, if you often worried that your partner didn't really love you or didn't want to stay with you, if you wanted to merge completely with someone else, and if that sometimes scared others away.

The three attachment styles were supposedly modelled on Ainsworth's Strange Situation classifications, but they didn't have a huge amount in common.

Ainsworth defined security in terms of having access to a safe haven when needed. And she thought this happened when Someone Important understood and interpreted what you told them and then responded appropriately and without too much delay. In other words, when they were sensitive to your needs. However, instead of a positive definition, Shaver and Hazan defined it as the absence of two things: a discomfort about being close to someone and a worry about being abandoned. But worries about abandonment didn't feature in Ainsworth's classification at all.

According to the Love Quiz, avoidance involved nervousness about being close to someone, but this didn't feature in Ainsworth's work either. Instead, Ainsworth thought avoidance involved distracting yourself from things that might make you upset and want Someone Important, because you weren't sure they'd be there if you needed them. And the definition of anxious attachment missed things that Ainsworth thought were hugely important – like being angry or passive.

The Love Quiz, like other questionnaires, relies on how people choose to describe themselves. Social psychologists often used self-report measures like this, but they were controversial among attachment researchers. Ainsworth had tried using self-report but found that people who weren't secure still described themselves as such.

She believed that self-report assessed our general, storytelling memory, which could consist of things that were told to us, rather than the memory that accesses specific events or moments in time. So if there was any discrepancy between these two types, Ainsworth thought self-report would only give you part of the picture – the distorted part.

Take Amos, for example. When he relied on his storytelling memory, he described his mother as loving and present. But when asked for specifics to back that up, his 'episodic' memory couldn't provide anything. And when I asked if he remembered being rejected as a child, he said no – even though he'd described lots of specific examples of rejection shortly before. If Ainsworth was right, asking Amos to do a self-report would simply (and incorrectly) tell the story of an ideal childhood. Whereas observing him could capture both his memory systems plus the way they interacted.

Shaver knew that Ainsworth and other developmental psychologists didn't like self-report, so he tried to find ways to show that it could tap into our unconscious. He used a self-report measure before asking people to describe their dreams or interpret blots of ink on a page. And he worked with the incredibly inventive Mario Mikulincer on a variety of studies. My personal favourite involved using self-report before getting people to hold a snake and see how they coped with it.

Despite the major differences between the Love Quiz and Ainsworth's Strange Situation classifications, the quiz led to some interesting results. People with different attachment styles reacted in different ways to what was going on around them, from coping with emergencies and illness to everyday interactions with their romantic partner. And despite the differences in measurement, these findings were aligned with Bowlby and Ainsworth's theories.

But despite its success, Hazan and Shaver were clear that the Love Quiz was just a first attempt to assess attachment in this way. And throughout the 1990s, researchers created a bamboozling array of self-report attachment measures.

There were so, so many that when Shaver and his colleagues went through them all, they were left with a colossal mound of more than 300 different questions or statements. They turned these all into one giant questionnaire, which they asked more than 1,000 very patient people to answer.

They then used statistics to analyse the results and found two patterns. The first was avoidance, which involved being self-reliant and feeling uncomfortable with intimacy. The second was anxiety, which involved preoccupation and fear of abandonment and rejection. In other words, avoidance involves minimising the desire for closeness, and anxiety is a preoccupation with it.

Shaver, Brennan and Clark chose 36 of the statements and created the Experiences of Close Relationships questionnaire (or ECR). Statements included 'I worry a fair amount about losing my partner', 'I resent it when my partner spends time away from me' and 'I tell my partner just about everything'. You can easily find it online if you want to read the whole thing. It soon became the industry standard for assessing attachment using self-report, and the two 'styles' of avoidance and anxiety became the main model.

A few years later, Mikulincer and Shaver introduced a new category: fearful. You're classified as fearful if you have high scores of both avoidance and anxiety, which they essentially saw as opposites. So they interpreted high scores in both as a breakdown of attachment styles and the equivalent of disorganised attachment. Although they haven't come across many 'fearful' people in their research so far.

As well as doing AAIs with each of the interviewees, I also carried out the ECR with them.

Remember that Elija was unresolved in relation to childhood abuse in the AAI, with a secondary classification of preoccupied? Well, he couldn't have the equivalent of an unresolved classification because the ECR doesn't have one. And while it does have a fearful classification, Elija didn't meet the criteria for it. So we can't really compare Elija's ECR and AAI results.

Incidentally, the person who scored the highest for both anxiety and avoidance, and was therefore the closest to being classified as fearful, was Ray (the boy who was sent away). But his AAI was coded as secure. And Matt (the boy with the stiff upper lip), who was also secure in the AAI, had ECR scores that were moderately anxious and a bit avoidant.

Whereas Amos (the boy who couldn't remember) was pretty secure in the ECR – even though he was dismissive in the AAI.

The only person I interviewed who had the same classification in both assessments was Lily, who was secure in each. Every other interviewee had completely different classifications in the two measures – and this echoes research findings.

It's tempting to think that an avoidant attachment style is the same as a dismissive attachment pattern, and that anxious is the same as preoccupied because they sound pretty similar. But a review of nearly a thousand people found nothing more than a 'trivial' link between attachment style measures and the AAI. And in another study, researchers found *no* link between the ECR and either the AAI *or* the Strange Situation.

So, how can we make any sense of this? Is there a way to explain why the interviewees had totally different results in the two measures?

Given that the aim of the ECR is to assess how someone is currently functioning in relationships, I suspect Ray's results were massively impacted by going through a divorce. This is *not* what the AAI is looking at at all. So it's no surprise his ECR and AAI results were different and he was insecure in one and secure in the other. I wonder what his ECR results would have been had he done one years earlier before divorce was on the cards.

And what about Amos? Remember when I said that
Ainsworth had found that people who were *in*secure described
themselves as secure when using self-report? Amos's relatively
secure ECR score echoes his glowing memories in the AAI.
But these glowing memories were contradicted by his specific
memories, memories that weren't picked up by the ECR. So,
as Ainsworth predicted, when Amos used self-report, all he
gave was the idealised picture without the contradictions.

And how do we explain Matt (the boy with the stiff upper
lip), who was secure in the AAI but moderately anxious and
slightly avoidant on the ECR? Matt's relationship strategy
throughout life had been to behave in 'avoidant' ways. His
notes from his therapy sessions confirmed that he didn't show
emotions, and that he held back and protected himself in
relationships – all of which are avoidant in the ECR. It's also
something Lily recognised in their relationship, saying that
he still had a desire to be perfect and to present that to her.
So, given that the aim of the ECR is to assess how someone
is currently functioning in relationships, being a little bit
avoidant makes sense in the context of Matt's life and
marriage.

As for anxiety, when Matt was filling out the ECR, he read
one of the statements aloud. It said, 'I'm afraid that I will lose
my partner's love.' He explained that being in a relationship
where he was emotionally vulnerable made him worry – he
worried that something might go wrong and he worried about
what he would do without Lily. Without access to a safe haven
for much of his childhood, he'd learned not to show
vulnerability. So it makes sense that he might worry about
losing the one person he'd learned to share it with and turn to
when he needed comfort and support.

None of this is assessed in the AAI. Matt's AAI score doesn't
tell you how his current relationships are going or how he
behaves in them. It explores how he processes information
about Important People. Getting a secure classification in the
AAI means he could freely think, talk about and remember

things to do with his childhood relationships. And that was my experience of interviewing him.

So, sometimes the differences in the interviewees' ECR and AAI results did make sense. But that didn't take away from the fact that, other than Lily, no one I interviewed had the same classification in both.

What are we measuring?

So in light of all this, can we really say the ECR and AAI are measuring the same things? And if not, does that mean there are two different attachment theories?

Social psychologists often see attachment as two styles – avoidant and anxious – that can be measured by asking people to describe themselves. They see security as the lack of avoidance or anxiety and don't usually delve into the impact of adversity.

Most developmental psychologists, on the other hand, see attachment as three patterns plus a fourth category or status that they call unresolved or disorganised. They usually avoid self-report and are keen to explore the impact of adversity.

These two groups have differed big time. And that makes talking about attachment theory in a neat and straightforward way incredibly difficult because they're essentially measuring different things. Yet much of what's written about attachment theory conflates the two and treats them as if they're the same group of people measuring the same thing, when they're not.

Social psychologists have carried out research that delves into adult relationships and how people with an avoidant style are more likely to do one thing, while those with anxious attachment will probably do another. But given that people often have totally different results in the ECR and AAI, it's tricky to apply those findings to the version of attachment theory we've been learning about in the book so far.

But despite the differences between the two measures, and as contradictory as this sounds … they might still be measuring different aspects of the same thing.

Mikulincer, Shaver and their colleague Omri Gillath asked people to read a string of letters and figure out whether those letters made a word or not. Some of them spelt names of their Important People – people whose job it was to provide a safe haven, and who it would be stressful to be separated from. Some letters spelt out names of other (less important) people, and some letters spelt the names of strangers.

Before being shown the letter strings, a neutral word ('hat') or a threatening word (like 'failure' or 'separation') flashed on a screen for 20 milliseconds – long enough to have an effect but not long enough for people to consciously clock it.

Seeing the word 'hat' had no impact on how quick people were at spotting their Important People's names. But when anxious people were subliminally primed with the word 'separation', they were faster at spotting the names of the people they would find it very stressful to be separated from. And when avoidant people were subliminally primed with the same word, they were *slower*. This reminds me of the avoidant child in the Strange Situation who turns *not* to their Important Person after being separated but to the toys in an attempt to avoid getting upset.

Mikulincer, Shaver and Gillath argued that the *only* way to explain their findings was the attachment system in action in adulthood. And this is what the ECR measures.

If Mikulincer, Shaver and Gillath are right, perhaps the ECR and the AAI are actually measuring the same thing – namely, whether or not we feel we have a safe haven when we need it. And how we feel about that might impact how we process information (as measured by the AAI), but also how we see ourselves and how we operate in romantic relationships (as measured by the ECR).

So, despite their differences, perhaps the two camps do actually agree on something fundamental – namely that, as humans, we all need a safe haven in times of stress. And that's the case all the way from the cradle to the grave.

Amos

The boy who couldn't remember
Attachment pattern: dismissive

I fell in love continuously. And I never broke up with anybody.
I was always rejected.

It was all about what other people thought of me. Like, 'Yes,
I can tell people I have a girlfriend!'

I was always very in love in the beginning. Then I'd get a bit
bored after a while. Sometimes I'd feel jealous and anxious,
sometimes not at all. With all of them I felt pretty insecure.
Then, after breaking up, I'd feel self-loathing and get really
depressed.

But I never asked for support. I would reject my friends' calls
or not want to go out. If I did, I wouldn't address the topic. I
didn't open up emotionally with anyone.

Then I met Daniela. I was immediately impressed. We went
to a bar. It was my first online date, she had done maybe 100.
She told me engaging stories, her conversation was great and
she cracked me up. After four, five hours, I was in love.

She was seductive, flirtatious. It made me really insecure,
because she could've been like that with others as well. But it
was also really attractive. It made me curious. It didn't make
me feel safe. But it made me really drawn to her, I wanted to
know more.

We exchanged numbers and kissed. If I kiss somebody, of course I want to date them, no? So, obviously we were going to meet again.

I felt a lot of sexual attraction. I couldn't think about anything else. I didn't really work that year. I was persecuted by images of having sex with her.

She said she liked me from the start. We went out a lot, did lots of funny things. Every weekend something different. I remember being on her little balcony, having drinks and talking and smoking. I so enjoyed conversations with her that we didn't watch a film until we were a year and a half into our relationship.

I never realised how jealous I was before I met Daniela. She would talk about people fancying her and I was so jealous, I started having physical symptoms. This is too much information. But I had diarrhoea for the first time in a decade. It was very painful.

I went to therapy again after this, to another therapist. And after three sessions, the therapist really helped me feel my anger towards my mother. It was so helpful.

I realised that every time I felt jealousy, I felt anxious because I might not have the love I needed. 'If I'm not special, I'm not going to be loved. Every time she looks in a different direction, she might fancy another guy …'

My therapist asked me to imagine being angry at my mum, especially as a child when my mum would comment on other children being cuter or better than me. Suddenly, I was aware of the anger for the first time. And I didn't have anxiety anymore.

From then on, mine and Daniela's relationship really changed because I wasn't jealous. Instead, the dominant feeling was unresolved anger with my mother. It's almost like I was taking back the anger but experiencing it inside. It was very helpful.

I was a lot less jealous. Daniela was a lot less distant. And gradually it became a real relationship.

Daniela's the opposite of how you would depict somebody 'anxious', because she really needs her space. She has many female friends she's close with. So I don't doubt she can feel closeness. But she's guarded with men, and that includes me. So, she was always mysterious. And she's not as affectionate as I would like her to be. I just can't put her in a box somehow.

Very soon I started sleeping at her place, and then I asked her if she wanted to move some place bigger. She said yes.

But even though we live together, I don't know how to explain it. I feel I can never catch Daniela. She's somehow always outside of my realm. Does that make sense?

And I think she would say those things about me.

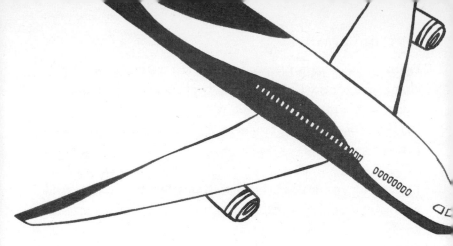

Ray

The boy who was sent away
Attachment pattern: secure

After a couple of years together, Ayumi told me in no uncertain terms that she was ready to be asked to get married.

I was absolutely ecstatic, because she'd basically committed to something that would be hard to get out of. And I think that's what marriage is about sometimes, isn't it? That's why people feel secure with it – 'It would be such a faff to get out of it, you must love me!'

We worked hard, saved money, bought a house. No fly-tipping, no lorry wrecks. We'd made our way to 'made it' street. We visited friends abroad, learned to dive, went to jazz concerts. We even occasionally talked to each other a bit about what we felt.

Then, after a number of horrendous miscarriages, we finally had twins, Elsie and Ayda.

Ayumi bore the disproportionate brunt of parenting, let alone carrying the twins and giving birth to them. The hormonal changes, the changes to independence and status affected her more than me, completely. She found having kids brilliant, but with a load of caveats.

Whereas I just found it absolutely bloody brilliant. Never, at any point, did I think, 'God wouldn't it be great if you guys weren't here or I saw less of you.' It was always a case of 'I can't get enough of you. I'll walk you to school, I'll drive you to school, I'll pick you up from here, I'll pick you up from there, take you to the airport, drive you to the ruddy country you're going to if I could ... I'll watch everything you go and play, do, sing.' I was there for almost everything I was eligible to be there for.

Ayumi and I had always been in alignment on how parenting should be done. We saw it as a job. And we were both predisposed to doing jobs as well as we could.

Suddenly our relationship went from being all about love and fun and being carefree to, 'We've got a job to do now, which is: be a bloody good parent, provide, and keep up appearances for all our friends.'

We didn't consciously do this coldly and ruthlessly like I'm talking about it now, but with hindsight I think that's what we did.

I didn't want to replicate what my parents had in any way. They divorced. They argued. And they did it in front of us. I didn't want to do any of those things. I wanted to be as different from my parents, especially my dad, as I could possibly be.

So Ayumi and I proceeded to divert all our attention to parenting and did a bloody good job.

We did whatever was required to maintain our relationship so it did not fall apart, and tried not to lose sight of the fact that we were supposed to be a couple. But our communication disappeared – it was all about doing the job. What did our daughters need? What did we need from the supermarket? Who should we see at Christmas? Where should we go on holiday?

That is not communication. We think it is, but it's not.

In all that time, we never had a major serious argument. We got by being extremely civil to each other in a very suppressed way.

It was a bit like my relationship with my dad. I know he wants me around, but he'll only call me about work or money because he can't talk about anything else. So he manufactures situations where he needs advice on these things. That's his way of having a relationship.

My dad will quite happily sit in silence with me and then say, 'It was nice to see you. See you next week and we can have another silent pizza together.'

And to some extent Ayumi and I did a version of that in our marriage.

CHAPTER SIX

Looking for Answers

Matt
The boy with the stiff upper lip
Attachment pattern: possibly insecure

Zimbabwe 17c

Lily hadn't ever seen a therapist before, but because she is wonderful and open-minded, she agreed.

Finances were really tight, but I felt that we needed to resolve issues, mainly on my side. I was calling it mostly for me.

What those sessions unfurled is that Lily's great, she's completely secure, but I don't say how I feel. It's that stiff upper lip again.

I was really struggling with being unemployed. I couldn't find anything, I wasn't getting traction with employers and it was really, really hard. I think there's a certain pressure in society that as a bloke you need to be a major breadwinner and do well. I definitely felt that pressure on my shoulders, so when I couldn't find a job, I felt really down and wasn't able to share it. My self-esteem was plummeting but I wasn't communicating that with her because I worried that if I told her how down I felt, she would think less of me. So I stonewalled her rather than bringing her in.

Unemployment was particularly difficult because, while I thought I was learning to be independent at boarding school, what I was actually doing was learning to hold myself to very high standards because I was always having to excel. Excelling was also how I got through my suicidal thoughts. It's also the only thing my dad values himself on. To me, excelling meant having a good job, so unemployment felt like failure – and I couldn't turn to excelling in my career to cope with it.

What I learned from our therapy sessions was that I should be more open with how I feel about things, more vulnerable or weak or however you want to describe it. To say it's weak to talk about feelings is crazy, but that's how I saw it.

Therapy enabled me to test what it was like to say how I actually felt in a secure environment with a therapist present. He asked me what was making me feel down, and I said, 'I'm finding it very difficult getting a job but I don't feel I can talk about it. I'm scared that if I'm honest Lily will feel less attracted to me and run a mile.'

Lily was sat there listening to all of this. And when he asked her how this made her feel, she said, 'It doesn't make me want to run a mile – I'm here to support you and it's important you share how you're feeling.'

The sessions helped me overcome being able to talk about how vulnerable I felt. They helped me see that it was okay for Lily to hear that and that she wouldn't want to leave – in fact, ironically, the opposite happened and it drew us closer together. Our sessions gave me the confidence to talk about difficult things more openly.

They also reminded me that I tend to push relationships until they snap. It's something that came up when I first saw my therapist, before I met Lily. He basically thought I would take relationships to breaking point by being a bit of a dickhead and only at that point, when the girl said, 'Enough is enough, I'm off,' would I think, 'Oh, no! But I didn't really mean it!' Then I would reel her back in, even if it wasn't the right thing to do.

I have notes from those first sessions about it:

> *I want them to meet my exacting standards. Only when they cave in and break up with me do I feel something for them. It's as if I want to see how far I can push them before they break. When the relationship is at the lowest point and I know it can't go lower, I recover. Then I have a sense of regret for treating them badly and want to get back with them as soon as I realise what I've lost.*

So maybe I was auto-piloting a bit back on to that.

But I haven't felt that since, at all, and it's been years now.

Therapy helped us massively. It helped me understand my background much more and also helped me reflect on all of this. I'd say 60 per cent of my ability to be reflective is down to the first load of psychologist sessions and 40 per cent the ones I did with Lily. I'm not sure we'd still be together if we hadn't had them.

I wish it was more acceptable in society to see a therapist or a psychologist. You get your car checked up once a year to make sure all the nuts and bolts are working, why not have a marriage MOT each year?

In terms of our marriage, I'm now fully committed, emotionally. The 'd' word, divorce, is never mentioned, it's never tabled, it's not allowed to be discussed. I feel quite strongly about it. It's not an option. As soon as it becomes one or is even mentioned in passing, you've planted a seed in someone's head. I also don't think it even should be joked about. It's completely off the table.

It means we can have blazing rows but we resolve them. And we feel safe.

The blazing rows happen every two or three months. I always reflect back on them and think they're stupid. I usually do something stupid, Lily disagrees, we both hold our ground, she gets really angry and I find that really funny. Then she storms off and you get doors slamming and all the rest of it.

Having been really angry and seen the red mist, a few seconds later I will be in fits of laughter and completely forget about it. But it lasts longer for Lily. It's pretty much always me swallowing my pride and saying sorry. Even if I'm right, which obviously I always am.

I've noticed that my avoidance flares up in difficult moments of conflict, as well as moments of low self-esteem. But I can 100 per cent call it faster than I used to, then deal with it faster.

When my avoidance reoccurs,
        there is a tightening, an unease. It's uncomfortable and unpleasant. Not nice at all.

It's such a visceral reaction. There's a tightening of the shoulders, tightening in the stomach, tightening in the neck. My arms are probably folded. They definitely feel folded metaphorically. And I'm really closed and guarded.

It must be hilarious for Lily, she can see in an instant that I'm either not telling the truth or I'm hiding something. It's blindingly obvious that I'm not engaging with her properly. I think it looks almost comical and she'll just call it.

I used to punch walls. Actual walls. Because it's stone and I   hit it with the soft bit of my hand, with my thumb, and   the pain jolts me back.

Obviously that's completely unhealthy. I just didn't have the capability to deal with the anger as it boiled up inside me.

I had one argument with Lily, I can't remember what it was, some usual, trivial thing. And, because she went out and slammed the door, I felt I should one-up her. So I punched the wall and created a hole. I didn't realise it was a plaster wall, so there's a massive gaping hole, she comes back in and says, 'What the hell? There's a hole in our wall?!'

I'm getting better at controlling it, controlling the rage – but it isn't easy because it flares up very, very quickly ... and then disappears just as fast.

Mindfulness has helped significantly, because I can feel it. Rage is something very visceral, I know it's coming and I can choose how to deal with it ... But it happens so quickly, I have to really catch it.

So that's anger. Depression is linked to self-esteem for me. I did have real ups and downs for a long time, but now I can't remember the last time when I felt down or depressed ... It was a very long time ago – which is quite incredible considering I used to feel down fairly often and then have really big episodes every couple of years when I was in my teens / early twenties.

Becoming more reflective and being with Lily have a lot to do with me feeling much happier. Lily and I spend a good hour or more a day chatting about things, so that's how I cope with a lot of things, including all the problems we've had trying to have kids. That, exercise and mindfulness.

Given how important it is to my well-being now, it's strange to think I spent most of my life not talking about anything emotional whatsoever.

My best friend Elsa could read me well enough that, when I'd been through several cycles of fertility treatment and was trying not to get my hopes up but still always getting them up, she would message every day and know or empathise with what that felt like. When it didn't go according to plan, she would say, 'Let's go for a cup of tea.'

I was regulated and monitored the whole time and had to have my bloods checked every couple of days to see where the egg was. I didn't want to tell my employer what I was doing so that meant trying to sneak to hospital in my lunch breaks. It was incredibly stressful.

When I needed someone to pick up drugs from hospital because I was stuck in a work meeting, Elsa was the one I called on because she understood how important it was to drop everything to help me do that. That type of reliance, which goes above and beyond the call of duty, which I would ask of family, I can ask of her.

Finally, after three very draining rounds of IVF and a protracted and painful two-day labour, Oli was born. There were lots of complications and I was in and out of hospital for a while, but Matt, Mum, Dad, Elsa and my aunt were hugely supportive. And it was worth it, as Oli was tiny and wrinkly and wonderful.

I was a bit nervous – no, nervous isn't the right word.

Matt has always said explicitly he wants to parent differently to the way his parents did, particularly the way his dad did. But at the same time, the way you are brought up teaches you behaviours that you don't even realise you have learned.

So I sometimes pondered how that tension would manifest itself if we had children.

But Matt is so different with Oli to how his parents are with him. He's so involved, I'm certainly less nervous of it than I was before he was born and it was all hypothetical.

We both enjoy parenthood and love Oli far more than we could have imagined. It's given both of us a general positivity, we both laugh much more than we did – and we were very happy beforehand. Oli is so funny, the whole time, and the experience of parenting is so hilariously ridiculous, it's given us both a joie de vivre. It's also given us a shared closeness that is not replicable in any other way. I mean, it is quite crazy that we made him.

There are also some downsides, of course. We end up focusing so much on day-to-day practicalities, it doesn't leave the space for some of the conversations that we used to have and for all of our needs to be met. We have ceased to be a two and have ended up being parents. That will only increase with two children – and I am eight months pregnant so double parenting isn't far away.

Parenthood has definitely made us reflect on our upbringings. Matt observes how he is as Oli changes and compares it to his memory of being parented, and that brings up a lot of conversations. I'm less analytical of how we parent, but we do talk about it a lot because we both have a desire to do the best for our son.

Matt's mum was clearly a very loving mother when Matt and his brothers were small because I can see how she interacts with Oli. She has a very intuitive grasp of what little people feel.

But it always feels like there is so much emotional repression that I can imagine when they got a bit older it was the army-style school of hard knocks.

I don't see how Matt and his brothers could have had a secure attachment once they went off to boarding school, didn't see their parents at weekends or half-terms and only came home for the big holidays … I suspect boarding school triggered an avoidance in Matt because there was very limited engagement from the moment he arrived. And I think Matt would agree.

If that was true, that might also explain the contradiction that in many ways Matt is. He is a very loving husband and dad, but has a lot of learned coping mechanisms that feel very avoidant or dismissive. Like his strong aversion to talking about anything emotional and his desire to focus on goal-setting when things are going wrong.

Parenthood has also made me reflect on my own upbringing. I'm sleep-deprived for two nights when Oli has a cough, so I look back on everything my parents were going through with my brother and think, 'Did they ever sleep?' I have asked them about it and I don't think they did. But I had just no sense of it. It was all down to the normalisation they did for me, which I think is amazing.

I remember when Charlie was in hospital in London for months. I now know what my brother was going through was really serious.

But all I remember is us going to the Natural History Museum. I'd been reading books about extinct animals and I remember thinking, 'This is epic! I'm in London. This is so cool. My brother got a cuddly crocodile toy and I'm going to the

Natural History Museum!' My mum managed to make everything feel so ordinary and safe.

The empathy I can now feel for her as a mother has brought us much, much closer. I've become much more aware of how difficult it must have been. Mum said the nurses were her best friends, there's a reason that we're still in contact with them. There is something important about the fact that she actively created those relationships and support networks. Mum also said that her and my dad talked very consciously about how they would manage his work schedule.

I wasn't aware of this at the time, but my dad agreed that he would never do business trips that were longer than one night. He would red-eye either side, often travelling overnight so that Mum was never left alone consistently and he was there for me as much as possible – at huge cost to sleep, I presume.

Mum said they also put in place strong strictures around me to make sure my life was normal – so they set certain parameters, like reading to me in bed every night and always sitting down together to eat family meals. They also put in place pick-up options with neighbours so I would never be the child abandoned at the gate. My mum was incredible in terms of arranging all of that – on top of everything that was going on with Charlie, she managed to make sure that I was always wrapped up in love. How Mum and Dad stayed together is beyond me.

Mum was there when Oli was born. She has talked about how being a grandmother has reminded her of the beautiful experience of having a healthy baby and what a pleasure it is and how happy and supportive everyone around her is.

I think being a very present grandmother to Oli has been a way for her to mourn the loss of a healthy second child.

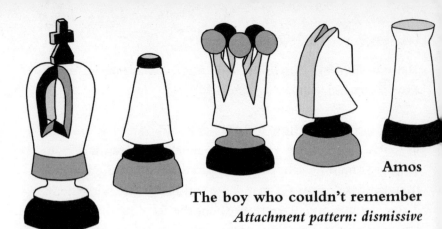

Amos

The boy who couldn't remember
Attachment pattern: dismissive

I think Daniela was seduced by me being avoidant to begin with. But now she finds it harder.

And when I'm tired or stressed, I'm more avoidant. It gets worse.

This is avoidant. Right? This is avoidant. Daniela is really angry that I haven't proposed. I have thought about asking at different points, but only because she wants to.

I'm really afraid of parties. This is avoidant. I very seldom arrange parties for myself. I'm really afraid people are not going to show up for me. Or not going to like the party. And I'm really afraid people will think I'm not a good choice for Daniela.

I haven't asked her to marry me because of this.

But I don't think I'm afraid of commitment … I would argue that because commitment means so little to somebody who's avoidant, they're less afraid of commitment than someone who is preoccupied, for whom a relationship means so much.

That's pretty profound.

So being in a relationship's not such a big deal.

But it's weird because in the rest of my life, I don't have this fear. It's specific to this wedding.

This is really dark stuff.

I think I should

                    talk in therapy about this.

Moving in together wasn't a problem. And having a child was amazing.

Before Daniela gave birth, people would say, 'How are you feeling?' And I'd say, 'I don't know … Well, a bit scared, because it means I can never break up with Daniela.' That was the only thing. So, commitment again.

We did a natural birth. I was the first one to see Bea coming out. It was so emotional. I remember she looked at me, and she had my eyes. A wave of crying and happiness went through my body. It was the best moment of my life.

I felt sadness for this girl who'd been alone for nine months in a cavity. I just wanted to hug her and be with her forever. And I also felt like she was me. I don't know how to explain it.

When I'm not with Bea, I miss her.

                        Once when she was 3 months, I went to Berlin for three days. I completely forgot that I was a father. And sometimes even when we were in the same house, I wouldn't see her for an hour, then I would turn and gasp in surprise.

But obviously with time, that has changed a lot. Now I don't want to be away from her. I miss her. I never expected to fall in love with my daughter that way.

But I don't feel any worry if we're apart, because if she's not with me, she's with Daniela or with my mum. I trust them completely when it comes to her. So I don't get worried. But I miss her.

I'm never angry with Bea. Sometimes I raise my voice because I have to put her to bed or change her. Then she runs around saying, 'Bea running, Bea running!' and it makes me laugh immediately. It's impossible to be angry with her for longer than 10 seconds. Maybe that will change when she gets older. But right now, I don't think anyone's got angry with her. I'm really proud of that.

My mum takes care of Bea a lot. She picks her up every day at nursery and is with her at least two hours every day. I've never seen her angry with Bea. She's different. She loves her.

I don't think she was angry or worried when I was Bea's age. At that age, you're pretty confined. You can't do anything crazy. And grandparents are usually better as grandparents than as parents. There's less responsibility. Less judgement. There's just the positive.

Bea is an easier baby than I was. She makes you feel really good about yourself. When she was 1 and a half, she would laugh at our jokes. Sometimes when Daniela and I had an argument, or Daniela was feeling sad, Bea would go to her and say, 'Mama, happy. Mama, no sad. Happy, happy.' And then Daniela would smile and say, 'Yeah! Happy!' and hug Bea.

She's easier to love than I was.

And I'm really happy with that. I don't say it with regret.

I'm really lucky to have her.

My mum still gets angry with me quite a lot, actually. And she did when I was a child. She would get angry for small things, like if I lost something.

I remember losing an earring of hers.

She got angry. Screaming and insulting, that kind of stuff.

But you know, it's okay.

If I closed the door with my hand in it, which I've done 20,000 times, my mum would help. But at the same time, she'd be angry at me for hurting myself.

My mum's still very angry with me very often. But somehow it doesn't get to me – because I'm not very responsive to her anger.

But I am always on guard about whether people are angry at me. That's stayed with me. 'If I screw this up, people are going to be angry.'

Or, 'If I don't get this job … it's okay, but life is not going to be as perfect.' The subtext is, 'Then no one will love me because my life is not perfect.'

I think that's related to my mum as well.

When I was a child, she would get mad at me if I didn't do things that made her look good. And if people criticised me, she didn't back me up.

But she praised me a lot when I did exceptional things. So, I thought that was the way to be loved by her.

Those are the headlines.

I never want to express anger to my daughter.

Expressing feelings is overrated because they're really vague.

If I say I'm angry, it doesn't mean anything. It's just a physiological state. Feelings aren't that important. They aren't good or bad. You've got them. It's like having feet. No?

Saying how I feel only means something if I say what's at the root of the emotion, my need that's unmet.

What's important is to express what your needs are. Like if I'm angry because I want to be listened to, or I'm angry because I want to be respected, I'm angry because I want to be loved. These are different forms of anger. Just saying 'I'm angry' doesn't help. Screaming doesn't help. Criticising or shouting or cutting other people off doesn't help.

And I don't think there's any benefit
        for a child to go through that.

Getting closer: building security

Inspired by the work of Ainsworth and other attachment researchers, Shaver and Mikulincer proposed that, in adulthood, the attachment system is made up of three modules.

Module 1 asks the question: are there signs of threat? Threats could include external dangers, like Someone Important suddenly being unavailable, or internal danger, like illness. Shaver and Mikulincer also thought that threats to status, identity or freedom would be relevant. This means that in the interviewees' adult lives, Module 1 might have been activated when Lily and Matt, and Ayumi and Ray (the boy who was sent away), got married; when Daniela made it clear she wanted to marry Amos (the boy who couldn't remember); when Matt became unemployed; and also in Lily's parents' lives as they tried to support two children, one of whom had a disability.

According to Shaver and Mikulincer, if as adults we think there's a threat, our attachment system is activated and makes us try to get close to Someone Important. They didn't mean physically close, as Bowlby did in his earlier work. They thought our Important Person might be alive but might also be someone that we've internalised within us.

This echoes the thinking of Bowlby, Ainsworth and Waters. In a secure script, when we encounter a problem, the first step is to communicate to Someone Important that we're upset and need comfort.

Shaver and Mikulincer thought that activating the attachment system in adulthood triggers Module 2, which asks the question: is Someone Important available? If they are and we manage to get close to them, we feel relieved, understood, cared about, confident and competent. This calibrates Module 1, essentially helping us chill out when it comes to sensing threat.

Mikulincer and Shaver called this the broaden-and-build cycle of attachment security. In terms of a secure script, this would be akin to an Important Person realising we're upset, supporting us in a useful way, and comforting and helping us regulate our emotions – and this happening on repeat.

According to Mikulincer and Shaver, Amos's attachment system would have been activated by the idea of getting married because it was a threat to his freedom. Amos himself recognised there was something 'weird' or 'dark' about how he felt about marriage – at the same time as trying to argue or intellectualise his way out of it – until he eventually admitted that he should speak to his therapist. In other words, he recognised that he should try to get close to Someone Important (his therapist) to deal with the threat to his freedom (getting married) and calibrate his attachment system so that Module 1 (which detects signs of threat) could chill out – and perhaps he might stop seeing marriage as a threat in the first place.

If Someone Important isn't available, Shaver and Mikulincer believe Module 3 is activated. This module asks the question: is trying to get close an option?

Hyperactivation

If the answer is yes, the attachment system is hyperactivated, and becomes extremely aware of anything to do with threat or attachment. This not only means the first two modules are activated more easily, but they're also harder to switch off. It's a double whammy – threats can seem scarier and it can be harder to be comforted.

Hyperactivation might involve feeling jealous, helpless or vulnerable, having pessimistic beliefs about whether you can cope alone, and seeing threatening things as uncontrollable or a product of your own vulnerability. It basically ramps up vigilance and can easily slip into a vicious cycle of thinking and worrying about threats or important relationships.

You might hyperactivate your attachment system when Someone Important emphasises your helplessness or you suffer trauma or abuse when you're separated from them. Or, as in the upbringings of Zsa Zsa (the girl who walked into fire) and Elija (the boy who was raised by wolves), when you don't get the care you need when you ask for it, or the care you're given punishes or prevents you from learning how to regulate yourself.

Deactivation

If trying to get close isn't an option, the attachment system is deactivated. This means you avoid anything to do with threats or important relationships. And anything that doesn't fit with deactivating the system is minimised or blocked.

Deactivating means you're unlikely to try to get Someone Important to be available. Instead, you're more likely to try to get distance from them – whether that's mental, emotional or physical. And instead of getting comfort from Someone Important, you get it from self-control. This might explain the way Ray behaved in order to make his relationship with Ayumi work. He recognised that she didn't want to talk about emotions and he was scared of arguing like his parents did. So he reverted to the script he learned growing up, namely not to ask for comfort or support and to try to rely on himself. Module 1 – are there signs of threat? Skip to Module 3 – deactivate. It might also have been what Ayumi had learned to do herself.

According to Mikulincer and Shaver, in order to deactivate your attachment system, you can change, block or repress information. Or you can dampen, redirect or postpone your response to whatever is threatening. But this doesn't just include negative emotions – it also includes joy and comfort. So someone might be radiating love to you, but when your attachment system is deactivated, you might only feel a dying ember of warmth.

Deactivating also means the first two modules are not only harder to activate, but they're also easier to switch off. So not only do threats seem less of a problem, they're also easier to shut down.

An example of the three modules in action is when Matt got married and went through a period of being unemployed. His freedom was under threat, as well as his status. Module 1: are signs of threat detected? Yes. He reacted by withdrawing from his Important Person, Lily. Module 2: is Someone Important available? No. Module 3: can you get close to them? No. Deactivate the attachment system.

So, Matt deactivated by stonewalling – instead of turning towards her, he turned away.

Except he then went back to Module 1: signs of threat detected? Yes. And he realised that the way he was behaving was threatening his marriage, so he went back to Module 2: is Someone Important available? This time, he turned to both Lily *and* his therapist, and together they discussed all the threats – to his status (caused by unemployment), his freedom (caused by marriage) and Someone Important being there for him (caused by the deactivation of his attachment system).

Through therapy, he learned that Lily was there when he needed her, and that he could share his feelings, something he'd learned during childhood to keep locked away. This helped calibrate Module 2: is Someone Important available? Yes.

Not only did he feel relief and security, but it also impacted how he reacted to threats in the first place. Loss of status or freedom didn't seem so overwhelming anymore, and if Module 1 did detect signs of threat, he was able to go straight to Lily. In other words, instead of assuming Someone Important *wouldn't* be there, and of deactivating, withdrawing and dealing with it on his own, he tried to get close to Lily and share how he was feeling.

This process echoes the ideas of Bowlby, Ainsworth and Waters. Namely that Matt slowly learned to change his expectations of important relationships. He came to learn that he could ask for support from Someone Important, that the support would be available and helpful and that his Important

Person would help him regulate his emotions. In other words, with lots of repetition and support, he was able to learn a secure script, despite having grown up without one (at least while he was at boarding school).

That's not to say that everyone needs a Lily. Shaver and Mikulincer thought there was too much emphasis on physically being with Important People – probably because Bowlby and Ainsworth studied young children who couldn't pick up a phone or send a message. Instead, Shaver and Mikulincer thought that, by adulthood, people could become more comfortable being on their own and could even benefit from it in creative ways. They put this down to broaden-and-build too.

You may be wondering, why didn't Matt just go to Lily in the first place? Module 1: signs of threat? Yes. Attachment system activated – try to get close to Someone Important. Module 2: are they available? Yes – job done.

Shaver and Mikulincer didn't think we only had one single relationship model in our minds. Instead, we have different attachment styles available depending on the particular relationship we're in, what's going on at the time, and our previous experiences and expectations. In Matt's case, he had come to learn that Important People wouldn't be available, that they wouldn't provide comfort or support and that the only person he could depend on was himself. So is it any surprise that was his go-to strategy?

Shaver and Mikulincer thought you might learn to deactivate your attachment system when you're rejected by Important People, for example when Amos's mum told him she wouldn't love him anymore; when they threaten to punish you or abuse you when you need comfort, as Elija and Zsa Zsa's fathers did; or when you find yourself in situations where you're encouraged to rely only on yourself, as Matt did. In other words, when you've learned that Important People won't be there when you need them, deactivation becomes your go-to when there are signs of threat.

But even though Shaver and Mikulincer argue that you see your current relationships through the lens of your attachment style, they don't think that that attachment style is fixed. Instead, they believe that we're continually changing our expectations about how relationships work. And this echoes both Bowlby and Ainsworth's views, as well as research into how attachment can change over time.

Of course, relationship patterns can be pretty consistent. Zsa Zsa and Elija spent years going for people who were dismissive. But sometimes we experience things in relationships that contradict our attachment style – like when Zsa Zsa and Elija dated Alex and Shelley, who were both loving, caring, available and able to talk about emotions. When this contradiction is repeated over and over again, or you start to see threat in different ways, relationships like those with Alex and Shelley can help shift the way our attachment system works.

That's how Matt explains the shift he's seen in his own attachment style. He thinks it's down to seeing a therapist and being in a relationship with Lily. Research backs him up. One of Mikulincer's students followed 73 couples for eight months. She observed how sensitive and responsive each partner was at the start, before assessing their attachment style at three different points. She found that, in the couples that were more sensitive and responsive, they became less insecure. And that makes sense because, in Ainsworth's mind, being sensitive and responsive were hallmarks of secure attachment.

But even though attachment styles can change over time, Bowlby thought that changing expectations of relationships would be slow and difficult. That doesn't mean it's impossible, and research suggests attachment isn't quite as consistent as Bowlby thought. But it doesn't mean it's quick and easy.

Bowlby also believed that someone who lacked support in childhood would start with lowered self-esteem. He thought they'd also expect less support and be less able to recognise and accept it than someone who grew up with strong support.

And this is exactly why Elija thought he sabotaged his loving and available relationship with Shelley, saying, 'I thought, "You want to be with me? What? No, you're lying, definitely lying … what do you want? What are you doing this for?"'

Perhaps low self-esteem is also why Amos's fears around getting married centred on people thinking he wasn't good enough for Daniela. And perhaps expecting less support is why, when Lily and Matt experienced difficulty, Matt's strategy was to stonewall, whereas Lily's strategy was to ask for help from trusted friends.

Even though attachment styles can change over time, it doesn't mean that, once changed, your hyperactivating or deactivating days are over. As both Amos and Matt recognised in themselves, avoidance flares up in times of stress. And that's exactly when you're least likely to notice what's happening – and when you most need support from others.

Ray

The boy who was sent away
Attachment pattern: secure

The children grew up. It all happened too fast. Even as they left home, I wanted to do everything for them. I wanted to blow their noses. I wanted to hug them. I wanted to take them to uni or work, and I wanted to make them packed lunches. I wanted to do everything.

And I had to stop and think, 'You don't do that in this century. Blokes aren't supposed to do that.'

But whenever I dropped Elsie off at uni or Ayda to her flat, a little bit of me broke a bit. Every time. It's pathetic.

I tried to be really cool with them. The way I did that is by appearing to be really busy with a great social life, lots of sport and lots of travel. So it looked like I didn't need anyone.

But I would drop everything, literally everything, if one of them coughed or suddenly wanted to come home.

Ayumi was always very stoic and very good at it. The girls know she's always available, she was very empathetic with them, but quite cool. Whereas I've always been trying to stifle my clinginess.

If I was to describe my ideal woman, it would be something close to Ayumi. She's incredibly kind-hearted, generous, intelligent, thorough and professional at everything she does, resilient and caring.

But as the kids got older, I noticed that Ayumi had more of a connection with them than she did with me. It made me jealous for two reasons. One, I'm frustrated Elsie and Ayda aren't like that with me, when I'm supposed to be the emotional one. Two is worse. Ayumi's relationship with them shows that she is capable of being emotional and open and considerate and loving, and always has been. Her emotional side was there for them, but never for me.

It's not that she was an ogre, or she had a flaming temper or threw food at me. It was nothing like that. But I was never told 'I love you'. I remember feeling alone, a lot, at times when I shouldn't have been. I remember having arguments on holiday about not communicating or being emotionally intimate enough. Kissing, the ultimate intimate act, was something she was reluctant to do.

It took me ages to work out that I was spending more and more time trying to entertain myself as she was preoccupied with her work and everyone else, her family, her friends, the children.

I gradually came to the conclusion that there was more love and intensity coming from me than from her. I started assuming that we were only together because it was convenient, it was too much of a faff not to be together.

But I decided not to bring it up because I didn't want to rock the boat and for it to finish. I wasn't ready for that when the girls were little. Don't ask the questions and have the conversations you're not prepared to have the answers for. Don't gamble with money you haven't got.

I wasn't in a position to lose the contact with the children, the stability. So I bumbled along and tried to do things that would make her say she loved me, want to hug me more, take my hand, or give me a spontaneous hug. But they didn't happen very much.

I didn't want us to split up because I didn't want any more separation in my life. I didn't want to change the timetable of our lives as it had been mapped out quite nicely. Even though it wasn't totally satisfactory, I was being given free rein to go off and pursue my hobbies and interests and read and do whatever I wanted.

And if we were in doubt, we had these odd friends who would come over and argue in front of us to make us feel like we were okay.

I think we were both very, very good at putting up with and surviving a situation that wasn't meeting both of our needs. But as I got older, the process of stifling what I was like inherently started to break down a bit. Our job had been to provide for and look after Elsie and Ayda, but they were growing up and moving out of home. The job had changed. And we both started to be what we really were a bit more.

I would say, 'Actually, I've never liked jazz and I don't want to go to another jazz concert ever.' That sort of thing started to happen a lot more on both sides, in a nice and respectful way. Then we were whittling through our lists and thinking, 'There isn't a huge amount left actually.'

So we went to counselling.

There was a real stigma about it. I'd often think, 'God, have we really been reduced to this?!' But it was the one time that we used to communicate regularly every week. The one time we could open up and actually talk about our feelings in a safe environment, which is what we had both worried about doing for decades.

We thought if we didn't do it in a safe, refereed environment, it would go pear-shaped and we would have a big row, but if we had it in a confined environment with a ref, it would be fine.

We didn't have any blazing rows. Unsurprising given I avoided conflict, arguments, to a very, very unhealthy degree. But we opened a can of worms, and we struggled to put them back. And I still have mixed feelings about that.

The worms were things like her saying, 'I might have loved you, but I'm not sure if I do now or not.'

Or when the counsellor said, 'Can you think of a list of things that you love about your spouse?' I found it dead easy. But Ayumi was really struggling. She put a few things down and I thought, 'Really? Is that what you think is good about me? "He keeps himself fit?!" For fuck's sake.'

Then we had a conversation, the dreaded conversation, about how she saw me not so much as a husband but as another child that she was mothering.

We tried to drill down into why she felt that way, so she made a list of all the things that bothered her – not doing the dishes, leaving stuff around the house, not leaving something clean. The sort of thing that teenage boys would do.

There was a large list of small and specific things, and some of them were not actually untrue. But I suspected there was more to it than that, that these were just excuses for something fundamental that was wrong.

So we went through the list and made sure that every gripe stopped happening. When we came back, the counsellor said, 'Has the situation improved?' Ayumi said, 'Yes, the things on the list are better.

But I don't feel any different.

> So it wasn't that.   It was never that.'

It wasn't about clean surfaces or certain parts of the house remaining uncluttered or putting the bins out. It wasn't ever about that.

In the end, we figured out what it was actually about when Ayumi said, 'I don't feel I can give you any love and affection the way you want it. I don't feel inclined to be intimate in any form, and I don't know why.'

She was quite closed about that. She couldn't change. Then the barriers would come down and nothing would come out.

That was the hardest moment.

Given the chance, the value in our relationship wasn't seen. The offer to work at it was indirectly made and it was rejected.

We had a coffee nearby and said, 'I can't believe I think we've just agreed to separate.'

And we had a moment of saying, 'We did a good a job, didn't we? It was good, wasn't it? And it was right, it was wonderful?'

Then it was, 'Okay, what do we do now?' And we had to work out whether we got divorced, how we split things, whether we sold the house, how we avoided it becoming acrimonious.

We eventually agreed on a split which involved selling the house. And we'd occasionally meet up in the neutral territory of a coffee shop and talk. Sometimes we'd be flippant and say, 'How do you see me in five years' time? How do I see you?' We'd make up joke scenarios of who we'd end up with and where we'd be living and talk about how it would be nice if we ended up remaining friends.

Then we tried to figure out how to tell the kids. We talked about timing it right to have the least devastating impact on them, then worked out how we were going to say it, and all the points that we would jointly present to pre-empt any questions they had.

We said it was something that happened relatively recently so that they didn't feel as though they were responsible for any of it. We said there was no fault, we'd just grown apart, we were heading in slightly different directions now that they'd left home. We would remain friends, we would co-parent and be there for key things together. Then we all had a group hug.

But after that, it was awful because everyone now knew it was happening. Our behaviour was different. When we were in the house, we were in different rooms all the time, watching different things, doing fewer things together.

It didn't become vile, but Ayumi and I were behaving like we'd already separated, trying to prep ourselves for the future. Friends cohabiting would have behaved better with each other.

Ayumi seemed to be in her element. 'Right, made that decision, now I'm going to cut all ties and buy separate food for the fridge, put it in separate compartments, do separate washing.'

We weren't talking about when we were going out or coming back, we just came and went as if we were strangers sharing an apartment. We weren't even friendly neighbours. That was the worst bit.

The worst bit.

Leaving our family home was devastating.

Ayumi found it easier. She was excited – she wanted to go somewhere new and have completely new furniture, a different type of house, rugs, pictures, frames, the works.

But I found it distressing. As things were moved into storage or taken off the walls, our 'made it' house looked like it was suffering a degenerative disease. It looked less and less as it did when it was at its peak.

Lampshades off, rooms empty, frame marks on the walls where pictures used to be – the life of this house was over.

I couldn't wait to get away.

Zsa Zsa

The girl who walked into fire
Attachment pattern: unresolved (primary),
preoccupied (secondary)

I was in hospital for two months when I was a baby, some kind of heart condition. I was really ill. And I had no idea. Literally, no idea. My parents never told me.

Maybe it's not relevant, but I can't ask them about it. I don't really speak to them now, so how would I say, 'Can you tell me about when I was sick when I was little?'

They'd say, 'How do you know you were sick?'

And I'd say, 'I requested my medical records to see if there was anything about the content of our family therapy to see if you tried to help me not want to kill myself anymore.'

I decided to get them because I wanted to check that I wasn't going mad. Having thought about it so much, I didn't want to second-guess myself anymore. The records say we went to the doctor. We were compelled to go to a family counselling thing, which my dad then appears to have cancelled because apparently he found his own counsellor.

Then I went to go and see a counsellor / therapist / God knows what and the only bit of information is the final letter at the end of our course of sessions, in which she writes that my father's taking a much greater interest in my life and I seem much better. I can't remember what my mum did. The records don't mention her.

It was interesting reading a letter from a therapist who's seen a 13-year-old child, and who concludes that they're better and don't need any more sessions.

I was surprised to see how close together the overdoses were. I thought that some months had elapsed between them, but my medical records suggest that everything was very quick. And I kept thinking ...   if a kid in a state school had taken two very quick overdoses, would the infrastructure around that child look quite different to how mine did?

Then I got in touch with my old teacher, Ursula, the one I went for walks with every week when I was at school.   She was a very solid and stable person for me at a really important time in my life. She really was. She was the only person that really felt like my ally.

It wasn't a fully conscious decision to reconnect with her, but things by that point had deteriorated quite substantially with my parents, and I thought being around her would be good. I think subconsciously, in the absence of any answers from my parents or medical notes, I wanted to know if she could give me some.

She got back to me so quickly when I reached out to her, and when we eventually met she said, 'I am just so pleased that you are still here.'

She meant it in a nice way. But it's hard to hear somebody you knew in your teenage years tell you that they weren't sure whether you'd still be alive.

Up until the last few years, I never thought I would be.

We spent five hours talking non-stop. It was quite draining. It was really hard. It was really hard, made me really sad.

I felt sad at myself that I reached out to her at a point when I felt really low, rather than in a happier time. I wish I'd reached out to her and said, 'Thank you for all you did to help me.'

Instead, it was almost like saying, 'When I was in a bit of a state, you really helped me. Then I had a decent stretch of life where things didn't feel so shit. Now I'm in a state again, so … Hi! I'm back! Can you agony aunt me?' Seventeen years later.

A lot of my memories of my parents are centred around photo albums. My parents had a lot of photo albums. So I don't know whether I actually recollect situations that really happened, or whether a lot of it is built around photo memories that I have created in my mind.

From the photos, it looks like we went on lots of holidays, it feels like it was one endless summer. We had a nice garden, there were lots of people coming over for lunch and playing tennis. From the photos, it seems I had a happy family life, everything was okay.

Talking to Ursula made me realise that it was blindingly fucking obvious that things weren't okay.

It was funny hearing her opinion on how things were and the fact that she had always worried about me
                        for years after.

'I always really tried hard to leave kids at school, but there were some I always wanted to take home with me. You were one of them.'

She meant it in a really lovely way. And she wasn't guarded in how she said things. There was a real honesty, in a nothing-to-hide kind of way. She said she carried me with her.

As a child I thought that nobody,   nobody saw me.
Until I met Ursula. I definitely felt seen by her, but I thought
my relationship was solely with her, she didn't have any
peripheral information.

But yet she had met my parents on multiple occasions and it
was   blindingly   obvious   that   she   knew   my   dad
was   dismissive and vacant and absent.

She'd obviously had some difficult conversations with him.
But he had made it clear to her that her input wasn't really
valid or required.

He must have felt jealous because I would go home and say
how wonderful this teacher was.   And this is a child
who   you know   he had a fractious relationship with.

It's the same as it would be for any abuser. You realise that
somebody else is important and suddenly feel vulnerable
because someone might find out what you've been
doing.   The curtain might twitch,   you might
not be so behind closed doors anymore …   what's
your daughter saying to this woman?

It's probably why my dad thinks that therapy is such a bad idea,
the idea that he might feature in it   but wouldn't be
there to defend himself and say that it was in fact all my fault.

When I first started seeing a therapist, my mum said, 'I think
that's a really good idea.' My dad said, 'That's a fucking waste
of money. That's just an absolute fucking waste of money. I
mean what do you even talk about?!'

I suppose the reason for having therapy is to try to find answers
to questions that I have for my parents that I know that they
will never be able to answer.

'Why didn't you stop Mum drinking? Why did you hit her?
Why did you hit me? Why, why, why, why, why?' My
expectation is that, because I have these questions, there must
be an answer. But in reality, the answers to those questions
don't exist   from him.

So therapy is about finding answers. Or understanding why I
think I need answers to questions that can't be answered. I
guess it's also about forgiving my dad in particular for his
inability to be self-aware enough to connect with his emotions
to give me any answers.

My dad would rather swim along on top of the water carrying
little boxes containing stories about his life. There's no room for
manoeuvre or chat, because that would mean he'd have to say
something about how he felt. Part of me wants to say to him,
'Do you want that to be how you live out your years? Or could
you be a bit more human and try to have a relationship with me?'

But it would just be met with, 'You're being very aggressive.'
When my dad says that, what he's actually saying is, 'Who are
you to criticise us?' and 'Don't you know what I've done for
you? You wouldn't be anything without me!'

I'm not not close to my parents because he hit me. That's not
why I don't want them in my life. It's nothing to do with that.
It's his actions that aren't violent that have made me not want
to have anything to do with him.

The thing is, I don't think he can do better or be better or be
kinder or be softer. Though I know he can be, with other people.

Unlike my dad, I think my mum's a really emotional person.
I feel a lot of empathy for her and what led her to be how she
is. But then she has also been the architect of some really,

really profoundly shitty moments in my life. All of her own design. And not just when she's been drunk.

I'm coming to the conclusion that there are no answers to some questions. You don't need to know the answers. You need to somehow process what they mean to you and why you might want those questions answered.

But also, in order to traverse your life on a day-to-day basis, you need to concentrate on things you have control over, like your own emotion and your own action, rather than feeling rage and fury at somebody else.

I just haven't managed that yet.

Ursula sent me a really nice message afterwards saying, 'It meant so much to me to see you,' and we agreed that we'd see each other again.

Then I didn't get back in contact.

Then she emailed again and I didn't respond. I don't really know what to do because now I'm embarrassed that months have gone by and I haven't even responded to an email.

I just get nervous about how much I put upon everyone in my life and I feel terrible reaching out to this woman who is clearly okay in her life and asking for her support, talking about difficult things, talking about suicide again, feeling I have so little to say that's good and I don't have anything to offer her in return.

So instead I think, 'I'll just put it back in the box.'

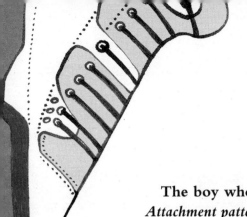

Elija

The boy who was raised by wolves
Attachment pattern: unresolved (primary),
preoccupied (secondary)

Earning money, becoming a man – I was on my own through all of it. My dad had disowned me and I didn't talk to my mum for nine years when she kicked me out. She had been the one solid thing in my life. And she never came to find me.

As I got a little bit older, I thought, 'Okay, you get one mum and dad. Let's just try to make the best of a bad situation.' So I went to find her and get things off my chest and ask what her reasons for doing it were.

She wanted to be loved, I get it. Some people say, 'How can you choose a man over your child?' But when you're in the moment, as I've come to realise in my life, you're blind to it. So it's not necessarily all my mum's fault – there was a man on the scene that broke things.

Over the years, trust has built up, we give each other hugs and kisses, I drop her a message every other day or so. But the trust is not 100 per cent there. It's definitely not 100 per cent at all.

I remember so much what my relationship was like with her before the trust was broken, and as much as we've worked on it, it's never, ever, ever, ever been the same. When you break that trust, you can build it back, but there are still cracks in the glass. Even now, there's this certain element in the air, a little reminder of what happened, every time I go home. Every single time.

I also made up with my dad. I didn't talk to him for 15 years after he disowned me. Then, when I was 31, I knocked on his door. And he said, 'Oh. What do you want?' After 15 years that was his response.

I went in and we had a chat, I had a lot of questions and I laid everything on the line:

> *Why did you beat me black and blue? Why did you pick me up and throw me across the room? Why did you emotionally torment me, to the point where you were running out of ideas and you made me sit in a cold bath for half an hour?*

> *When did you realise that that was all wrong? Or do you still think it's right, what you did? Why didn't you learn how to stop it? Did you even try to change?*

My dad answered the questions as best he could.

But he doesn't search within himself in any way, shape or form, so he can only give the answers that he knows, and they're not sufficient. Probably 25 per cent qualify as an answer.

So I have to fill the 75 per cent out. His dad is not here to go and talk to as he passed away, otherwise I would go to him.

The answer I've given myself is, 'My dad doesn't have answers. That means I'm never gonna get the answers.'

I'm okay with accepting that.

He was beaten as a kid, so that contributes to his insufficiency, his lack of answers. But I still wanna go, 'Give me some more, Dad!'

Or, 'What other things can I think of to pardon him for being insufficient?'

My dad carries everything difficult in boxes – we all do. But if you're not gonna visit those boxes, unlock them, explore what's in them, it's a weight that you carry around in your life. The what ifs, the sleepless nights, the crying, the wide-awake thinking about that one thing that happened 25 years ago. You remember a beating that you got or an incident that happened or someone that passed.

If you don't visit those boxes, you just leave them in the corner, then you will carry weight. A lot of people do – they don't even realise how much weight they're holding. Some people can't even find the door to the box, let alone open it.

There've been boxes that I've opened and a little weight's fallen off. Some I couldn't even notice the difference, really, but I've opened others and thought, 'That was so fucking heavy!' Now that I'm not carrying it no more, it's like I'm flying, I'm walking on the moon with enormous slow-motion steps. But every box is relevant, no matter how big or small.

I was super-frustrated about Dad's locked boxes for a long time. But I think I've come to terms with it and think, 'Okay, I'm never going to have the key to that box.' You can stay angry if you want to, or you can think, 'Ah, well, nothing can be done about it – he hasn't got the key.' And his dad's not here to give it to him. And my dad's self-analysis is non-existent. There's a lead barrier around him and you can't get in.

That's why my sister and my dad will never have a relationship – because for that to happen, they both have to go to places in themselves that they will never go.

My sister is emotionally scarred because of him. He never touched her, not once. But he beat all the people she loved and he turned her home into a place of terror.

You mention my dad to her, and she'll say, 'He's a fucking idiot.' Hatred, no, not having it, 'Don't say his name in front of me, I'm not gonna see him ever, ever, ever, ever.'

If I was still holding on to all of that, I probably wouldn't be able to walk because of the weight. And my sister's walking around with that. She hasn't released any of that tension. None at all.

It had a massive impact on my sister's childhood.
        If she was to open all those boxes,
                she would cry for years.

Boxes and self-preservation

When we experience something that we find threatening, we can find a way to shrink it or get rid of it – or at least that's what psychoanalysts think. They call this a 'defence'.

Ray, Zsa Zsa and Elija didn't use the word 'defence', but they did talk about boxes, cans of worms and lead barriers. Zsa Zsa described how both she and her dad used boxes to store things – her dad stored feelings and stories about his life, whereas she put difficult things in them. Elija talked about the weight of carrying boxes (even if you don't realise you have any) and the lightness he felt after opening his up. But he also discussed the difficulty of doing so – and thought his sister would cry for years if she were to open all the boxes she carried. Elija also spoke about the importance of accepting that some people, like his dad, will never open their boxes. They don't have the key.

It's not only the interviewees that talked about putting things away in our minds. Research has found that people with an avoidant attachment style don't usually show vulnerability, even after thinking about a break-up. But when Mikulincer, Shaver and their colleague asked them to remember a seven-digit number, thoughts relating to break-ups started popping up. It's as if, by doing the memory task, they used up some of the brainpower that they'd been using to keep their worries hidden in boxes. Which might explain why Elija felt lighter when he opened his up.

The research and the interviewees' words echo Bowlby's thinking on the topic. His ideas haven't been tested by researchers since, so there are no studies to prove or disprove his theory. But his thoughts are still worth exploring, not least as a way of looking at what came up in the interviews, but also because they reflect ideas that often come up in certain types of psychotherapy.

Bowlby thought that, while some forms of 'defence' are destructive, some can help you cope with what's going on around you. Zsa Zsa found it useful to put difficult things in a box sometimes. Ayumi's ability to shut off after she and Ray agreed to divorce may have helped her cope with one of life's hardest transitions. And if opening her boxes really would lead to crying for years, you can understand why Elija's sister might keep them locked up.

Bowlby also thought that, while some defences are conscious and controllable, others aren't. And this echoes the interviewees' experiences. Zsa Zsa described how, sometimes, she deliberately put things away in a box, whereas Elija thought his dad was incapable of opening them, given he had lost the keys.

To really dig down into a defence, Bowlby thought it was also useful to ask what the effects were on the individual – did it help or harm them? And what about their family? Or the community at large? But he thought that the psychoanalytic idea of defences was too overloaded and confused to even be able to ask these questions.

He thought the confusion was largely down to Sigmund Freud changing his explanation of defences over time. In his early career, Freud saw trauma as a pathogen that initiates defence in our bodies, and the memory of trauma as a foreign body that's still at work long after its entry. Twenty years later, he described it as a censor in the mind that excludes things it doesn't like from our consciousness. And his ideas continued to evolve over time.

But because they evolved, Bowlby thought that other psychoanalysts misunderstood what Freud meant. He also thought that most of them, including his former supervisor Melanie Klein, didn't distinguish between helpful coping strategies and unhelpful defences. With the exception of a handful of psychoanalysts, he thought their definition was often lazy, unclear and didn't describe important processes in our minds. So he came up with his own theory, which he called 'segregation'.

Bowlby thought that, in order to cope, we sometimes filter information out of our experience. We basically block it. This filtering might be flexible, so we may be able to drop it when we need to. But it might also be inflexible and block information over a long period, no matter what the circumstances. This inflexible form of segregation reminds me of Elija's description of a lead barrier and losing the key to the box.

Bowlby thought there were two types of segregation. The first involves excluding or not noticing certain things in the world. Or if we do notice them, we might not respond. A classic example of this is dismissive attachment. If, as both Ray and his therapist suspected, Ayumi was dismissive, then she might direct her attention away from things that could upset her and activate her attachment system. In doing so, she would be filtering that information out. Ainsworth saw this in action with little children in the Strange Situation who focused their attention on toys and away from their parent. The aim of this filtering is to avoid getting upset, because this means they don't have to look for a safe haven that, based on their experiences, they don't think will be there.

Bowlby's second type of segregation involves filtering and disconnecting memory. This means we might not be able to access certain memories, or if we can, they may not be tagged with accurate and well-defined meanings. This filtering or disconnection may explain why Amos doesn't have negative memories of hospital, even though his recurring nightmares suggest it wasn't as positive as he seems to think:

> I don't, I don't, I don't have any negative memory of hospital. Just positive ones of people bringing me presents, having a room with toys. My memories are about the toys.

> I had nightmares about dinosaurs eating me, people putting sharp things in my legs. And a recurring dream that my house would burn and I couldn't do anything about it ... But otherwise, I don't remember anything bad.

Amos's memories also seemed disconnected when he described his mum's anger towards him as a child. He initially described her as never being angry, saying, 'I don't think she was angry and worried when I was Bea's age.' But he then went on to talk about the many ways in which she got angry with him when he was young: 'She would get angry for small things, like if I lost something ... Screaming and insulting, that kind of stuff.'

Amos might be right, it might be that his mother wasn't angry in early childhood and became angry later (after the death of her mother, for example). But it might also echo the other possible inconsistencies in his memory.

Bowlby didn't think segregation was necessarily bad. In fact, he thought if it was flexible, it could sometimes be useful and help our long-term mental health. But he didn't think this was the case when it was inflexible. He saw segregation as similar to some types of illness, where the processes involved are helpful by their nature, but faulty in their amount. For example, your immune system usually fights infection, which is obviously a good thing. But in autoimmune diseases, it can go into overdrive. In rheumatoid arthritis, your immune system attacks the cells that line your joints by mistake – and can lead to a vast amount of pain. As with inflexible segregation, it's helpful by its nature, faulty in amount.

Flexible segregation strategies might include choosing to block thoughts, distractions and daydreams to help enable you to explore the world. Or choosing to keep worries out of your mind when you're trying to get to sleep. Or focusing your attention away from someone or something that might irritate you – by doing so, you lose some information, but you don't completely lose contact with reality. Or you might engross yourself in work, cooking or exercising when you might otherwise be mulling something over or feeling upset.

Bowlby thought there was another level of this sort of flexible strategy. You might, for example, joke about something incredibly painful. To Bowlby, you're acknowledging it, but the emotion is blocked off. So you're allowing the difficult experience, but only in part.

On the more inflexible end of segregation, you might block information if it's difficult to accept, dangerous or doesn't fit with your values. You might even completely exclude it from part of yourself. If, as a child, anger wasn't allowed or you were punished if you got angry, you might mute it altogether. You might even make it totally unreachable. This is what Ainsworth did, as her mother didn't allow angry behaviour when she was a child.

This has the benefit of avoiding punishment from the person or people that can't tolerate anger. But Bowlby warned that this sort of segregation might not just block anger, it might block lots of other important things too.

Bowlby described a young teacher in her mid-twenties who went to see an analyst called Jonathan Pedder. Initially she described her upbringing as idyllic. But Pedder soon discovered that when she was 18 months old, she was sent to stay with an aunt while her mum was pregnant. Six months later, she felt like her aunt was more of a mum to her than her actual mother – so having to go back home was very painful. From then on, she was petrified of being separated again, until she turned 10, when she told Pedder that she switched off her anxiety 'like a tap'. But she didn't just switch her anxiety off. She switched off most of her emotional life too.

Her story made me think of Ray being sent away as a child, then having to return once he had come to see his grandmother as his mother figure. And I wondered if, in the past, he'd adopted a similar approach to managing his feelings to protect himself from the overwhelming distress of separations. If so, that would account for the coder detecting dismissive aspects to his AAI. It might also mean that he switched off some of the rest of his emotional life too.

Bowlby thought this sort of inflexible, uncontrollable, lead wall type of segregation stops you from being able to learn from and enjoy the world. After all, if you block off all your emotions, how can you fully experience the joy in the world and in others? But this wasn't all. Bowlby also thought this sort of segregation could lead to major problems.

That's partly because he thought that when we segregate memories by holding them back, strong emotions can be disconnected from their original source. This means they can seem to appear out of nowhere or be linked with inappropriate things. Perhaps that's why Elija's dad's rage would erupt out of nowhere, like when Elija crossed the road to pick up his ball. As Elija explained, 'I've seen the emotion on my dad's face – it's like he needed an excuse to let his aggression out, to beat me more.' The emotions are in there, they're disconnected from their source and they can burst out at any time.

Dissociation

A more extreme form of segregation is dissociation, which can involve feeling disconnected from yourself and the world around you. Bowlby thought it might have evolved as a way for us to shut off and protect ourselves from extreme experiences or memories. But with dissociation, instead of segregating information, we segregate the way we see, hear, touch, smell and taste.

Bowlby thought that dissociation meant losing information about moments in time and place, not responding to the environment – and coming to afterwards. Perhaps that's what Elija was describing when his dad beat him for hours and 'was absolutely out of it'.

So, if Bowlby was right, as much as we try to block things, it doesn't always work. For example, if your parent punishes you if you get upset or ask for comfort, as Elija's and Zsa Zsa's dads did, you might try to block out upsetting information that could trigger your attachment system. You might ignore the pain if you get hurt, pretend it doesn't make you sad or focus your attention away from information about where your parent is to try to avoid going to them for comfort. You might persuade yourself you're fireproof, even though no human can be.

This reminded me of when Bowlby's colleague Robertson studied a small boy who'd been sent to hospital when he was 13 months old and stayed there for three years. Shortly after he went home, he burned his hand in the fire. He ignored the pain, pretended it didn't make him sad and didn't ask for comfort. Instead of howling and seeking comfort like an ordinary toddler, he smiled and kept it to himself.

It also reminded me of when Matt (the boy with the stiff upper lip) started having suicidal thoughts at school, and his strategy was to ignore his painful thoughts and feelings and focus his attention somewhere else. He said:

> If I did want [my parents'] support, all I had was those blue letters … they were very distant from me. I started thinking, 'There's no one I can talk to about any of this at all.' So I didn't … I just bottled it up and carried on through … I just refocused my energy on something else. Cricket, I think. I focused on doing well in that.

But this strategy won't always work. If your injury is particularly painful or upsetting, or Someone Important is actually available, you might find yourself conflicted between your attachment system and your attempts to avoid triggering it. Which is exactly what happened when Matt struggled with marriage and unemployment and stonewalled Lily – at the same time as wanting to ask for support.

Bowlby thought that our attachment system impacted our basic sense of self-worth, of being acceptable, and capable of being cherished. He also thought that forgotten wishes and disappointments from our childhood would be incorporated into both relationship expectations and how we act as adults. And if we segregate something in an inflexible, lead barrier sort of way, Bowlby thought that conflict might contribute to anxiety and depression later on.

So while some boxes can be helpful, or maybe even necessary sometimes, if they're made out of inflexible, heavy metal, the very boxes that we created to protect ourselves might end up boxing us in.

And perhaps one of the greatest challenges of growing up is to find a way to own and balance the different parts of ourselves, including anything we've hidden away.

Skyler

The girl wrapped in cotton wool
Attachment pattern: unresolved (primary),
preoccupied (secondary)

Most people couldn't fathom what I was going through. When I came back from Liam's funeral, a friend of mine said, 'How was your holiday?'

As time passed, some other friends were like, 'Well, it's been six months, that's longer than your actual relationship – why aren't you over it?'

A few weeks after he died, I went to a party with a bunch of his friends to celebrate his life. I got very drunk and ended up hooking up with one of his best friends. One of my friends was like, 'That is so disrespectful. I can't believe you would do that.'

I was not hooking up with his best friend to hook up with his best friend. We were both trying to feel closer to Liam. It wasn't, 'Well I haven't had sex in a while, may as well ...' We were not willing to accept the fact that Liam was no longer around and were trying to feel a connection to him. That's what I was doing when I was trying to replace him by dating anyone who looked remotely like him – I was trying not to acknowledge the fact that he's no longer alive.

It's tough to process a loss when there's no one around who has gone through something similar. I talked to a charity group for young widows, but even there I felt like I didn't have the right to grieve. They were open and accepting and made it clear that I was more than welcome, but it was hard because I hadn't been married and everyone else there had been.

I'd keep thinking, 'I'm going to solve this, I'm going to feel better.' But there are no books on it. There are no articles about it, no blogs.

Tonnes of books on how to deal with the loss of a spouse, millions of grief books, even about friends – 'How to Lose Your Friend When You're 15 and a Half', that's covered. But there's not a single article out there about what happens when you lose somebody that you have just fallen in love with but it's only just become official.

And my parents were not going to say, 'I know there are no books on this, but what you're feeling is real.' It's tough to process a loss when you've been raised to not talk about emotions, and haven't been allowed to feel.

So I thought, 'I'll go to therapy, that will make this go away.' That's what I did. I was so on top of it, I tried to get a therapist before the funeral even happened, but all the grief counsellors said, 'We don't see people for a month.' And I was like, 'But I want to be fixed now!'

I eventually got one, this 68-year-old man named Gerald. It was so uncomfortable. I felt like I was talking to my dad, and given I wanted to ask questions like, 'Is it cheating to sleep with someone else?' I just couldn't talk. Plus emotions weren't really something I did, particularly not with my dad or someone that looked like him.

So I got a different therapist. I went for someone who was younger and female and she was great. She helped a lot in terms of accepting my right to grieve. She made me acknowledge that emotions are not facts that are applicable to everybody and that, regardless of what they are, your emotions are the truth. Whatever you're feeling is what you're feeling, so your feelings can't be right or wrong.

That was the best thing that helped me process Liam's death. I still have issues with the right to grieve, but it was a lot worse right after it happened. A lot worse.

I saw my therapist for about a year. We talked about everything, she was non-judgemental, trustworthy, wise – I found our sessions together really useful.

And then she died.

She was 36.

I think it was an illness, but I didn't get a lot of information.

She was dead within a month.

CHAPTER SEVEN

Reflecting & Grieving

Ray

The boy who was sent away
Attachment pattern: secure

Grief doesn't go away. It's always there.

There are lots of types and you carry them around with you.

All you do is manage them better and learn how to put them in their boxes. But you carry the boxes around. Everyone's got little boxes of grief.

I've got ones for losing our family home, the kids growing up, my marriage ending, getting older. I carry a catalogue of griefs.

I underestimated the impact of all those losses.

Once I'd found somewhere to live, there was an element of excitement, but then the nitty-gritty of the divorce started to kick in. It wasn't quite as amicable as I'd hoped. We had arguments which came down to money and they undermined 24 years together and everything we'd invested in.

Then the loss of the house hit. That was our 'made it' house. We had it all. The house, the kids, the lifestyle. We don't have any of it now. It's all gone. I occasionally walk past and think, 'I used to live there.'

There's the loss of status in life, we made it, made it, made it … and then lost it. Snakes and ladders, you just hit a snake.

I lost my marriage. Spending time with each other's relatives, friends, all of that, which I didn't really value or factor in, has been lost. And then you start realising how much of that was important to you.

You have a conversation before and after a divorce and they're very different. Before a divorce, it's, 'We had so little in common, we had such differences that we've been stifling. Confronted with how different we were, it was inevitable that we would have to go different ways.'

The people you talk to say, 'I always thought you two were different, I was surprised you stayed together that long.' And you believe it and you go through the process and you divorce.

And within months of the finality, you start thinking, 'Actually, the thing I quite liked was when we just hung out or had ramen or went to the cinema or for a long walk or watched TV together and laughed at the same programme.'

You start realising there were all these other little things that you had in common that you never valued because they were never, ever bigged up in society or the media as things that are relevant or important. But those tiny, tiny little things, those innocuous things, which there are millions of, all add up. Then they're compounded by the biggest thing of all, which is shared experience of life.

I think a lot of people divorce and then realise those little things, that shared history, are worth so much. But maybe they're worth a lot more to someone who has an anxious attachment pattern, and a lot less to someone who's avoidant.

My dad, my unemotional dad, summed it up quite well. He said, 'It's such a waste. You are now in the position where you've got your time back, you can travel and do stuff together with a lot less pressure financially than you could have done before. It's just such a waste.'

He wasn't just talking about my divorce – he was also reflecting on his decision to divorce my mum. The only time he becomes even slightly emotional is when he says, 'How's your mum these days?' Or, 'Is there any way you could have a word with her and see if she would be up for meeting up, just to talk things through?' I suspect part of him thinks, 'Might life have been so much easier if we had just stuck it out?'

Because there's the sheer logistics of seeing your children and your grandchildren twice as often as you would if you split up. Even as adults, when they come over, when they've got spare time, they've got to choose between one or the other. They might divide it equally, but that is half the time you would get if you hadn't broken up.

No one says that. No one tells you about that when you're thinking about getting divorced. They say, 'The kids are all grown up now, it's fine.' But it's not.

And if they go on to have their own kids, you'll get half the time you could have with your grandchildren.

But at the same time, although I saw the kids more before the divorce, my contribution was not as emotional because it was dominated by Ayumi.

I was the silent, quiet, going-along-with-things dad.

If there's one good thing about getting divorced, it's that my kids won't see the toxic nature of the relationship anymore. That apathy. It wasn't violent or horrific or abusive, it was just slow-burn toxic.

Up to now my kids have been brought up on a diet of a false dad. Obviously, there's been elements of my true character in there, but how to conduct relationships is not one of the life lessons I would like to have left them with.

I think we could have done a lot, lot worse. And there's a very strong argument that what we did, and how we did it, was right for us. Who knows what would have happened if we'd gone, 'Let's explore our feelings' a lot earlier. But I'm really fearful of giving my kids a template for relationships based on us because I don't think there was enough emotion there.

Life's too short to be false. For me, being false meant being very fiercely independent, not needing anyone, not saying how I felt, wanting to be alone and have a lot of 'me' time. These are things I've convinced myself or others that I was.

It all starts with getting rid of all the things you're not, all the things that you've been doing that are not really you. And once you've got rid of those, then you realise what's left is what you could never define before, which is you.

I don't want to ever not argue or say what I feel, or carry something around like emotional baggage. Time's too short and I don't want to waste it anymore.

So I confront and say what I think and feel a lot more.

I just wish I'd done that much sooner.

Yes, I have less time with my kids, but it's of a higher quality.

I don't want to be like my dad. I don't want to be talking about the weather or bank accounts with them, I want to be talking about how their jobs are, what their partners are like, how exciting their lives are, whether they are following their dreams, how they feel.

And I want them to be brave enough to express their emotions, and not be stifled like I was. I want them
to never have to pretend to be
someone they're not.

I don't think it's an accident that as I've become more myself, my friendships have been improving. And I've also been on a few dates with someone who is very good at expressing their emotions and very, very well versed in attachment theory ...

Her name is Veronica, she's a friend of my brother's and we get on like a house on fire.

She went through a very messy divorce nine years ago – she was messed about by her husband, who was an alcoholic with a gambling problem. It was traumatic.

She was bitter and angry for a long time, still is. Partly because she thinks, 'I wasted my time on him,' partly because she didn't have any children. She keeps saying to me, 'At least you've got two kids from your relationship.'

I think she's pretty 'sorted' – I've known her a long time and she's seen a therapist, so she feels like a safe person to entrust my emotions with. She's the complete opposite of Ayumi. That's obviously one of the things we've been talking about – how different we are from our exes. We're convinced that our exes are both avoidant.

If I were to compare the two ... Ayumi would be like the savannah. Beautiful and attractive in its own bleak, barren way. Veronica is almost a Hawaiian sunset. Which just makes me a bit sceptical because I think, 'I haven't seen one of those for ages ... And I'd settle for a nice day down in Brighton.'

She's very, very open and intelligent and genuine about her emotions. And she hasn't been short of offers, so I'm flattered that she is interested in me. In my head, she's a bit like my very first girlfriend, Debbie, the one who came to visit me in hospital every week when I had leukaemia.

We've gone on about a dozen dates. And we've snogged. It was brilliant. Absolutely brilliant.

When we first did it, I almost thought I'd forgotten, I thought, 'Right, here she is, she's coming in for the move ... Shit, now what do I do? Am I doing this right?' I felt like I was about 16. I realised I hadn't kissed someone for 20 years.

I like to think that the older I've got, the better I am at assessing people. And I think, having made a reasonably quick assessment, that this is probably it. Or it never will be – I have contemplated the scenario of not going out with anyone again. It's not the end of the world.

I haven't told anyone about this. The girls don't know, the ex-wife certainly doesn't. I only mentioned it to my therapist for the first time last week.

I brought it up because I've got a track record of throwing myself into something new, and I'm conscious of not doing that as a way of avoiding the grief.

I explained all of this to my therapist, who sat and very patiently listened. Then after about 20 minutes of me talking at her, she said,

'Ray, you've lived in the savannah for years.
Enjoy the Hawaiian sunset.'

Zsa Zsa

The girl who walked into fire
*Attachment pattern: unresolved (primary),
preoccupied (secondary)*

My current relationship with my parents is   pretty bad.

I mean, I don't really have a relationship with either of them now.   I can't remember the last time I had any meaningful interaction with either of them.

My parents have changed. They've got worse. I used to believe my dad was largely responsible for my mum, that it was his lack of compassion and kindness and his desire to be seen as provider of all things that led to the degradation of my mum's integrity as a human.

But now, my mum   can be   horrible. The things she's said to me in recent years have been vitriolic.

She's a mean person now.

My dad thinks he's got her drinking under control, but it's now tragic in a way that it never used to be.
              It just looks tragic.   And feels tragic.

It feels like she now has no control.

I don't know if she ever did have any control, but now it just feels like   a slow crawl to the bottom.

Part of me thinks if I don't spend any time with her, she'll drink herself into an early grave. Though I feel like she's doing that anyway.

Part of me thinks if I spend time with her now,
              she might just not drink as much when she sees
me, because she knows how much it upsets me.

And part of me knows that she won't be able to stop herself.

The last time I saw her, I took her to a tennis tournament. She
was absolutely legless. Legless. My dad had put her in a taxi
knowing she was like that, and then admitted to me that they
both knew she was drunk when she left.

This was the one time we were going to spend time together.
I met her at the entrance and she'd already necked two gin
and tonics and she,
                     she could hardly stand up.

'You knew you were coming to meet me.
            You know   I can't cope with you drinking.
         It's nothing new.   And yet,
at that moment of deciding whether or not you were gonna
skull a few gins before you got in the cab …
                                you chose booze.'

By that point, I'd not been near her for more than a few
minutes in a year. I'd forgotten just how bad it was.
         I saw her and realised, 'What was I thinking? This
was a bad idea. Why didn't we go for breakfast?!'

I feel suicidal most of the time. Suicidal thoughts are integrated
into how I live my life. I can't imagine how I'll stay alive, but
I'm not …   I'm not currently going to kill myself. I
have to say it with laughter.

I don't feel like I'm clinically depressed, I feel like I'm
chronically dissatisfied with my own level of satisfaction in
life and therefore, I feel very sad.   I constantly think,
              'I'm so sad.'

The way I talk about it with my therapist is that, for years, I feel like I've totally conditioned myself to work really hard and maintain friendships and drink lots and do things.   So most people just see the side of me that says, 'Everything's fine.'

It's not like I feel sad all the time. It's taken me years to accept that I can still laugh really heartily and still be okay,   while also having a deferred equilibrium of general misery.

People say, 'You can't be depressed, you're always laughing, you're always out and about.' And I think, 'Then I go home and cry, but you don't need to know that.' I just have to learn to live with it in a way where I get on with it.

In the last few years I've been stripping layers away from my life. Not just relationships that failed but other things like work that have forced me to stand back and think, 'I'll probably need to deal with some of that, I can't just keep glossing over it.' By 'it', I mean everything.

Then I suddenly realise, 'It's always been like this. Maybe I should go back to just hiding it, all the dark matter, because I don't think I can fix it.'

I know hiding it costs a lot of energy, but then you get to the end of your life and then you die. I just worry that I'm going to run out of steam.

I've pulled apart parts of my life to try to understand more and then I don't have energy to put it back together ...   then I find that I'm living in a world of fragments.   How many layers do you strip off trying to process something that you don't have answers for?

I think I have come to the realisation that I need to grieve,   actually,   profoundly grieve the parents I wish I'd had.

But where am I going to find the energy to do that? It's as if I have a bank of energy and it's finite. I wake up and think, 'Okay, right, let's do today.' But there's only so much in the bank.

I can't put down the things that I have to carry round but I also can't keep walking with them. So I don't really know what to do.

Sorry.   Sounds very miserable, doesn't it?

The objective part of me, my rational mind, thinks, 'Grieving – it's what you need to do. It's not going to last forever. It's not that bad. You have people that love you.'

It's not that the voice doesn't exist in my head, it's just overtaken by,   'How much more can you really do? Are you sure you haven't tried enough already?'

I mean, why would you willingly mourn something?
        It sounds horrific. You begin and you don't know where it ends, you don't know what will happen at the end of it.

I have got to the point where I think, 'Okay, I must stabilise and find an equilibrium on some level. There must be some solid ground somewhere that I can just stand on for a bit, without constantly feeling like I'm running out on to an icy lake.' Which is currently how I feel like I start every day.

It's fine.

        I just have to walk really fast.

Boxing off emotions: attachment and grief

Bowlby developed a theory of loss, grief and mourning that's still one of the most comprehensive around. He thought grief was the inescapable risk of loving relationships, of caring for someone. And he thought that the same psychological mechanisms are involved in separations that are brief or permanent. In other words, the same processes are at work whether we're bereaved or temporarily separated from Important People in our lives.

The interviewees suffered a number of separations and bereavements. When Zsa Zsa was little, her mum left repeatedly, leaving her in the care of her abusive father. Elija (the boy who was raised by wolves) was disowned by both his dad and his mum, and spent years separated from both. Ray (the boy who was sent away) was sent abroad for three years when he was 2 years old and was disowned by his father as a teen. Then as an adult, he went through a divorce, which meant separating from not just Ayumi but also her friends and family, as well as seeing less of his daughters. Amos (the boy who couldn't remember) lost his grandmother and spent a lot of time in hospital as a child. Lily (the girl who was wrapped in love) was separated from her parents when she went to boarding school as a teen, although she was in daily contact with them. Matt (the boy with the stiff upper lip) was separated from his parents on repeat when he was sent to boarding school with very limited contact. He also stopped seeing his grandma, who was a major loving presence in his life. And when he was 12, she died.

It wasn't just the interviewees who lost Important People – so did their parents. Skyler (the girl who was wrapped in cotton wool) had a colossal amount of loss in her family. Her mum lost her dad when she was 12, and Skyler's dad lost his brother in his teens. Her parents also lost their newborn daughter – and Skyler lost her sister. Skyler also lost her partner, Liam, and then the therapist she went to see about her loss. And Amos's mother lost her mum shortly after Amos was admitted into hospital as a child.

But loss isn't just about separation and death. You also suffer the loss of what you never had. This might be the loving and available parents you – and every child – deserve, a healthy parental relationship, a safe haven of a home, or a healthy child like Lily's mum. And as with any loss, these also require acknowledgement and mourning. It's difficult to mourn something that was always absent, but from a psychotherapist's perspective, that's what's needed.

Bowlby thought grief was normal and necessary. And as he did throughout his career, he looked to animals so that he could better understand it in humans.

In the 1960s, Harry Harlow and his colleagues separated 5-month-old rhesus monkeys from their mums. At first, the baby monkeys were agitated and protested, screeching and trying to break the barriers that separated them from their mothers. But when this failed, they became lethargic and withdrawn. Later work with elephants found similar reactions.

And when ethologist Konrad Lorenz studied greylag geese who had lost their mate, he noticed that they frantically searched and called. This eventually gave way to a lack of energy, slow movements, looser feathers and eyes that seemed smaller. They carried their head and neck less upright, they were less social and they were less willing to fly. Bereaved geese were generally ignored by others, and females were hardly ever courted by males, even though there was a shortage of them.

Bowlby thought this was amazingly similar to the observations his colleague James Robertson had made of young children who were hospitalised and separated from their parents. For example, he'd described how the eyes of young children seemed to become small and narrow, and their hair lank and lifeless. Bowlby came to believe that humans and animals behave in similar ways after loss and separation – and that adult humans go through a series of reactions similar to those seen in young children.

Phases of mourning

Bowlby suggested that there were different phases of mourning. People criticised him for this, arguing that humans don't experience rigid phases and that they vary massively in how they respond to loss. But Bowlby's phases weren't rigid. He didn't think we needed to go through one phase after another in sequence. Nor did he think they were mutually exclusive. And he also thought we could oscillate between them.

He noticed that people who had recently been bereaved often failed to register their loss, presumably because it seemed incomprehensible or was too painful to accept. He called this first phase 'numbing', and he thought it could be interrupted by intense anguish or anger.

He called the second phase 'protest', which he thought involved yearning and searching for your Important Person. As a child, you don't always know whether a separation will be permanent or not. And given that you depend on your Important Person for your safety and survival, it makes evolutionary sense to try everything you can to get them back.

Once you realise your Important Person is gone, Bowlby thought the third phase was inevitable. He called it 'despair'. He also thought it involved mental and physiological disorganisation – a painful inability to stick to your normal, organised patterns. Unhelpfully, this is another example where attachment thinkers use the same word in different ways … This type of disorganisation has nothing to do with being classified as disorganised in the Strange Situation.

The fourth and final phase was reorganisation – which is basically trying to make sense of the world and your place in it without that Important Person. This might involve finding a way to integrate their legacy, memory and presence into your own identity, plans and life, or having a continuing bond with the Important Person you've lost.

The impact of attachment patterns

Bowlby had two major aims in writing about grief. While some people might see disbelief, anger, searching, and having an ongoing bond with Someone Important after they die as irrational or immature reactions to loss, Bowlby wanted to show that they were very understandable if you looked through an evolutionary or ethological lens. So in Bowlby's mind, Skyler's reactions to Liam's death were totally understandable. In fact, her experiences echo much of what Bowlby outlined in his phases of mourning: she couldn't do anything for months, she wasn't able to accept that Liam had died, and she tried to get him back by dating anyone who looked remotely like him.

Bowlby also wanted to show that our own attachment patterns influence how we respond to the loss of Someone Important. He thought people who were secure would find it easier than others to adapt – the idea being that they hadn't only learned that Important People would be available, but that they themselves were loveable and valuable. And this helped them in the face of grief.

It's not that you escape grief if you're secure. Instead, you allow yourself to be swept by its pangs, and share your upset and yearning with others, seeking their support. But as the months and years pass, Bowlby thought you'd probably be able to organise life, perhaps helped by a sense of your Important Person's continuing and loving presence.

But Skyler hadn't grown up with Important People that were emotionally available. Instead, she learned that emotions couldn't be talked about, and that if she needed comfort, she wouldn't get it. She also grew up feeling that she wasn't enough.

According to Bowlby, this may have made it harder for her to feel she was allowed or entitled to grieve Liam's loss – made worse by the very vocal presence of his ex-girlfriend, and the belief of others around her that the value of a relationship lies in its duration.

When she did try to share her grief with her mum on the way back from the funeral, her mother didn't provide comfort.

Instead, she told Skyler she should be grateful, happy even, because at least Liam hadn't cheated on her.

Recognising that she needed support in processing her loss, Skyler went to see a therapist. Finally, she had Someone Important she could talk through her emotions with – Someone Important who was available. Except her therapist also died, unexpectedly, in her thirties. She was dead within a month.

In light of the barrage of losses that Skyler endured, it's easy to understand why she was classified as unresolved in her AAI. And given the lack of comfort and support she received growing up, her secondary classification, preoccupied, is also understandable. According to Bowlby, her preoccupied classification may have made her experience of grief even harder.

Bowlby thought that people classified as anxious/ ambivalent or preoccupied might do everything they can to avoid being separated from Someone Important – and keep searching for them when they are. In the face of separation or bereavement, he thought they would find extreme anxiety and sorrow difficult to avoid. He also thought this could lead to 'chronic grief'.

Whereas he thought people with an avoidant or dismissive pattern might show a complete lack of grief. This reminded me of the way Ayumi seemed 'in her element' once the divorce had been agreed. She seemed at ease with cutting all ties, and Ray suddenly felt like they were strangers sharing an apartment.

Bowlby thought that people who were compulsively self-reliant might not grieve at all. He thought this stemmed from growing up with Important People who didn't value relationships, discouraged or disallowed emotional expression, or rejected attachment behaviour as childish or weak. This made me wonder how Matt's mum (who physically couldn't tolerate emotional conversation) reacted after the death of her mother, who Matt spent most of his school holidays with. It also made me wonder whether Matt's dad had ever grieved the loss of his own father when he was a child.

Bowlby thought that, if you didn't consciously grieve for a long time after someone's death, you might be defending yourself against the emotions of loss, but this defence could subsequently break down and give in to intense feelings of grief and sorrow. He also thought it could be bad for your physical health. This is how he explained the gastric pains, nausea and heart palpitations that Charles Darwin suffered throughout his life. He thought the cause was suppressed grief – Darwin lost his mother when he was 8, but his father didn't allow him to talk about her after she'd died.

He also believed those hidden thoughts and feelings would influence your emotions and behaviour, even if you had no idea it was happening. Perhaps the silenced bereavement of Skyler's family, layered on top of more silence surrounding the sudden and traumatic bereavements that each of her parents had already suffered, influenced the way they felt and behaved. In particular, this may have contributed to their difficulty in providing comfort when Skyler needed it, as well as her mother's continual pattern of smothering her in cotton wool. But if Bowlby was right, then Skyler's mum and dad may have had no idea that the boxed-off grief from their losses was influencing them in any way.

And perhaps one of the reasons Skyler's mum was unable to comfort Skyler when Liam died is that this would mean engaging with the colossal grief that not only her daughter was experiencing but she herself may have walled off in relation to the loss of both her father and her child.

Keeping painful things walled off usually means you haven't worked through them. And as a result, Bowlby thought that small, subtle things could summon fragmented memories and leave you feeling anxious, upset and disoriented. Maybe this was behind Matt's mother's sporadic bursts of crying, her visible discomfort when emotions were discussed and her refusal to watch anything vaguely emotional on TV. Bowlby thought the key was to work through those emotions and memories, to integrate them into your life and understanding of the world. And he thought that if you did, small, subtle things might not trigger sadness in the same way.

Working within limits

Bowlby was limited by the research that existed at the time. Most of the work he based his theory on came from groups of relatively young people from North America, Australia and Great Britain. And he recognised that this research had limitations and couldn't be used to generalise beyond those groups of people.

The Minnesota Study was only just starting and there weren't many large-scale studies around. So he often relied on specific case studies. But by looking at a handful of people that had been to therapy, Bowlby wasn't seeing the full picture. He wasn't looking at people who didn't see a therapist, for example.

Despite these limitations, recent research has backed up his theory. Social psychologists found that people who are relatively secure adapt to loss with the fewest complications – whereas people who have relatively high attachment anxiety have a higher risk of severe grief symptoms, depression and anxiety, which are often seen as signs of complicated grief.

And when hundreds of people did an online survey that assessed their attachment style (among other things), people who were more avoidant were more likely to describe long-term difficulties in adjusting to loss.

Why mourn?

In her interview, Zsa Zsa asked an important question: 'Why would you willingly mourn something? It sounds horrific. You begin and you don't know where it ends, you don't know what will happen at the end of it.'

She's right. It does sound horrific. And lots of thinkers agree. The psychoanalyst Melanie Klein thought mourning meant rebuilding your inner world. And she thought the rebuilding would be done in anguish, and that, as a consequence, your inner world would feel as if it were in danger of collapse.

Bowlby was a firm believer that people don't really want to mourn, saying that anyone who's treated patients knows how reluctant humans are to face disorganisation and depression. Instead, they cling desperately to their defences. So while mourning could eventually lead to something better, defences are at the very least organised.

He also thought that disorganisation wasn't just intensely painful, it was also alarming.

Zsa Zsa gave a brilliant explanation of what disorganisation might feel like:

> I've pulled apart parts of my life ... and then I don't have energy to put it back together ...   then I find that I'm living in a world of fragments.   I have got to the point where I think ... 'How many layers do you strip off trying to process something that you don't have answers for?   There must be some solid ground somewhere that I can just stand on for a bit, without constantly feeling like I'm running out on to an icy lake.'

Given quite how painful Bowlby and others thought disorganisation could be, and given Zsa Zsa's experience of it – is it any wonder that people try to avoid going through it, no matter how unhelpful their defences are?

Grief in childhood

Bowlby also talked about grief and mourning in young people. He thought that, as children, sometimes we *have* to use self-protection because our minds haven't developed enough to cope with the work of mourning. And this is relevant to both Ray's and Matt's fathers, as well as to Skyler and Skyler's mum, who were all bereaved as children.

With the exception of Skyler, they each lost an Important Person whose job it was to provide them with a safe haven. And that meant losing access to their comfort and support at exactly the time they needed it most – in the face of profound loss.

But what if their Important People didn't provide them with a safe haven? When that's the case, you not only lose

Someone Important, but the hope of a better relationship. That's a huge amount of loss for a child to cope with. And that's before even considering the effects of the loss on others in the family and the larger context. In Skyler's mum's case, for example, the death of her father not only meant losing an Important Person but being catapulted into poverty.

If Bowlby was right, Ray's and Matt's fathers, Skyler and Skyler's mum would each have had to deploy self-protective mechanisms in order to cope with their loss as they were too young to be able to mourn. In the face of what may have been a multitude of losses, they were doing the best they could. And, if Bowlby was right, these self-protective mechanisms share similar processes with pathological mourning in adulthood.

He described a child that he and Robertson studied as part of their work with hospitalised children. The child was 3 and a half, and played a repetitive game by himself. At first sight, he seemed to be quite happy. He was bowing, turning his head to the left and lifting his arm. But when Robertson got closer to him, he heard the child muttering to himself, 'My mummy's coming soon – my mummy's coming soon – my mummy's coming soon.' When the little boy was lifting his arm, he wasn't gleefully playing a game, he was pointing to the door he thought his mother would come through. And Bowlby thought that his tic was a way for the little boy to try to control his expressions of grief.

Earlier in the book, I described a child who severely burned himself in a fire but didn't cry. As you would over the course of three years in hospital, the little boy got to know the ward sister and many of the children very well. But when he went back six months after being discharged, he said he'd never been to the hospital or met any of the staff or children before. And when he got home, he simply said he'd been for a car ride, and didn't mention going to hospital. Bowlby thought it was as though the child had two lives and an iron curtain separated one from the other.

If Bowlby is right, when we put these self-protective mechanisms in place at such an early age, we're just doing the best we can in the face of something our brains can't yet process, something so hideous that many adults would rather avoid it at all and any cost. Then, once those mechanisms are established, we have years and years to practise and repeat them. And this can make them all the harder to reverse. It's even harder still if we're taught during our childhood not to think about emotions or relationships because to do so would be to break a rule that our Important People have set. So if Ray's and Matt's fathers, Skyler and Skyler's mum were taught *not* to think about emotions or relationships, any self-protective mechanisms they had may have become even more entrenched.

But there's only so much that self-protective mechanisms can take before they break. Skyler was very young when her baby sister died, and she wasn't allowed to talk about her loss. In Bowlby's mind, the combination of these things meant Skyler probably used protective mechanisms to cope. But these defences might have been overwhelmed when Liam died. And if so, then his death may have been even harder to process because Skyler was effectively mourning two losses – those of Liam *and* her baby sister.

Although Bowlby thought it was a 'whopping great job', he thought that seeing a therapist could help try to reorganise your internal world – as Skyler did. It could enable you to examine the whole history of a relationship, with all its satisfactions and deficiencies, the things that were done and those that were left undone. He also thought they could help you sort out your hopes, regrets, despair, guilt and anger, and have compassion for your bewilderment, anxiety and pain.

But he thought it was essential that therapists didn't go faster than their patient was able to, because if they brought up painful topics too insistently, they would stir their patient's fear and provoke their anger or resentment.

He also thought that some people would need much longer in therapy, especially if they'd developed a very organised false self and become compulsively self-reliant or given to the caretaking of others.

Reviewing Bowlby's writings on grief, I realised that Zsa Zsa was right – you don't know where the process of mourning ends. And staring down the barrel of never-ending grief and disorganisation is nothing short of petrifying.

But although you don't know what'll happen at the end of this process, Bowlby thought it was worth the pain, disorganisation and hard work involved in having to deconstruct and rebuild ourselves. He likened it to a child destroying his Meccano construction before he could use the pieces again. In a similar way, we have to allow parts of ourselves to be seen and dismantled before we can reorganise them – preferably with the support of someone who provides us with a safe haven.

Bowlby also thought that inflexible segregation costs energy, and that by boxing off grief and mourning, you might also be boxing off joy. In fact, he used similar words to Elija and talked about a protective shell. In some people, he thought the shell becomes so thick that they don't engage; they blunt their experiences in relationships, which become reduced to a point at which loss doesn't mean that much.

And he thought that this could have a devastating impact. Particularly if, as he believed, our attachments to other people are the hub around which our lives revolve, the store from which we draw our strength and enjoyment of life, and what enables us to give strength and enjoyment to others. So when we box off grief, we can end up depriving not only ourselves but also the Important People in our life – just as some of the interviewees' Important People deprived them when they were children by barely talking to them.

Of course, there are benefits to putting things in a box. You can avoid uncertainty. You can avoid disorganisation. You can avoid the unfamiliar. You can almost avoid mourning.

But, Bowlby asked, at what price?

Matt
The boy with the stiff upper lip
Attachment pattern: possibly insecure

Zimbabwe
17c

BY AIR MAIL
PAR AVION

I think I have had to grieve about not having parents who were more available emotionally. I think I am still grieving a bit about   that.

It's a combination of frustration and anger.
I recognise and accept the choices that they had to make,
I just don't understand the way they went about things.

My parents decided boarding school was the best education for us. It wasn't done in a malicious way. But going there impacted the way I am as an adult. Definitely.

I had a wonderful time, but I wouldn't send a child there before the age of 13. I wouldn't send Oli there.

By doing so, you are trading off   the ability as a parent to be there emotionally for your children in person.   Sure, comms are easier now, but even so, having a phone or video call is not the same as spending time face to face, giving your child a hug.

326 PLEASE FIND ATTACHED

I've seen people from secure homes who have gone through boarding school aged 13 to 18. They still had a loving, caring relationship, their parents still listened to and dealt with the emotional difficulties they were going through. You could chat every day, send messages or emails, see your parents every weekend, spend the holidays together. So I think you can go to boarding school and get emotional nourishment.

Clearly I didn't have that with my parents.

At the same time, if you were the sort of person who called home every day, you weren't called a mummy's boy ... but people did think, 'Really? Do you need to speak to your parents every day?'

Now I'm a bit older and more mature, I think actually that's normal, or that should be. When it comes to relationships and developing the emotional side of children, there is an element of frequency in providing stability, so regular contact with someone who loves you is important.

Even if I had gone to a day school, I doubt it would have changed my dynamic with my parents massively because of the nature of who they are.

I really want to listen to my son more than my parents listened to me. I want to ask open questions, be more involved with things he's studying and how he's navigating through things. I hope that whatever interests Oli has, we can explore them together and see where they go. I hope I can be a big part of his life, but not in an overbearing way.

I'm definitely more cuddly with him than my parents were with me. I guess I want to have more physical connection, more hugs, because I didn't have much of that growing up.

I really hope Oli's relationship with me is similar to the one Lily has with her dad, one where he can message and talk to me about anything he wants and know that I am always there and that he always has that emotional support, in a proactive way. Lily's dad is a phenomenal role model for me and he gives me something to aspire towards, not just in terms of having a relationship with children, but also how to manage work–life balance, be present and navigate the relationship all the way through. He's done an incredible job.

I'm learning from Lily's parents constantly and always aspiring to be better. It's difficult for me to have an argument with my parents, but it's very easy with my in-laws – in a constructive way. It could be as banal as something relating to cricket or the royal family, but it will flare up, we'll chat it through and it's fine.

When I go to my parents, it's completely opposite.

The   recent   relationship   dynamic   between   them   is really   stand-offish and not open to talking about feelings. And I see,

I see the past in front of me.

This is why it's very difficult for me to visit my parents now. I just see how things were, how it was run, how it's not open – it's closed. It's like there's smoke all around and I'm going to get stabbed. It's really an intense, difficult environment.

Becoming secure has made me drift further from my parents because I can't engage with them emotionally. It makes it difficult for me to go back to see them.

I hope they will change, but being realistic, I should probably accept they won't. When I have subtly raised things before, particularly with my dad, he said, 'Yeah, your mother and I should see a therapist, there's lots of unresolved things there …' But I don't think they ever would. It's my biggest frustration.

I wish they would see a therapist so I would feel okay to visit there more, so that my son Oli could have a better relationship with them, so he could have a brilliant relationship with them in the way that I did with my grandparents.

But it's now such a hostile environment, it's like warfare.

Although my brother took up a lot of my parents' emotional time, and I was very aware of that, my parents were very, very, very supportive all the time.

But even so,   growing up, I remember quite vividly having to take up less space. For example, an ambulance would be outside the house to pick up my brother and I would go to my room and read a book, that kind of thing.

I remember going with my brother to doctor and dentist check-ups, and my medical appointments would take two minutes compared to my brother's hour. My mum would trot out all the medical conditions again and again and again. So it would have been highly complicated if I had taken any more time than 'Fine, check!'

I remember at family gatherings everyone would always ask how my brother was.

I always felt really boring and that no one was ever very interested in me because I was always the one who was ... fine.

Because of the emotional and physical time my brother took up, I think I'm used to being 'the good one'.

But I don't think I wish anything had been different. I don't think I need to mourn the loss of a healthy sibling.

We played so much together in our own particular way that even now I don't wish he was more active or healthy. I don't really know why.

Maybe it's because I see so many different sibling dynamics, I don't think I was deprived. Instead, I would think, 'Well, I had a brother who I was very close to who had some physical limitations, but someone else had one brother six years older who they never saw, another person had a twin sister and they were always competing.' So there was no real role model version that we were all aspiring to. Even though we were very different and he took up a lot of the space, I think we had and have a great relationship.

Overall, I had the most vanilla childhood. I haven't suffered any great trauma. I haven't lost anyone really important. I mean, I experienced the loss of two of my grandparents, but we weren't close enough to acknowledge it in a very emotional way.

The closest I've come to experiencing grief is the homesickness I felt when I went to boarding school. I imagine grief is like an extreme version of that.

So I'm really lucky as I haven't really experienced grief. And I haven't lost anyone.

Touch wood.

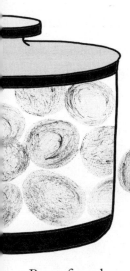

Skyler

The girl wrapped in cotton wool
*Attachment pattern: unresolved (primary),
preoccupied (secondary)*

Part of me knows it's not fully my fault that Liam died. His friend that was supposed to be helping him move the day after I left could have said something, or his sister, who he spoke to all the time.

But even if I don't take 100 per cent of the blame, maybe I still could have stopped it.

And that won't ever change.

Unless I somehow miraculously got proof that he died instantly, the second that phone cut out.

His death had a massive impact on me. In a weird way, I learned to trust my own feelings more, but I also have a field of deep regret for not calling anybody earlier than I did. If I was following my gut, I would have said something on the Thursday. Or maybe even the Wednesday when our phone call got cut off. But I didn't.

His death has also made me value life more. And fear death. I have a lot of anxiety about safety now. If I don't hear from somebody, I'm worried something has happened to them.

I was probably always a bit worried about that. When I was dating Karim and I got anxious about his safety or what was going to happen, I was always trying to hold on to something, afraid of losing it.

But after Liam's death, that anxiety got worse. I've started dating someone new, Charlie, and I am petrified that she is going to die or that something bad is going to happen. I'm petrified that I'm going to lose her. I have to consciously tell myself that it will be okay.

Charlie and I decided to move in together around the beginning of the pandemic. And when you spend 24 hours a day with nothing but a goldfish and 15 tomato plants, you start to get to know somebody on a deeper level.

It's the first relationship I've had where I've felt fully respected and cared for, other than with Liam. It makes me very sad for my former self, grieving the amount of disrespect and horrible treatment that I've put up with, knowing that this is what a healthy relationship is.

I always worry about her well-being and safety. I worry most when I am feeling anxious in real life. Sometimes, when I am sad about relationships with my friends or am feeling unworthy about my career progression, it feels like I'm screaming but nobody can hear me. And my reaction is to cling. If your upbringing led you to feel like you weren't good enough, how do you change that?

By 'clinging', I mean I try to take care of Charlie quite a lot. I worry I do it too much. I know it's bad, but it's so comforting that I just keep going back – a bit like when I keep going back for cookie after cookie after cookie. I know I shouldn't do it but it makes me feel secure. Then again, if I'm just looking after somebody, that's not what a relationship is. I'm just piling on the cotton wool.

I guess it's understandable I'm so worried about Charlie's safety because

Liam was not supposed to die when he did.

Grandparents are supposed to die, I'm not saying it's not tragic when they do, but they are supposed to die as they get older. Liam was not supposed to die. It's like when a parent loses a child. It's not supposed to happen.

But maybe it's even more than that.

I've never really thought about
   how much loss there was in my life. Liam is the only one that I really ever acknowledged.

But my first childhood memory was my sister dying. I grew up with a dad who lost his brother when he was 19. I lost the first proper boyfriend I ever had. And then I lost the therapist I went to see about his death.

So I guess it's reasonable that I'm afraid of me and the people in my life dying. That fear is grounded. I hadn't really realised how much death is around me.

And there's even more loss than that. My mom hasn't shared a lot about her life — I could probably remember every anecdote she's told me. But I know that her dad died in a fire when she was 12 and her mom, who was blind, raised five kids on her own.

Things were really difficult when her dad died. Everything was very tight financially before he passed away, but then it got much worse. She has told me a couple of stories of being bullied by her brothers. She shares so little, but those are the stories she chose to share rather than happier ones.

Then, as soon as she was old enough, she became a nurse in the navy to escape living at home. That's when she met my father and ... that's it. They had my sister, me, and my younger sister, who died.

I don't think I've made this connection before, but maybe the experience of losing someone who wasn't supposed to die is why she is so overprotective and unbearable. Unbearably overprotective.

And as well as losing someone who wasn't supposed to die, I was bullied and then moved to this country to try to escape. That's exactly what my mom did. I've never really realised that before.

My mom hasn't processed any of the loss she has suffered. Any of it. And I think the way she treats me and acts in her life is a manifestation of that.

It's not easy growing up with a parent who hasn't processed loss, because it means they can't possibly provide you with the ability to understand your emotions, as they can't understand their own.

She's definitely unresolved.

I find it insulting that she still tells me to wear a seat belt and can't trust me enough to take care of myself.

But at the same time, I have the same level of worry about Charlie. And it's not that I don't trust her. It's just that I'm worried something bad is going to happen or I will lose her. But it probably feels like I'm smothering her in blankets just like my mom does.

I suddenly feel a lot more understanding of the way my mom has treated me, now that I know why. And it seems so obvious looking back.

When I learned about my dad's horrible relationship with his father and that he lost his brother when he was young, it helped me have more compassion for him. But with my mom, even though I knew about her dad dying so young, I never really put two and two together.

Maybe that will help me to be less angry with her in the same way it did with my dad.

I've always wondered why my mom treated me and my sister differently. Thinking about it now, I remember my mom told me I had quite a similar personality to her dad. And he was also a singer, like me.

Maybe I remind her of him.

And maybe that's why she is so worried that I'll die unexpectedly – just like he did.

Amos

The boy who couldn't remember
Attachment pattern: dismissive

Growing up I really had a sense that death was everywhere in our family. My mum lost her mother when I was little. My dad had lost his father. After being in hospital as a young child, I started writing a lot of poems about death. Which can't be normal, surely.

I don't know how to explain it. Death was everywhere.

I was 4 and a half when my grandmother died. I don't remember much about her, maybe a couple of holidays together, being in the garden. I think she made me feel really good about myself. But I don't remember.

She had been sick for a long time. The day before she died, I remember saying, 'Are they curing you?'

I don't remember sadness or anything.

I feel weirdly sad about it now, even if I don't remember her. It's like the sadness has stayed.

There was a funeral, but I wasn't there. Then we went to the cemetery every year for the following 20 years.

My mum was devastated. Everyone was. I think, in retrospect, it might be why she was so angry at me all the time.

She didn't get depressed.

She got angry.

My grandmother was 58 when she died. That was pretty young. So, my mum felt it was really unfair, I think.

She had a lot of grief. She didn't speak about her mother much. She couldn't.

She never told me that she died. She said, 'She's left to buy her medicine.'

I would ask, 'When is Grandma coming back? Why can't we find the medicines for her?'

Even now, I have nightmares where I think she's still going to get medicine and wondering where she's gone. Insane, right?

For decades, my mum wasn't able to say her mother had died.

We went to a chess tournament when I was in my twenties, my mum and me. I had been thinking about all of this in psychoanalysis, and I said, 'You never told me that Grandma died.' And she froze.

I said, 'Come on, tell me now. Tell me, "Your grandmother died." Please. Can you please tell me?'

And my mum started crying.

She said, 'I can't do it.'

Twenty-plus years of grieving is very long. Something got stuck.

One thing she kept saying was, 'Your grandmother really loved you. Really loved you.'

I mean, every grandmother loves their grandchildren, no?

My mum's always told me really positive things about her mother. But I get the impression her upbringing was quite harsh. A lot of discipline. And corporal punishment.

I have had a number of losses, like the loss of my grandmother, my aunt, my nanny. And I didn't feel anything. I don't feel like I've had massive grief. I really accepted the losses.

So weird.

Recently, my nanny died. She looked after me four days a week when I was little.

I went to the funeral. I don't know what to say about it.

I cried a lot. I never cry. Something about thinking about her really makes me cry.

But I feel okay.

I'm not devastated.

Same with being in hospital as a child.

It was fine.

Although I still have nightmares. One is that somebody shoots an arrow on my wrist. And I wake up and still feel the pain there. I told my therapist, and she asked what it reminded me of. And I remembered the IV drip that they put in me in hospital.

I had it for months.

It's so crazy because *boom*, I had the full picture and bodily feeling and illness like a time machine.

What I'm saying is that I remember only the positives of being in hospital. But there are a lot of things telling me that maybe I was a little scared.

Actually, I've just remembered that I asked my mum at the time, 'Why is this happening to me? Why me?' I remember where I asked it. We were in the square down from our apartment. I don't remember what she said.

Now that I'm thinking about this, I had the sense of falling from grace. Or that there was a mythical past. That I'd done something wrong, that's why I was in hospital. Before, I was more obedient, more beautiful, better.

Now I was this 'thing'.

It obviously wasn't conscious. And I carried on with my life on most days okay.

I didn't think about emotions until very late in life.

Daniela has been a huge help. She really helped me feel anger. Because I've never been angry with anybody as much as I feel anger with her. It's like murderous rage.

When I'm in the situation, it's horrible. Believe me. But overall, I think it's positive. It keeps me aware.

I grew up not being able to experience and communicate anger. Or even let sadness come out and cry. I was unable to communicate emotions, because I grew up with a family that wasn't emotionally supportive.

My dad's not very articulate on an emotional level. That's how he is.

He's a really good person. He's just not

capable of interacting at that level. So I never got that kind of interaction.

But my parents were great, otherwise.

I've worked to move past it, but it's still with me.

There are positive aspects — I don't get upset easily. I'm intellectually independent.

But I'm trying to work on recognising how my behaviour impacts others. And knowing that the key to suffering is fear of emotion.

I'm pretty good with negative emotions now. I don't often feel very anxious. And I don't feel depressed. I am aware of the emotions I'm trying to avoid and I'm able to face them. And that cures it.

My parents not believing in me, always doubting what I was saying, and my sense that people don't trust me means I don't look for other people's support. I am very independent. My upbringing led to self-reliance. And I don't think I can learn from other people.

Daniela gets angry with me for it.

I understand. I didn't feel very trusted growing up. I would often tell my parents something and they always disagreed with me or doubted it – especially my dad. My dad doubts everything.

I know why he does it and I forgive him, because I do it too. I don't believe anything because I'm dismissive like him. But it's painful nonetheless.

My dad can't speak about emotions. He is insanely dismissive. But sometimes reaching inside is helpful. It gives you confidence. You have a more cohesive story of who you are.

So I've really worked on being reflective.

Freedom through reflection

In 1987 Bowlby invited three researchers to train to do the AAI with Main and Hesse.

Their names were Peter Fonagy and Howard and Miriam Steele.

Fonagy had grown up in communist Hungary, until he turned 14, when he was sent to school in London on his own. He was bullied, spoke no English, had no friends and, within three years, was suicidal. So he went for psychoanalysis with someone called Anne Hurry, whose strategy was to help him feel understood and recognise how he was feeling. It saved his life. He went on to become a professor at University College London, where two of his graduate students, Howard and Miriam Steele, introduced him to attachment theory.

Fonagy and the Steeles began the UCL Parent–Child Project, which lasted for 17 years. They started by doing AAIs with 100 expectant mums and dads, and then the Strange Situation when the children were 12 or 18 months old. And they found powerful connections across generations.

In Chapter Four I explored coherence, which basically means that the different parts of someone's story in their AAI fit together to create a logical whole. A parent's coherence was clearly linked to whether their relationship with their child was secure or not. Most kids whose mums or dads gave very coherent AAIs were classified as secure. And most kids whose mums had incoherent AAIs were insecure.

Coherence was clearly a big deal. But when they dug deeper, Fonagy and the Steeles noticed that a key feature was the way people used language to describe beliefs and desires and give meaning to their experience. They saw this as evidence of something they called 'reflective function'. And they defined it as the ability to think about the thoughts, feelings, intentions and behaviour of Important People and themselves.

Fonagy and the Steeles thought reflective function was relevant throughout the AAI, but especially in response to two questions about what motivates and influences your parents – and yourself. To give you a sense of what different answers might look like, I'll share two from Matt (the boy with the stiff upper lip) and Zsa Zsa (the girl who walked into fire).

The question I asked from the AAI was, 'Why do you think your parents behaved as they did during your childhood?'

Matt answered, 'My dad lost his dad from a young age and had no father figure role model. Also, that generation was a bit more old-school. And my mum went to boarding school from age 8, an all-female boarding school, and was close to her dad who was pretty stoic as well. So I think those are the reasons why.'

When I asked Zsa Zsa the same question, she said:

Umm …

I wonder whether or not they ever had a conversation about what it would mean to be parents, like, 'What do we want for our kids?' They got on a train as parents, and they did the thing that people did.

They had a nice life in London. My dad had bought a flat. He had a motorbike. He was a self-made, successful man. My mum was intelligent, had a good job. And they had kids, because that's what people did. And then they moved out of London, 'cause that's what people did. And they lived in a big house and got dogs and chickens and …

There were always tick boxes, things that you have to do as parents. One of them was 'Send the kids to a private school – if we do that, we've done our bit.'

There are two stories my parents tell about me when I was very young. The first is, 'We were at a dinner party and your mum had gone into labour. So we got a taxi to the hospital.

'I dropped your mother off and I paid the cabby. And when I came into the reception area, I said, "Have you seen my wife?" And they

said, "No."' And he said, 'Your mother had waddled off down the street.'

'I caught her, and I said, "What are you doing?! You're going into labour."'

Now, it's a funny story when you tell it in a funny way. But what you realise also in the detail is that she must've been drinking and that they find it funny that they were about to have a child.

The other story they tell was when, in the days before mobile phones, they'd been at a lunch party, and all the kids in their fucking – what do you call the things that you put kids in and carry them – carriers? Bags? Holdall? Whatever.

They'd been at this long lunch. And they said it's only when they got home and they could hear the phone ringing at the flat and my dad went, 'Fuck. We've forgotten Zsa Zsa.' They'd left me at a lunch … And someone was calling to tell them. They got all the way home without realising they'd forgotten their child.

And again, my dad thinks this is funny. But if, if, if I was that young at that time, my mother must have been breastfeeding. And again, she must've been drinking.

Drinking and driving in those days wasn't a problem. Drinking and parenting apparently wasn't a problem in those days either.

So I kind of … I'm … I've gone off what the exact point of the question is …

Matt clearly and succinctly described what had gone on in his parents' upbringings that might explain why they thought and acted as they did. Whereas Zsa Zsa got lost in her anger for her parents.

And that's not surprising given where Fonagy thinks reflective function comes from – namely our relationships with Important People growing up.

Fonagy thought it would have a major impact on our personality, relationships and ability to understand ourselves and regulate our emotions. In other words, Fonagy thought we develop our sense of who we are based on our childhood experiences with Important People.

Many children aren't lucky enough to grow up in a family that helps them understand themselves, like Lily's. Some have Important People who lack empathy, aren't consistent and don't provide them with a safe haven, like Skyler's mum. Some are capable of only very hollow relationships with their children, like Matt's father. Some are unloving and cruel, like Elija's dad. Some inflict physical or sexual abuse, or other forms of trauma, on their children.

Fonagy thought these would all make reflecting harder. In fact, in some circumstances, thinking about what was going on in an Important Person's mind would be so awful, it would be unbearable. This made me think of Zsa Zsa. How can anyone hospitalised for a suicide attempt make sense of their parent treating it as an inconvenience – let alone a child?

But the way we cope in childhood isn't always helpful later in life. In the long term, Fonagy thought that being able to identify and reflect on our beliefs and desires was fundamental for our relationships and mental health. And blocking it would make it harder to have satisfying relationships, empathise with others and identify and regulate our own feelings. He also thought it would affect our sense of who we are.

Fonagy saw our capacity for reflection as *so* important that he thought helping someone reflect was the key ingredient in therapy. Reflection is something Matt focused on with his therapist, having grown up with a complete lack of it. He attributed 60 per cent of his ability to be reflective to his first therapy sessions and 40 per cent to the ones he did with Lily. Although I'd argue that being in a relationship with Lily, as well as the influence of his loving grandmother, probably also played a role.

Whatever the causes, Matt scored very highly on Fonagy's 'reflective function scale'. Scoring this doesn't just mean counting the number of times someone mentions a thought or feeling. If Matt had just said, 'I felt rage,' that wouldn't count as reflective. Whereas when he said, 'I'm getting better at controlling ... the rage – but it isn't easy because it flares up very, very quickly,' it suggests that he's actually thought about the feelings involved. Perhaps that's why he scored 8 out of 9 overall.

Having created the reflective function scale, Fonagy and the Steeles analysed the AAIs they'd done for the UCL Parent–Child Project. And they found something important.

Inspired by Main, attachment researchers had long thought security in the AAI was all about coherence – a sticking together of someone's story. But once they included reflective function in their statistical analysis, Fonagy and the Steeles found no link between a parent's coherence in the AAI and their child's security in the Strange Situation.

They reached the conclusion that being coherent comes from being able to observe your own mind and those of others. And that that reflectiveness directly impacts a parent's relationship with their child.

They thought that a child would develop a secure relationship if, based on their experience, they could assume that their Important Person would reflect on and respond to their mental states appropriately. This meant they could feel safe having ideas and desires, feel secure about their own internal world and be more likely to feel they had a safe haven when they needed one.

An example of reflective function is Ray explaining his dad's behaviour. 'I know he wants me around, but he'll only call me about work or money because he can't talk about anything else. So he manufactures situations where he needs advice on these things. That's his way of having a relationship.' Ray could've thought nothing about his dad's behaviour, or taken it at face value, thinking that he really did need advice about money or work. But Ray looked beyond that and imagined what might be motivating his dad's behaviour, as well as the thoughts and feelings behind that motivation – namely an inability to talk about emotions and a desire to talk to and spend time with his son.

Another example of reflective function is when Lily describes her dad's behaviour when she went to boarding school:

> In the run-up to me going, Dad told me every day, 'You can call home any time you want. And you can come home. You can come home in the first week. You can come home in the second week.' He was probably projecting his own emotions on to me. But also wanting to make me feel secure that I could go back to them anytime I wanted. I remember him being very anxious about dropping me off, and mirroring that a bit.

Lily could simply have thought nothing of her dad's behaviour. But instead she imagined what he might be feeling (anxious) and why he might be saying that (to reassure her) – as well as imagined how that all impacted her (encouraging her to mirror his anxiety).

Initially, Fonagy and his colleague Mary Target put a lot of weight on early childhood experiences. But they expanded their idea of reflective function to acknowledge how people other than our parents can also be important – like grandparents, older siblings, friends and teachers.

This means a child isn't doomed if they're born into a situation with zero reflection. They can still learn to sense and imagine what's going on in their own minds if other people around them behave in a way that suggests they have thoughts, feelings, motivations and intentions. Like Zsa Zsa's teacher, Ursula. Zsa Zsa couldn't remember what they spoke about but she remembered that Ursula's primary motivation was Zsa Zsa's emotional well-being and that she showed care and compassion. I don't doubt that this played a huge role in helping her understand what was going on in her own mind and the minds of others. As Zsa Zsa put it, 'As a child I thought that nobody, nobody saw me. Until I met Ursula. I definitely felt seen by her.'

And, much like the idea of developmental pathways, the idea that other people in a child's life can help them develop their ability to reflect allows for hope.

Fonagy and Target thought reflective function was *so* important that it was only through learning how to do it that mental health problems could improve. And they also thought it was essential in breaking the 'cycle of abuse'.

The idea of a cycle of abuse came about in 1984, when the Minnesota Group found that people who had been abused were more likely to abuse their own children. Except it was more nuanced than that. They noticed that mums who had been abused but did not go on to abuse their own child had been through at least one of three experiences: some had been in therapy, some were in a supportive and stable romantic relationship and some had received emotional support from a non-abusive adult while growing up.

Fonagy and Target thought these experiences all had one thing in common – they increased a parent's reflective function. And this meant they could interrupt responses that could otherwise have predisposed them to abuse or neglect their own child.

In other words, developing reflective function helped them avoid repeating damaging patterns and behaviours from their past.

And this flash of hope reminded me of Elija.

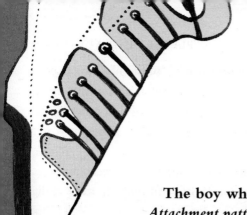

Elija

The boy who was raised by wolves
*Attachment pattern: unresolved (primary),
preoccupied (secondary)*

I couldn't tell you exactly what my dad's upbringing was like because he doesn't talk about it, but I do know it was strict. He would get beaten, and the only thing he had as an outlet was basketball.

I think my dad had a real, real, real lack of love in his life, even from his mum.

Looking at people that I know that have had a lack of love, they don't really love many things. They don't really like people sometimes. My dad's the same – he'll happily cut somebody off for doing something really minor. He's quite cut-throat.

The lack of love from only one parent, which is the background I have, wouldn't necessarily do that to you. But I think the lack of love from both parents would push you to be that way.

My mum and me had our differences at a point in life, but for the rest of it, she loved me to pieces and I loved her to pieces. And that's helped me stay on the straight and narrow. There's some hope when you get cuddled after something like that.

'Why is my dad beating me? …   My mum's giving me a cuddle now, everything's going to be okay.'

If I didn't have love from my mum, woah, I don't know what would be happening right now. I couldn't even comprehend that. If my dad beat me and then my mum beat me afterwards, maybe I would be beating people up for a living, who knows.

When I was growing up, I would think, 'Is this really happening to me?' And as I've grown, I'm like, 'Yeah, that happened to me. I did actually live it.' It's a slight feeling of disbelief. Not everybody goes through that. Why did it happen to me?

The PTSD is definitely inside, but it doesn't burden me. It's less now, the nightmares. And the feelings. It doesn't weigh on me so heavy.

Sometimes I'll have moments, not so much now, but in my early twenties I was a bit all over the place, in terms of becoming a man. That's when I really started to see things like fathers supporting their sons and daughters and families and I thought, 'All right, well, where was mine?'

I felt like he was empty inside. He wasn't able to give love, care, attention, understanding, all the things that parents are supposed to give. It left me empty – I had to learn everything myself. I never got anything from him in order to set me up.

I've always felt a few years behind everybody, even to this day. It's been an emotional roller coaster across the board: how to travel, how to save money, how to buy a house, finances, tax, de-de-duh, emotional support, how to change careers ... He broke me in many different areas of my life. I didn't know how traumatic that was until now I'm trying to find somebody to maybe start a family.

'Even if you did teach me everything I needed to know in basketball, you really fucked up the female side of things, badly. Badly.'

I missed out a lot on that, which might suggest why I struggle a little bit now with relationships.

A lot of my friends got married, they bought houses, they've had kids and all that kind of stuff. I can say, 'I've focused on my career so that's why I haven't had kids yet.'

But in my twenties, when I made mistakes 15 times and still didn't learn from them, there was never that male figure to say, 'Stop that, don't do it 15 times, do it 5 times and then learn.' I never had that. I had to go through all 15 times to be like, 'You've learned that, Elija, stop now.'

In literally every single scenario I messed up so many times, so many times, 'cause I had no guidance. That's why I choose the word 'empty'. He literally left me with nothing. I can't pinpoint anything my dad has given me that's benefited me.

When as a parent, from what I've come to understand, you give your child the base and then they build on top of it. Or that's how it should be. But there was no base there from Dad. There was a massive base from Mum, but no base from a male figure.

I've missed so much in family, in learning about life, about work, how to deal with certain emotions when people upset you, how to deal with upsetting people.

I didn't realise Dad's abuse wasn't about me until probably about four years ago.

I didn't know as a child. I've got tears in my eyes now because it's so late, it's so late to realise. I didn't realise that it was about him.

It was always, always about me. 'What did I do wrong?' I'd go to bed with my arse bright red, shaking it was hurting so much because he'd beaten the hell out of me and I'd just sit there and say, 'Why?'

You don't have answers at that age. You don't say, 'My dad's got issues with his dad, he needs to fucking sort them out.'

It was never me that had the issue. It was always, always his to deal with. But he never dealt with it, which is probably why it continued for such a long time.

When you don't deal with issues, they don't go away. They just follow you around. You keep carrying the boxes.

It was very, very, very late that I realised it wasn't about me.

I didn't deserve to be beat up. Okay, I wasn't allowed across the road as a kid, but who the hell gets out of the van, shouts at their kid in front of all their friends, says, 'Get in the house now,' and then takes you upstairs and beats you with the belt just because you'd crossed the road to get to the ball?

It's not normal.

This is not normal.

I wasn't asking the why's until I'd done some deep, deep searching. Through my gymnastics career, I ignored a lot of these emotions. I was busy, I was touring, I was dealing with girls, I was doing this city, that city, I wasn't doing self-assessment. And then it all slowed down and I become based somewhere – I was still doing gymnastics, but it was only then, when I was 30, 31, I started looking inside and I realised, 'It's not my fault.'

How do you grieve something that you have no answers to? How do you process and get over it?

If you don't have answers, or you don't have a key, or you've lost the box, you don't know where the box is, I think you have to try and find your way to be okay with not knowing. And I am.

I'm just trying to fix everything in myself as much as I can before I have a little kiddiewink. I can't fix everything, it will still be there, but I will do my best when he or she arrives. If they arrive.

I just don't want them to grow up with a pack of wolves like I did.

I would like to be a little bit more stable on the love front. There are moments where I've been like, 'Oh my God, what's gonna happen to me? Somebody tell me? Somebody give me a girlfriend! Anybody got one?'

First step – the lead walls have gotta stop. 'Stop head-butting the lead walls, Elija!'

But I'm quite prepared to be on my own just in case nobody can love me.

Everybody I meet, I say good morning to, I'm always lifting people up, I'm always asking, 'What do you need?'

So one of the most recent thoughts that I've had is, 'Maybe I'm not here to be loved this time around. Maybe I'm here to put love into the world.'

And next time, because nobody knows for sure ...
Maybe next time I will receive it in abundance.

Epilogue

We've come a long way in terms of how we think about children, their relationships and the adults they become.

Only a few decades ago, we separated hospitalised children from their Important People. And only a few decades ago, we thought children could tolerate whatever was thrown at them, including abuse. Some went a step further, thinking abuse was actually good for them.

We now understand that staying in hospital is precisely when children need a safe haven the most. We know resilience is born out of positive relationships that protect a child, rather than being a magical armour every baby is born with. And there are now thousands of studies showing a clear link between child maltreatment and mental and physical health problems in later life.

But we still have a long way to go.

If attachment theory teaches us anything, it's that you can't understand young people (or the Important People in their lives) if you don't understand their context. You can't understand Zsa Zsa's suicide attempts unless you know what was going on in her family. And you can't understand why Ray's parents sent him away unless you know that they were living in poverty and working multiple jobs, struggling to survive.

Providing a safe haven requires Someone Important to be present, pay attention, respond, and regulate their own emotions as well as those of a child. That's a big ask if they're isolated, exhausted or overwhelmed, living in poverty or conflict, or frightened by their own trauma – or when they didn't have a safe haven themselves growing up. And this is something Zsa Zsa reflected on when I spoke to her (and the others) four years after our first interview:

> *In another life, I would like to be a parent, a life where money is no object, I have a house with a garden, job stability. But to me parenting seems like quicksand. And childhood trauma can be like a rip that's cracked open when you have your own kids. Parenting involves so much that's unmanageable and unpredictable that unless every practical element is taken care of, I won't find the space and emotional bandwidth to be present for a child or have what I would need emotionally in that situation. It would be a whirlpool.*

Ideally, we would live in a world where Important People didn't have to cope with extremely difficult circumstances while trying to look after children, a world where healthy relationships were valued far more than they are. Ideally, we would live in a world where poverty, conflict and inequality didn't heap so much stress on parents and partners that it was a struggle to survive, let alone provide the love and support that every child needs and deserves.

But until significant structural changes in societies take place, there are easier, more manageable things we can do to change the lives of both Important People and their children. Like parenting interventions.

The ABC stands for Attachment Biobehavioral Catch-up and was created by Mary Dozier and her colleagues. It consists of 10 sessions in which a coach teaches Someone Important about attachment theory and talks about their past experiences and what they expect of both themselves and their children. This is important as it can unfurl unhelpful thoughts like 'being harsh helps a child toughen up' or 'being too loving can spoil them'.

Important People watch and discuss films of others responding to their children in helpful and unhelpful ways, before playing with their own children and being filmed themselves. The intervention ends with a montage of video clips celebrating when they behaved in nurturing ways or when they followed the child's lead.

Throughout the sessions, coaches give feedback up to 60 times an hour(!). They do this to achieve three things. Bowlby thought it was crucial for a child to feel confident that Someone Important would be there for them when they were upset. So the first focus of the ABC is to help Important People be nurturing when a child's distressed.

Ainsworth thought it was vital to be 'sensitive' to a child's needs, so the second focus is to help Important People pay attention and respond to children's signals. And the third is to help them avoid behaving in harsh, intrusive or frightening ways – because Main and Hesse thought that this disrupts a child's ability to use their Important Person as a safe haven.

By building on the thinking of Bowlby, Ainsworth, Main and Hesse, the ABC builds on mountains of research. And because it's so focused and specific, training takes just two days, and most people that want to become a coach can. And while it's not a golden bullet, the intervention can make a big difference to both Important People and their children, a difference that can be seen years after the ABC took place.

Supporting Important People makes financial, as well as emotional, sense. Researchers have studied young people that behaved in antisocial ways from an early age, and calculated the cost of the health, education and social care services used. They found it cost £3,300 more per year if the young person had an insecure, rather than secure, relationship with their mum. And that went up to £12,650 more per year when they had an insecure, rather than secure, attachment with their dad. Just to be clear, that's not a total cost, that's per year – and with inflation, those numbers would be closer to £5,000 and £21,000 in 2024.

It's not that securely attached children are happy all the time. But when they're upset, they have one question in their mind – 'Where's my Important Person?' Whereas insecure children have several – 'Where's my Important Person? Is it safe to approach them? Do I have to shout to get their attention or deal with it on my own?'

Changing society and educating and supporting parents are only part of the puzzle. There are also important things we can do as individuals to create change. That might mean recognising our own ability to provide a safe haven for the children in our lives, just as teachers, family friends and neighbours did in the lives of the interviewees. And it might mean changing the way we treat ourselves.

Ray (the boy who was sent away) explained:

> You can talk yourself into being a sort of person based on what other people tell you you are. I was starting to do that. 'I'm a bit touchy, feely, needy. Maybe I should suppress it a bit more, or tell people and apologise for it.' But now I realise, 'No, that's me – and actually I'm not that needy, I'm quite happy and secure in myself.' I just need to find the people that match.

> Life circumstances change. Lenses aren't always correct. And they're fluid. That means you can change them. You aren't necessarily what you are branded to be.

And Zsa Zsa (the girl who walked into fire) said:

> I try to avoid fires now. My default thinking is always, 'I've probably done something wrong, I'm probably in trouble, I'm not that great a person,' or being surprised that people love me or want to spend time

with me. The only thing I can do is live a life that respects the nicest parts of me and be kinder to myself.

I don't see my parents very often and I've shrunk my circle of friends beyond belief. I just don't want to feel bad anymore. Now I'm only close with people that expect me to be myself. And the good version of myself when I can be.

I'm much more aware of myself; not drinking and not doing drugs help. And I accept that my cup isn't full all the time. And when it isn't, I'm fine. Life is doable and bearable and sometimes joyous, but sometimes also still shit.

And Elija (the boy who was raised by wolves) said:

I've cut contact with my dad. I realised every time I have interactions with him, it's bad. It's always bad. He was still trying to pull the strings even though I was a grown man. And I need to move forward in my life.

No one talks to me about my dad anymore. And after trying to have a relationship with him, my sister cut contact too, for different reasons. I didn't even realise how much of a weight he was in my life until I let the weight go.

I gave him 37 years of chances, that is more than enough for anybody. The only reason he had that many is that he came with the title 'Dad'. But not everybody deserves that title. You still have to earn it, uphold it. He didn't. Ever.

You can't control what you were born into, but you can control what you choose now.

And it's a choice not to change. It comes down to you. It's one of the hardest things to look in the mirror.

Existential thinkers have long argued that life is about choices. In the context of attachment theory, one of the most important choices we can make is to recognise the value of having and creating safe havens. And that means surrounding ourselves with Important People who can provide them – and providing them to people who can be trusted with our love.

Matt (the boy with the stiff upper lip) explained:

We had our second child, Jack, and we decided to move closer to Lily's parents. Now, our kids see their grandparents the whole time. And Lily's aunt. Our family unit has grown to include them, and we think a lot about their end-of-life care, how we would look after them and Lily's brother.

We could have moved closer to my parents, but we didn't because they're not involved at all. My mum has visited once in three years. They're a 45-minute drive away, and she visited once after Jack was born and that was it. Maybe old age brings out extremities, but the more we become a better family, the more it highlights how much less functional my parents' family unit is. And I find that really sad.

Lily (the girl wrapped up in love) added:

This process has really made me reflect on the importance of being there and being the Important Person. My dad always said we can talk about anything any time and I've always found that really comforting. And now I know that's something really important to impress on our children.

Matt and I have come a long way from our struggles in early marriage, we are in a very different place in terms of unity and strength, and parenting has supported and enabled that. There's just a great deal of contentment. But I wouldn't want to sugar-coat it – it's been two steps forward and one step back. Parenting puts its own pressures on, but we have a toolkit to help us navigate that. It may not always function perfectly, but we have trust and security. We value and trust each other.

But while the interviewees and research both agree on the importance of having a safe haven, it's precisely when we need a safe haven the most that it can be the hardest to create one.

Amos (the boy who couldn't remember) said:

Daniela and I lost a child. After four years of suffering, we have to face the waning chances of having another child.

I'm not being super-close to Daniela because I'm busy and thinking about work a lot. I'm doing a job I really like, but no sports, I'm not eating well, I don't see friends ever, and I stopped seeing my therapist because I have no time to go.

But I don't think I feel depressed. I would say I'm doing okay.

When Daniela is upset, she's quite aggressive. And when I feel attacked, I withdraw. I rarely counterattack, but I do withdraw.

I know that she's gone through a lot. I've been to all the doctor appointments with her. It's harder on her for sure. That doesn't mean I'm able to not feel frustration if she attacks me. I'm just a human being. I feel triggered when she insults me, when I'm unwell and she hasn't even asked how I am.

On the one hand, life is full of choices, like the choice to seek and provide comfort and support. But on the other, old patterns die hard, like the tendency to attack or withdraw instead of connect. In times of crisis, precisely when we need a safe haven the most, it's all too easy to fall back on attachment patterns learned in childhood that can make achieving that more difficult.

Those patterns shouldn't be stigmatised. They're often the best we could do as children in the circumstances we were born into. Lily's strategy of going to her Important People when she was sad wouldn't have worked for Elija, who was beaten for crying. But the patterns we develop when we're little don't always serve us well when we're big.

Ainsworth thought human relationships were a need. Bowlby thought they were the store from which we draw our strength and happiness. And Sroufe and Egeland thought that resilience was born out of relationships. If they're right, then no matter what our attachment patterns are determined to do, we need to be even more determined to create a safe haven, both for ourselves and for our loved ones.

And the interviewees were doing just that.

Ray (the boy who was sent away) explained:

I'm about to move in with Veronica, the Hawaiian sunset. I feel guilty for having such a good time and that it's all working out for me. Part of me thinks, 'I don't know if I deserve it.'

I sometimes find myself thinking, 'This is so brilliant because I'm getting all this continuous affection and love,' and then my bad brain thinks, 'But are you really fully aligned on all fronts?' and tries to undermine it and find faults. But nothing is ever going to be perfect.

I still wake up every morning and miss Ayumi. I still have an immense amount of respect for her and love her to bits. I still have dreams involving her as a friend, going out, having dinner with the twins. Even in my dreams, I'm still sad about our having broken up.

Part of me thinks, 'Could I have changed the outcome? Could I have told her I loved her whether she liked it or not?' I would have said, 'I'm sorry, this is how I am. I'm tactile. I tell you how I feel when I feel it. If you find it smothering, that's fine, that's your issue. I'll walk away. But I'm not going to stifle it.' I would probe what was going on in her head a lot more. I would have said, 'I don't know why you're like this, but it's not healthy. You need to tell me what you're thinking and why. You need to bring yourself to the relationship more.' And then I would work on it continuously until she talked and brought it all out.

But we both knew full well that if we brought any of this up, we would open a Pandora's box that we couldn't close. We were brilliant parents. We provided a safe, secure background for the kids. We did it really well. And there were very rare but wonderful moments of tenderness, which I treasure. But I could count them on one hand.

When I told my daughters I'd met someone, I made sure they knew they were still my absolute priority, and that I didn't want them to think I would ever neglect them. They were both really happy for me and have asked after Veronica ever since. It's lovely. They're lovely.

And I don't think I've totally messed them up when it comes to relationships, as I had feared. I'm going away with Elsie and her boyfriend this weekend. Her boyfriend is so grounded, so loving, so the perfect boyfriend for her. They're tactile, they say they love each other. I feel like my job is done.

Skyler (the girl wrapped in cotton wool) explained:

Since this project started, Charlie and I have got married and bought a home together. The telling thing is that I'm able to be honest when I'm upset about something. And not only am I with someone that respects and cares about me, but I'm also sticking up for what I want out of a relationship and what I deserve. And that's really nice.

My relationship with my dad has got so much better. And I'm much less angry with my mom. I've accepted that she's not going to change, which has helped. And I'm trying to be really patient, with varying degrees of success. Charlie gets on well with her, which makes it easier for me to. But frustratingly, she still smothers me with cotton wool.

Having such a good relationship with Charlie has helped me process Liam's death more. It will always make me sad. But there were certain things I was holding on to, memorialising: a card that somebody wrote me, a box of mints that I was given when I was with him. I didn't want to seem disrespectful by letting things go, but I don't need to hang on to old lingerie I bought to wear for him. It wasn't until Charlie and I moved in together that I got rid of them.

I'm never going to look back and smile about the fact that this amazing person died. But I've processed it more. I am now okay. I don't think I was when this project started. I might still be a little paranoid about death. It's not that I let it affect my daily life. But death is something that happens. And in my life, it's happened a lot.

Zsa Zsa (the girl who walked into fire) explained:

> *I have just moved in with my girlfriend, Belinda. She's probably the first person I've dated who is open and aware enough of their own mental health and their history. She's lovely. She's kind. And she's very, very thoughtful. She cares about me very deeply and I care about her very deeply.*
>
> *I worry all the time I'm not making her happy. And I walk on eggshells because I'm worried that letting little angry Zsa Zsa bubble up will cost me my relationship. I am also inherently resistant to the idea that somebody is going to be my partner. But we're pretty good at talking about where we are with things and how we feel and what we're doing for each other. I just hope she doesn't fuck off.*
>
> *I also have Rosie, my miniature schnauzer, who is always eternally and endlessly happy to see me. When I wake up, she's there staring at me, tail wagging, because she's thrilled that I exist. This tiny, amazing thing that I love, loves me. It's so simple.*
>
> *We've turned into a little family. When I wake up in the morning with Belinda and Rosie, I think 'I don't want anything else, I don't need to be anywhere, I just want my little family.'*

And despite thinking that he might not find love, Elija (the boy who was raised by wolves) was also in a relationship:

> *I've been going out with someone called Leila for eight months now. She's emotionally right there, she's emotionally available. She's sturdy. She's not a lead wall.*
>
> *She's training to be a counsellor, so she's done a lot of work on herself. She knows herself very well. And people that know themselves don't push and pull you with emotions because they're unsure of who they are. She was neglected to the high heavens growing up. But she's grown.*
>
> *She has two children. I was never in my life prepared for two children to arrive on my doorstep. So, I had to think about it for a long, long time.*

I don't want to dip in and out of a family home. Kids form attachments. And if those attachments go, it plays havoc. So, we're taking it very slowly. In a year, I have only been to hers once while the kids were there. And I went as her friend.

Leila allows her kids to express so much, she never raises her voice, she doesn't hit them, she spends time with them. She says things like, 'I'm annoyed with you, you cannot hit your brother. But it's okay to be angry, and I still love you.'

The way she parents is so different compared to what I grew up with. It's almost alien to me. I didn't have anyone I could confide in, and her kids come to her with their problems. I couldn't express emotions growing up, but she explains to her children what anger is. I didn't know I could be angry and that my mum would still love me. If I was ever angry, my dad would come at me.

There's a pattern in my family that parents shirk their duties at the most critical time.

I'm doing everything I can to break that pattern. That pattern stops with me.

There's no handbook for bringing up kids. But if you're not taught how to have a safe haven growing up, you have to learn it. You have to choose to learn it. And that's what I'm doing.

Postscript

A few months after our final catch-up, Amos called. Which was unusual, as my experience of him wasn't as someone that enjoyed speaking on the phone.

He said:

I wanted to give you an update on me and Daniela.

I realised that we were both falling into old patterns, that it was going to destroy our relationship, and that I needed to stop withdrawing.

I should have proposed earlier but I didn't because of my fear of commitment.

And I knew that proposing would help make her feel safe.

So I proposed.

> *And she said yes.*

Daniela is deliriously happy, which is lovely. And of course, that makes me really happy. But what I didn't anticipate is that getting engaged has also made me feel safer.

So I wanted to tell you.

> *Because I love books with a happy ending!*

> *Especially when there's a wedding ...*

Acknowledgements

My first thank-you has to be to the interviewees. Thank you for being searingly honest with the most difficult parts of your lives, for sitting with me for so many days over so many years and, above all, for your trust. Thank you for helping me, and hopefully anyone who reads this book, understand the very different childhoods that people lead, what the micro-moments of those childhoods can feel like, and quite how much they can influence us in later life. This book wouldn't have story and heart at its core if it wasn't for your generosity and courage.

Thanks also to the interviewees who embarked on the project but couldn't continue. Thank you for being willing to take part and for your time and trust in speaking to me.

My second thank-you is to the consultants – Kate White, Linda Cundy and Robbie Duschinsky.

Kate, thank you for speaking to me at all hours of the day and night when I needed your wisdom, for reading AAIs, questions and book drafts, for your epic knowledge of attachment theory, for digging out journals and books and articles, and for always being unwaveringly calm. Your support, encouragement and belief in both me and the project were fundamental to its completion – and my sanity. Thank you. And thank you, Daisy!

Linda, thank you thank you thank you for taking the time (SO much time!) to help me prep questions and talk through how to ensure the interviewees were as protected as possible throughout the process. Thank you for bringing your mega-therapeutic experience and skill to the project, for reading AAIs, outlines and book drafts and for helping me make sense of things and ask the right questions. Your humanity, expertise and effortless insight were invaluable.

Robbie, you are a genius – and I don't use the word lightly. Thank you for doing SO much research in writing *Cornerstones of Attachment Research*, for knowing SO much about attachment theory and child health and development, and for being SO generous with your knowledge and time. Thank you for helping me make the book as accurate and up to date as possible, for welcoming me into your research group and for giving me a holistic understanding of child development, far beyond the remit of attachment theory.

Which leads me to the Cambridge Child Health and Development Group. Thank you for hosting and sharing reading groups, writing sessions and meetings and for attending conferences. Your expertise has transformed my understanding of what we can be doing to improve the lives of children. Also, writing books is an isolated business – you each brought me in and welcomed me into your very excellent crew. Thank you.

Thanks also to:
Harriet Poland at Audible for approaching me in the first place to create the audio version, and the literary brains of Harry Scoble, Victoria Haslam, Madeleine Feeny, Imogen Pelham, Jack Ramm and Imogen Papworth. Imogen, this was an intense and complicated project to inherit halfway through – thank you for always being enthusiastic, supportive and available. A huge thanks also to the exceptional Jim Martin and Sarah Lambert at Bloomsbury for their epic editorial brains on the paperback, endless patience in adding *just* the right amount of white space – and for being brave enough to publish another one of my books!

The production team at Audible, Nicola Wall and Yuki Parmar, for taking the time to understand the project and offer mental health support for interviewees, and all the audio engineers that carefully set up recording studios so that AAIs and follow-up interviews could take place in privacy.

The typesetters, the brilliant, brilliant typesetters! And the marketing and publicity teams at Audible and Bloomsbury, special shout out to the excellent Rachel Nicholson, Gracia Lumboko and Jessica Gray.

My children's agents and editors, Caroline Walsh, Christabel McKinley, Victoria England, Tegen Evans and Isobel Doster, for your patience and understanding when I was subsumed by this project, and for listening to me talk about this book for YEARS.

Marinus van IJzendoorn, Marian Bakermans-Kranenburg, Samantha Reisz, Najette Ayadi-O'Donell, Ursula Du Sauzay, Malcom Scoales, John Donohue, Catherine Holland, Harry Strawson and Deane Dozier for your expertise and insights.

Bea Longmore, Diana Mucha, Barbara Plaxton, Ed Ryland, Sam Michell and Catherine Deveson for reading some or all of the book and your incredibly helpful edits.

My friends and family for being so supportive, I can't list you ALL here as these acknowledgements would never end … Vanessa Morgan, for creating the space in which I could write this book, the Smith family, Sapana Agrawal, Tara Button, Charlotte Hacking, Jon Ball, George Bednar, Jula Dettke, Lana Dettke, Krysia Mucha, Laura Wade, Jenny Nelson, Susan Okereke, Jenny Andrews, Daniela Stawinoga-Carrington, Rahima Laird and Veronica Strom.

And finally, my husband, son and mum. Thank you for doing things like buy loo roll and breakfast when I was too overwhelmed by this to remember. Thank you for cooking and cleaning and listening and understanding and supporting and tolerating my less-than-optimal self around book deadlines. Thank you also for helping remind me why I was doing this when I was exhausted and overwhelmed and needed reminding. You were secure attachment in action.

Recommended Reading

Allen, B. 2023. *The Science and Clinical Practice of Attachment Theory: A Guide from Infancy to Adulthood*. APA, Washington, DC.

Cassidy, J. & Shaver, P. R. eds. 2016. *Handbook of Attachment: Theory, Research, and Clinical Applications*. 3rd edn, Guilford Press, New York and London.

Dozier, M. & Bernard, K. 2019. *Coaching Parents of Vulnerable Infants: The Attachment and Biobehavioral Catch-Up Approach*. Guilford Press, New York and London.

Duschinsky, R. 2020. *Cornerstones of Attachment Research*. Oxford University Press, Oxford.

Duschinsky, R., Forslund, T. & Granqvist, P. 2023. *The Psychology of Attachment*. Routledge, Oxon and New York.

Index